Jonathan Edwards was one of the most i T0008251
to ever walk the planet. He lived with a
within these pages. He knew intense highs and lows – personally, professionally, physically, and spiritually. But unlike most others, who ignore, deny, or medicate themselves through life's most difficult moments, Edwards faced them head-on and took them seriously as markers of his progress as a man and as a Christian. While on assignment in New York in the bloom of his youth, he began to make and keep what became seventy vows that ensured this way of life. Called his *Resolutions* today, they continue to inspire us to greater spiritual authenticity. This book by John Gillespie is a sure guide to these vows. Read it earnestly, prayerfully, with Edwardsean intensity. I bet God will use it to renovate your life.

DOUGLAS A. SWEENEY

Dean, Beeson Divinity School, Samford University, Birmingham, Alabama; author, *The Essential Jonathan Edwards: An Introduction to the Life and Teaching of American's Greatest Theologian*

The *Resolutions* of Jonathan Edwards is one of the most thought provoking and convicting documents to come out of his illustrious publishing ministry. While the *Resolutions* are impossible to keep, they nevertheless form a useful tool to stir Christians on toward thoughtful and virtuous aspirations in the Christian life. John Gillespie has helpfully reintroduced the modern audience to an old, yet timeless, document. In simple fashion, he has provided a devotional which tethers the *Resolutions* to the pages of Scripture. I'm certain many Christians will benefit from this work.

PETER SAMMONS

Assistant Faculty in Theology, The Master's Seminary, Los Angeles, California; author, *The Forgotten Attributes of God*

'Resolved, to live with all my might while I do live.' This short statement has changed my life more than any sentence outside the covers of my leather Bible ever has. It encourages me, convicts me, rebukes me, and reminds me of both the brevity and beauty of life. With this and sixty-some other *Resolutions*, Jonathan Edwards

(1703–1758) helps us focus our mortal eyes on eternity by reminding us of what it means to live the Christian life. I am so glad that John Gillespie has guided readers through these *Resolutions* again in a fresh way!

MATTHEW EVERHARD

Pastor, Gospel Fellowship PCA, Valencia, Pennsylvania;
contributor, *The Jonathan Edwards Encyclopedia*

I've known John Gillespie for many years, and haven't come across anyone more passionate for the glory of Jesus than he is. The words of this book are matched by the quality of his life and his service for Christ. They will search our hearts and challenge our cool responses. They will bring to our present day situation the genius of Jonathan Edwards and apply his *Resolutions* to the lives we lead. Get ready to be challenged!

ANDY PATERSON

Associate Pastor, Charlotte Chapel, Edinburgh;
author, *Ready: Evangelism for Everyone*

Following
Jesus
in an
Age of Quitters

JOHN D. GILLESPIE

Following Jesus

in an

Age of Quitters

THE *RESOLUTIONS* OF JONATHAN EDWARDS FOR TODAY

CHRISTIAN
FOCUS

Copyright © Myrrh Books 2024

paperback ISBN 978-1-5271-1094-6

ebook ISBN 978-1-5271-1120-2

10 9 8 7 6 5 4 3 2 1

Published in 2024

by

Christian Focus Publications Ltd,

Geanies House, Fearn, Ross-shire,

IV20 1TW, Great Britain.

www.christianfocus.com

Cover design by Pete Barnsley (CreativeHoot.com)

Printed and bound by Bell & Bain, Glasgow

Contents

To Bruce Montgomery,
who first showed me how to
follow Jesus.

Foreword

Trace Thurlby[1]

Quitting is easy.

From emphatically ejecting to subtly disengaging, quitting takes many forms and has many faces. Look around. People quit all the time, and it goes beyond superficial quitting on diets or gym memberships. Leaders are quitting on sacred promises and commitments like marriage, family, and ministry. From Judas' betrayal to this year's headlines, history is filled with the stories of men who walked closely with Jesus for a time but did not finish well.

Somewhere along the way, it seems they quit relying on His promises and power. They stopped following. The results are tragic, easy to criticize, and even mock. Other times, quitting hits too close to home. Our relationships fail. Our families fracture. Our heroes fall. In moments of doubt and pain, we're left questioning whether we, too, are destined to quit.

As a young man, surrounded by this sobering reality, I asked myself if it was even possible to follow Jesus to the end. The answer is a resounding 'Yes!'

Exhortation and encouragement are part of the solution. Words matter. In response to our desperate need for the Truth of Jesus Christ distilled in words, Pastor John tees up Kingdom treasure, tying together Jonathan Edwards' *Resolutions* with practical application for lives of personal holiness. As thankful as I am for this book, I am even more grateful for John's example. The world needs men who follow Jesus faithfully. By God's grace, Pastor John Gillespie is such a man. He does not quit, though he has had many opportunities to do so.

In 1994, pastoring in the United Kingdom, John could have quit when his church denomination ousted him for holding the line on an authoritative view of Scripture. The British press picked up the story. It went national. John got his 15 minutes of fame and could have walked off the playing field with his head held high. Instead, he stayed local, went across town, started over, and kept teaching the Word.

Later, John taught God's Word to pastors in some of the most underserved and under-resourced countries on earth. Year after year, he endured tens of thousands of miles of travel, spartan accommodations, foreign food, time away from family, and varying attendance with no fanfare. One hot, Haitian afternoon, I sat in an unconditioned, cinder block room as John led dozens of pastors, most of whom never had the opportunity to go to seminary, through the challenging book of *Romans*.

In that setting, with his brothers in Christ, John was fully alive! He loved it but was again faced with a significant challenge when his heart failed a few years ago. God brought healing, extending his life, while at the same time removing John's capacity to go to the ends of the earth. Once more, he could have hung it up, retired, and finally gotten serious about his golf game. Instead, he embraced a call to return to the pulpit, teach the Word, and shepherd Westbrooke, a faithful church in Overland Park, Kansas.

For 41 years, John has faithfully loved his wife, Tessa, and his ever-growing family of seven children, their spouses and 22 grandchildren. Watching his family walk with the Lord brings him great joy. He has written eight books, preached more than 6,000 sermons, baptizing and discipling many along the way. I know because I am one of them.

Obviously, I love and respect John greatly. One of the most encouraging things about him is that, in so many respects, he is a normal guy. In addition to having a sweet golf swing, he likes to bike, lift weights, talk and play guitars, and have a good laugh.

Most importantly, John is fully convinced that he has no hope of following Jesus faithfully without the supernatural, abundant grace of God. His awareness of this personal need comes across clearly in his exploration of these *Resolutions*. The overriding desire of John's heart is a deeper relationship with Jesus, for himself and for others. The process of writing imprints truth in the author's heart and mind as much (or more) as reading does in ours, and that's part of why he writes.

In 1975, Paul Simon wrote a hit song about just how easy it is to quit on relationships. "50 Ways to Leave Your Lover" was right in one respect. There are at least that many ways to quit. But it was quite wrong in another. Quitting is not the way to 'get yourself free'. True freedom is found in following Jesus: in leaning in – not walking away.

In a world where it often feels like *we can't* – where excuses are the norm – the truth is, *we can!* In the power of the Holy Spirit, we can resolve to follow Jesus, like Jonathan Edwards did and like John Gillespie does. I am so grateful for him showing us how – in word and deed.

Lean in!

I have been crucified with Christ and I no longer live, but Christ lives in me. The life I now live in the body, I live by faith in the Son of God, who loved me and gave himself for me.

Galatians 2:20

Welcome

Dear Friends,

I have known failure. I have at times been a quitter. Jesus has been so, *so* gracious to me.

He has not defined me by my failure but by His faithfulness.

And He has given me grace to want to rise above the spirit of my age ... a spirit that gives up quickly. He has put many men and women into my life who have inspired me to get back up and keep running the race. One is a young man who lived three hundred years ago. For years now, I have been wrestling with him. I have tried to escape, but this youngster keeps taking me down to the mat and I think he has all but pinned me. So ...

Come back with me to the year 1722. Brace yourself. We are going to meet an eighteen-year-old man. (Notice I do not say boy. These days we would rarely refer to an eighteen-year-old as a man, but not in those days.) He was a new follower of Jesus. He had exchanged death for life, darkness for light, lies for truth. God had begun a work of transforming grace in his young life.

Born in 1703, Jonathan Edwards was to become perhaps the greatest thinker and theologian in American history. His life was not only useful in his own day; his influence has grown over the centuries. But his development was no accident. This young man applied himself to Christ. Jonathan Edwards lived an extraordinary life because he was a normal Christian (never confuse average or common for normal).

In his nineteenth year, Edwards began to set down seventy *Resolutions* to which, by the grace of God, he held himself accountable for the rest of his life. The first thirty-four *Resolutions* were conceived and written in just two sittings. The rest came into being over the following year and a half. The fact that he wrote these over the course of eighteen months indicates that they were not just reflecting a fleeting mood, but arose from a deeply convinced disposition. Thus, by 1723, Edwards had committed himself to these seventy *Resolutions*: to read them prayerfully once a week, for the sake of his soul, for the sake of his usefulness, for the sake of his walk with Jesus. This he did for the next 35 years (that is, over eighteen-hundred times!) until his death in 1758.

So, what I want to attempt is to open up each *Resolution* to us, so that we can explore it in the light of Scripture, and have our lives impacted by it, by Jonathan, and ultimately by God.

But beware! A warning should be attached:

These *Resolutions* will be hazardous to our love of ease, comfort, and self.

We are about to explore the heart of a man who did well. The jury is in on him, but still out on us. The ancient warning from Israel's King to the overconfident Ben-Hadad is timely for us as we embark:

One who puts on his armour should not boast like one who takes it off.
(1 Kings 20:11)

So, we will approach with reverence, humility, readiness, and confidence in the Lord as we, together, see the resolve of one uncommon but not abnormal brother in Christ. These will not be for the casual, the shallow, the indifferent. They are for those who, knowing they have been apprehended by grace, set out to run well the race marked out before them.

I offer these simple expositions upon Edwards' *Resolutions* in the hope that something of the robust Jesus-following of his life may be birthed in us. May they serve to provoke us to valiant, dangerous, radical, world-defying – in short, normal – Christianity.

As to my method: Jonathan's *Resolutions* came from his heart in no special order. They did not arrive in neat categories. Themes are repeated. Nothing is systematized. I thought about trying to collate them to eliminate the repeats but I finally thought it best to take them all as they come ... from Jonathan's heart to ours. If he thought it necessary to repeat a theme, then perhaps we need to see something again in a slightly different light, take another dose of the medicine, or enjoy another slice of the pie. So, I make no apologies for any repeats. Take them not as redundant but as needed. Will you join me on this journey? If you are ready and willing you might want to begin by praying the simple and profound prayer of Augustine:

'O God, command what you will, and give what you command'.

Excited!

John Gillespie

***

A few warnings before you proceed:

1) Beware of the modern cry of 'legalism' to anything that approaches diligence. The two are not the same. They are not even remotely related. Diligence is a worthy response to the empowering grace of God. Legalism is labour in ignorance of the grace of God. These *Resolutions* are not the efforts of a religious man trying to find favour with a distant God. They are the proper responses of a man who has received God's favour.

2) Beware of the emergent attitude which dares to suggest that we have arrived at some new understanding of discipleship while chuckling at the past. Humility is called for here. A teachable attitude which values history and honours those who have gone before will accomplish far more than a closed mind which disdains anything more than five years old.

3) Beware of confusing grace with licence. Grace empowers to change. Licence excuses the refusal to change. The prevailing attitude today is that 'grace' means 'sin really does not matter', and that the Gospel is God saying, 'Aw shucks, don't worry about it'. Nothing could be further from the truth. Old-timers understood that sin is

truly wicked, God is truly holy, Hell is truly deserved, that the Gospel is truly amazing, and that one's salvation, while never earned, is always proven by the pursuit of holiness empowered by grace.

4) Beware of trying to live these out 'solo'. The Christian life is meant to be lived and experienced within Christian community. If 'it takes a village to raise a child', it takes a church to raise a Jesus-follower. You will fail on your own. You need the discipline, direction, and love of a faithful family of believers around you.

5) Never forget that, in the end, you will be as holy and as happy as you want to be. God is not short on the supply of grace. His promises are sure and His willingness to work in you to your good and His Glory is not in question. Laziness will be rewarded with little joy and little transformation. Diligence will be rewarded with much joy and much transformation.

Finally, this book has not been written by an authority on Edwards, but just a Jesus Follower who has found Jonathan Edwards to be helpful in his journey. I have tried to be faithful to his theology throughout, but if you find a departure here or there, forgive me. I think the sentiments of John Newton well sum up my heart toward this work:

> If the LORD, whom I serve, has been pleased to favour me with that mediocrity of talent, which may qualify me for usefulness to the weak and poor of his flock, without quite disgusting persons of superior discernment, I have reason to be satisfied.
> (John Newton, Preface to *Olney Hymns*, 1779)

* * *

Grateful thanks to the wonderful congregation at Westbrooke Church, Overland Park, Kansas who first received these devotionals as my weekly Pastoral Letters, especially to those of you who week by week encouraged me to keep writing them. Thanks to Mark Whiting for his early editing of those letters. Thanks to Dee Molton for her numerous rounds of deep editing of the completed manuscript. Special thanks to my dear wife Tessa for her years of constant encouragement, and for being my partner in following Jesus in an age of quitters. I am so eternally grateful for our – to use Jonathan's words for his life with Sarah – 'uncommon union'.

Being sensible that I am unable to do anything without God's help, I do humbly entreat Him by His grace to enable me to keep these *Resolutions*, so far as they are agreeable to His will, for Christ's sake.

Jonathan Edwards

Resolution 1

Resolved, before all else, to do whatever will promote God's Glory, and my own good, profit and joy. And, as my happy duty, resolved to promote the good, profit and joy of others. I resolve to do this for the whole of my life, no matter how long it takes and no matter what challenges come my way, from now and into eternity.[2]

Whoever finds their life will lose it, and whoever loses their life, for my sake, will find it. (Matt. 10:39)

Friends,

These *Resolutions* tumble from Jonathan's heart like precious gems spilled from a purse. We will take them as they come, warts and all (they are not Scripture!), knowing that they helped shape the soul of a good and useful servant of Jesus. May they do the same for us!

Our young Jonathan gets it right from the start: The goal and purpose of life is to live to and promote the Glory of God. To live for anything less (worldly comfort, acclaim, pleasure) is to live beneath our purpose. It is idolatry to seek to exalt anything above God and His Glory in our lives. And, since idols are impossible to please, idolatry always leads to brokenness. We are created and redeemed from sin so that we can promote, declare, and *enjoy* the wonder and goodness of God.

Look what Jonathan puts together, right in the same sentence: the Glory of God *and* his own good, profit, and joy. How can that be? How can we live for the Glory of God *and*, at the same time, live for our own pleasure? Are we not called to deny ourselves, take up our cross, and follow Jesus?

Yes! Absolutely! But here is the wonder of this Christian Life: As we battle to dethrone *all* lesser 'gods' and enthrone Jesus solely and supremely in our lives – repenting with tears, refusing all pretenders and false lords to the thrones of our hearts – we discover *Jesus is the source and supply of all true joy, good, profit, and pleasure.* There is no conflict between *true* pleasure and pleasure in God. There is great conflict between all lesser contenders for our hearts' affections and happiness in God.

We were *made* for joy as certainly as we were made for Jesus. We were *made* for pleasure as surely as we were made for God Himself. It is when we seek joy and pleasure apart from having God enthroned and glorified in our hearts and lives that the pursuit of our pleasure, profit, and good becomes idolatrous and destructive.

If we 'delight [ourselves] in the Lord', He will give us the 'desires of [our] heart[s]' (Ps. 37:4). *And* if we are delighted in Him, He will be the desire of our hearts that we receive!

The *Westminster Catechism* in 1648 said it perfectly:

Question: What is the chief end [grand purpose] of Man?
Answer: Man's chief end is to glorify God *and enjoy Him forever.*

C.S. Lewis famously put it as only he can:

It would seem that Our Lord finds our desires not too strong, but too weak. We are half-hearted creatures, fooling about with drink and sex and ambition when infinite joy is offered us, like an ignorant child who wants to go on making mud pies in a slum because he cannot imagine what is meant by the offer of a holiday at the sea. We are far too easily pleased.[3]

George Muller put it this way:

The first great and primary business to which I ought to attend every day is to have my soul happy in the Lord.[4]

Friend, go after the Glory of God! Go after the unrivalled pre-eminence of Jesus Christ – in every area of your life! Seek to promote the same in the lives and culture around you! Refuse all lesser rivals and pretenders! Battle for this daily, no matter how long it takes, how much repenting, refusing, and re-focusing it requires! Your true joy, good, and profit will be the inevitable and fitting result of your pursuit of God being rightly honoured in every facet of your life.

Let nothing deter, discourage, or distract you from seeking all your joy and profit in the promotion of the Lordship of Jesus in every corner of your life, and every corner of this world.

That marvellous Christian! He loses everything to gain all things. He goes down to go up. He is slave to all and slave to none. He is bound to Christ and yet the freest of all. He dies that he might live. He denies himself yet discovers himself. He despises his own glory as he pursues God's, and yet discovers total joy in the journey.

That marvellous Christian!

You make known to me the path of life; you will fill me with joy in your presence, with eternal pleasures at your right hand.

(Ps. 16:11)

Resolution 2

Resolved to be always discovering new ways to Glorify God in my life and increase both my joy in Jesus and that of others.

The kingdom of heaven is like treasure hidden in a field. When a man found it, he hid it again, and then in his joy went and sold all he had and bought that field. (Matt. 13:44)

Dear Glory Seekers,

I want to begin with a caution.

I can almost hear someone charging young Jonathan with over-active zeal, perhaps chuckling a bit at the youthful idealism he expresses. For this I have two thoughts:

First, perhaps Jonathan, at times, needs some balance. Who doesn't? But I caution against any of *us* (modern, Western Christians) being too quick to judge Christians of previous generations or contemporary Christians living elsewhere. *We* are not the 'Gold Standard' by which true discipleship is measured. Sorry if that hurts, but it is true. Jonathan (and perhaps your grandmother) was probably closer to a *normal* Christian than we are. What we write off as idealism may be just what Jesus meant when he likened the Kingdom-life to a merchant who *joyfully* sold all he had to buy a treasure-laden field. And Jonathan's 'over-active zeal' might match Jesus' when He declared that all comers must be self-denying cross bearers (Luke 9:23).

But secondly, when I read and think on Jonny's youthful resolve, I remember a time when I too, as a young Jesus-follower, was like him – before I became 'mature' and 'balanced' (horrible, self-conscious words!). During my middle years I would have read these *Resolutions* and thought, 'A bit much, these. Calm yourself, Jonathan!' But now that my earthly life is – statistically – 6/7ths *over*, I find myself thinking like Jonathan once again: Life is brief; Heaven is near; the Kingdom of God is what counts; Jesus is worth my very best all the time and in every way. Nowadays, I read Jonny's *Resolutions* and say a hearty, 'Yes! Way to go, Jonny!' I need a good dose of his zeal and idealism!

We love, we admire, we applaud a 'go get 'em' attitude in a businessman, a mind for discovery in a scientist, creativity in an artist, or an urge to climb higher in an adventurer. Well, here is a young man who is applying just such an attitude toward the most wonderful thing in all the universe: God.

Do you see the sense of *adventure* in this *Resolution*? He is not lamenting, 'Why do I *have* to pursue God and His Glory?' He is not complaining, 'Why do I *have* to seek my good, joy, and profit in *Jesus*?' He is not moaning, 'Why *must* I seek that others discover their fullness in Christ?' Just the opposite! He is saying, 'I *want* to forever be finding new ways to discover, and be discovered by, the wonders of God! I *want* my Bible open and my mind engaged. I am *ready* to repent when I find sin within, and on the lookout for joy-robbing, God-dishonouring idols. I *do not want anything* to keep me from loving God, my own soul, and others, and I want to always be discovering how I can better promote the Glory of God in myself and in my world'.

He has *seen something*. He is *in the grip of something*. He is on a journey of discovery and the object is not a woman, a hobby, a passing treasure. It is nothing other than the Eternal God. Now get this: As *uncommon* as this may be to our time-bound values, it is *normal* for the child of grace. It is what we have been created and redeemed for. A hunger for God, for Him to capture our hearts and those of our fellows, should be the *normal* desire of the child of grace.

But you don't have to take it from me!

Take it from King David:

One thing I ask from the Lord,
this only do I seek:
that I may dwell in the house of the Lord
all the days of my life,
to gaze on the beauty of the Lord
and to seek him in his temple.
(Ps. 27:4)

Take it from Paul:

My goal is ... that they may know the mystery of God, namely, Christ,
in whom are hidden all the treasures of wisdom and knowledge.
(Col. 2:2–3)

Take it from Jesus in his beautiful parable of the field of treasure.

Friends, let's get back a sense of *adventure* in our pursuit of the Glory of God and our joy in Him! We dare not drag our feet as though we were being reluctantly hauled into the doctor's office! We are being invited into an eternity-long journey of discovery. Any reluctance betrays a poor view of God and an over-love of lesser things. I promise you, the most learned theologian, the most advanced follower of Jesus, has barely begun this glorious journey of discovery. May we join with Jonathan and stir our hearts heavenward. May we always be discovering new ways to glorify God in our lives and increase both our joy in Jesus and that of others.

'Now the Lord give you that grace to be humble; and then, according to his promise, he will make you rich in every other grace.
(Philip Henry to his son Matthew)[5]

Resolution 3

Resolved that, if and when I become lazy or dull and begin to neglect my spiritual well-being and these *Resolutions*, I will earnestly and quickly repent.

Godly sorrow brings repentance that leads to salvation and leaves no regret, but worldly sorrow brings death. (2 Cor. 7:10)

He restores my soul ... (Ps. 23:1)

Friend,

I have some very good news for you: God's Grace is not in short supply. We have a willing God and an open Heaven. God's supply is not a puddle, not even a lake, but an unending river of grace. And grace gives power: power to live life to the Glory of God.

Diligence with your heart will be repaid a thousand times over. No man or woman has got, or ever will get to the end of their earthly journey and say, 'Dang! I was too diligent with my soul. I should have been less careful!'

But there is a need for watchfulness, carefulness over our hearts. It is dangerously easy to become lazy, dull, negligent, and distracted. Hopefully, none of us will ever flat-out deny Jesus, but all of us face the very real danger of neglecting Him, being lazy, and taking our eyes off the ball. Nothing prospers without input. No garden thrives without attention. No one's body is healthy without deliberate intent. Laziness might not keep you from Heaven, but it will keep you from *fullness*. Carelessness is costly. Jonathan knows himself. He is not so brash, so brave, as to believe that he cannot grow dull in his pursuit of God's Glory and his joy in Jesus. He knows that he can grow cold. Distractions abound. Sickness of soul often begins with neglect. It does not take outright rebellion to take one off course. So, he factors *repentance* into his *Resolutions* right from the start.

I once asked a pilot, 'If you left London bound for New York, and began *one degree* off course, left uncorrected, how far would you be amiss of JFK airport at the end of the flight?'

'Three hundred miles.'

Would you be happy to be a passenger on *that* plane?

Let's remember, diligence is not legalism. It is a fitting response to the wonderful saving work of God. So, Jonathan resolves to repent when he finds himself growing lazy and dull. He has not committed adultery! He has not robbed a bank – yet! But he realizes that 'gross sin' begins with little acts of neglect. So, rather than let things get out of hand, he wisely resolves to be diligent with the little habits of life.

So, let's ask ourselves a few questions. These do not represent rules. They represent *responses* to Jesus.

– How is my daily prayer time? Am I opening my heart to Heaven every day, even as I open my mouth to food?

– How is my time in God's Word? Am I renewing my mind with Truth or am I neglecting to do so, allowing the world to shape my thinking?

– With whom am I keeping company? Am I running with the wise or stumbling with the foolish?

– How is my private world? Am I doing anything in secret that I would be ashamed to have known in public?

– How is my conversation? Is it sweet and edifying, or bitter and discouraging? Am I remembering that I will give an account for every careless word spoken?

– How is my thought life? Am I seeking to honour Jesus with the meditations of my heart? If my thought life were a movie, what would it be rated?

If I find myself slacking in these right and good responses to the love of God, I need to quickly correct my course. Listen – to know yourself, to examine your life, is not over-doing it. It is *basic discipleship,* and it bears sweet fruit.

The renowned violinist, Jascha Heifetz, said, 'If I don't practice one day, I know it; two days, the critics know it; three days, the public knows it'.

King David ... who certainly knew what it was like to get careless with his heart and make a huge mess of things, put it this way:

Search me, God, and know my heart,
  test me and know my anxious thoughts.
See if there is any offensive way in me,
  and lead me in the way everlasting ...
(Ps. 139:23–24)

Oh Friend, let us learn the wonderful help of repenting quickly! Let us never be too afraid, ashamed, proud, or slow to run to Jesus with our sin! Let us learn and understand our hearts and become accustomed to the sound of sin's stealthy approaches. Let us believe that big failings begin in the small places: little words, secret thoughts, prayerless days.

God has such joy for us, such purpose, abundant goodness! He *wants* us to be captivated by Him and pursue Him. I cannot tell you, with any degree of confidence or accuracy, what God has in store for this nation. But I can say with *certainty* what God will do for you, and for me: If we will be desirous of Him above all else and live a life where repentance from the little sins that lead to the big sins marks our way, then I am sure that He will show Himself to us and lead us into a usefulness and fullness that will bring Him much Glory and much good to us and those around us.

But one thing I do: forgetting what is behind and straining towards what is ahead, I press on towards the goal to win the prize for which God has called me heavenwards in Christ Jesus. (Phil. 3:13–14)

Many sensational gifts and talents don't mean much over the long haul. The longer I live, the more I treasure people who just keep walking with God.[6]
(Jim Cymbala)

31

Resolution 4

Resolved to do all things with my whole being, body and soul, big or small, to the Glory of God, and, so far as possible, to avoid anything which offends God and His Glory.

And whatever you do, whether in word or deed, do it all in the name of the Lord Jesus, giving thanks to God the Father through him.(Col. 3:17)

Question:

How does a young man on the frontier of civilization, far from the power centres of his world, with little money and few worldly helps, rise to become a shaper not only of his generation, but of generations and even nations to come? What was it about this man that made him so useful to God? How was it that the Gospel advanced so much in his hands? How did Jonathan Edwards become Jonathan Edwards?

I am not sure if the Gospel has ever prospered and gone forward because Christians had plenty of money and worldly power. The Gospel prospers when Christians really know Jesus, go deep with Him, and resolve to live their whole lives for His Glory, regardless of all else. If we are as concerned with spiritual riches and power as we are with material riches and power, we can be world-changers. Even a surface knowledge of the history of missions will reveal the wondrous fact that the Gospel has prospered through those who concerned themselves not with stuff, but with Christ.

Meet C.T. Studd (1860–1931). He was an English cricket star. For you 'Yanks', cricket is the Englishman's answer to baseball. (If you think baseball is slow ...) He gave away a fortune and went on the mission field. He knew Jesus deeply. The spiritually shallow come out with sayings like: 'If only God would save the rich and famous, then we would see the Kingdom come'. But God just does not seem to work that way. Studd *was* rich and famous when Jesus grabbed him, and he made himself nothing so that Christ could be something in him. It would be like Patrick Mahomes or David Beckham giving up their fame and their riches, at the height of their physical powers, to go to some totally obscure place for the sake of the Gospel. Studd went to India and then Africa. People thought that was crazy, but God did not, and the history of Christian missions (far more important than the history of cricket or football) has vindicated him.

Hear him:

> How could I spend the best years of my life in living for the honours of this world, when thousands of souls are perishing every day?[7]

> Some want to live within the sound of church or chapel bell; I want to run a rescue shop within a yard of hell.[8]

Studd became a world-changer. I know we use that term a lot. But he really did. He founded WEC International, which has trained and sent out thousands into the mission field. Only eternity will reveal the true impact of his decision to do all things with his whole being, body and soul, big or small, to the Glory of God.

The history of Christian missions is loaded with amazing stories of nobodies who lived for the Glory of God and thus became world-shakers:

George Muller, Hudson Taylor, Amy Carmichael, Henry Martyn, Catherine Booth. Spiritual giants. Spiritual billionaires. They lived for God's Glory, not their own.

Will *your* name be added to that list? Will *mine*?

Spiritual wealth is the currency of the Kingdom. By spiritual wealth I mean:

A true and genuine knowledge of Jesus Christ,
   A heart for holiness,
      A charitable spirit,
         A love for the lost,
            A hunger for truth,

A life lived for the Glory of God.

To be rich in such things is to be truly rich. It is to be powerful in the things that matter. God's way is so different than ours! To Him, a widow's two pennies are worth more than all the cash of the world's rich (Luke 21:2). God can do amazing things through the 'surrendered simple'.

When our young Jonathan writes this *Resolution*, he is pursuing spiritual wealth; he is exercising spiritual muscle; he is purchasing shares in the Kingdom of God; he is choosing true riches over temporary riches.

This is a rich *Resolution*.

Captivated by Christ and His Gospel, wooed by things unseen, this young man – barely old enough to shave – brings to mind Moses, the young prince of Egypt, who *'refused to be known as the son of Pharaoh's daughter' [and] regarded disgrace for the sake of Christ as of greater value than the treasures of Egypt, because he was looking ahead to his reward. [He] persevered because he saw him who is invisible* (Heb. 11:24–27).

So, I say again, if we are as concerned with spiritual riches as we are with material, we will be world-changers. To resolve to live for the Glory of God, both in soul and body, that is, in the secret place of the heart, and in the public place of one's actions, is to embark upon a life of spiritual power and purpose. Go deep with Christ. Seek to become a giant in spiritual things. Determine that the currency of the Kingdom will be your treasure. In an age of material wealth at the price of spiritual poverty, by God's grace, determine that yours will be a life marked by something more than fleeting fancies. Determine that yours will be a life marked by the currency of the Kingdom.

> I sometimes think that the Lord was looking for someone weak
> enough and small enough to use, so that all the glory would go to
> Him and not to a man, and that He found me.[9]
>
> (Hudson Taylor)

Resolution 5

Resolved never to lose one moment of time but to use each moment
in the most profitable way I possibly can.

*Be very careful, then, how you live – not as unwise but as wise, making
the most of every opportunity, because the days are evil. Therefore, do
not be foolish, but understand what the Lord's will is.* (Eph. 5:15–17)

*Come to me, all you who are weary and burdened, and I will give you
rest. Take my yoke upon you and learn from me, for I am gentle and
humble in heart, and you will find rest for your souls. For my yoke is
easy and my burden is light.* (Matt. 11:29–30)

Dear Friend in Jesus,

Before we *dare* venture farther down this *Resolutions* highway
with Jonathan, I need to have a heart-to-heart with you. Stop what
you are doing and lean in with me. I must ask you a question. It is
the most urgent question I can ever ask you: Are you fully, totally,
desperately, joyfully trusting in all that Jesus Christ is and all He has
done for your salvation? Have you harboured your soul in Him and
His Gospel? Do you rejoice that Jesus lived the sinless life that God
required of you? Do you rejoice that He died the sinner's death that
God required of you?

Yes?

Are you sure and certain that all your hope is in Christ and
Christ *alone*?

OK! That being settled, we can proceed!

Why did I press you so? Why did I ask you the same question

five different ways? Because unless we are living out of the fullness of Christ crucified for our sins and risen for our justification, this *Resolution* will produce legalistic despair in us. But from the position of security in Jesus, this *Resolution* has the power to deliver us from the tyranny of the urgent and unto the freedom of walking in God's daily purposes for us. Submitting our time – our moments and our days – to the Lordship of Jesus will actually set us free from bondage to our own agenda. *Our* timetable inevitably wearies and burdens. *His* timetable actually ensures our fruitfulness *and* provides rest for our souls – for He is gentle and humble.

So, from that place of safety in Jesus and His wonderful Gospel, here we go!

Life is short! Soon we will be called to give account to our Lord and Saviour for our lives, our years, our days, our hours, our minutes! I think here of the Psalmist's wise prayers:

> *Teach us to number our days, that we may gain a heart of wisdom ...*
> *... Show me, Lord, my life's end, and the number of my days; let me*
> *know how fleeting my life is.* (Pss 90:12; 39:4)

I know Jonathan's words have a whiff of youthful zeal about them. I want to say, 'Learn to relax a bit, son! You resolve to "never lose one moment of time"? Really?' I feel the temptation to excuse Jonny for his overzealousness and thereby let us off the hook. But that would be too easy. Remember, he held himself to this *Resolution* for the next 35 years. It was not so much an expression of his youthful zeal as of his life-long resolve to not waste *any* of his earthly days. So, let's take the medicine. Our generation is a wasteful (the Bible word for wasteful is *prodigal*) generation. We have more leisure than any culture has ever imagined. We have it so good *now* that rarely do we contemplate the fast approach of death and our day of account. *We are wasters.* We waste food, we waste stuff, but worst of all, we waste *time.* Would we not do well to live with life's end in view? Would we not benefit from living with an eye on Heaven? Would it not help us to 'make the most of every opportunity' if we remembered every day that life is brief and soon our wonderful Lord and Saviour will call us to give our account?

Oh, if I could have some days back! I mourn the days I spent being irritable instead of cheerful, selfish instead of giving, wallowing instead of worshipping! How often I have wasted grace! I need to press in here and – with repentance in my heart – ask Jesus to give me grace to 'make the most of every opportunity', or, as the King James Version says, to 'redeem the time'. And I need to be motivated by joy. I need to *want* to use my moments and my days for Jesus and for others; I need to *want* to not waste my time.

Our Bible passage at the top of this letter from Ephesians 5 reminds us of our great Gospel reason for being diligent with our time: 'because the days are evil'. We are in a war! How dare we play and snooze our way through the battle! Opportunities are abounding for us to spread the fame of Jesus for the joy of all peoples. These are *our days*. We should be as earnest – and excited – as a farmer at harvest or a fisherman before a bountiful sea. It is our time to grasp opportunities. Not all of us are as gifted as Jonathan Edwards was. His output was profound. It was as though he packed two lifetimes into his 54 years. Not all of us can 'go' as hard as he did. (He usually spent 13 hours a day in study, counsel, teaching, preaching, and writing, on top of caring for his family of eleven children.) I am thankful for times of leisure that Jesus gives me. Sometimes resting and re-creating *is* the best use of my time. That is OK! But the challenge here is for us to live each day in the light of 'That Day' as accountable stewards of the life and gifts that God has given to us.

Jesus is not a slavedriver! He is actually easy to please. *His* yoke is easy and His burden is light. In fact, I am confident that we will find *His* Lordship over our time far more 'do-able' and pleasant than *our* lordship over our time. So, in a spirit of Gospel joy, from one who has been redeemed from sin and slavery to safety in Jesus, here is my offering to you: Let's receive this challenge from Jonathan to bring, *deliberately, actively, and happily,* our days and moments – including our hobbies and leisure times – under the lordship of Jesus Christ. My best advice is that we begin each and every day by lifting our hearts to the Lord Jesus and *asking Him for grace* to live that day as He would have us live it – including our work, our rest, our play, our chores, our engagements. If we make this our life habit, we will find deliverance from the tyranny of the urgent into the freedom of the purposes of our good, gracious, and generous God.

Time is given us to use in view of eternity.[10] (Harry Ironside)

Resolution 6

Resolved to live with all my might, for all of my life.

For Christ's love compels us. (2 Cor. 5:14)

Friends,

From 1936 to 1951 – excluding the three years that he spent in the U.S. Military during World War II – Joe DiMaggio played more than 2000 Major League Baseball games for the New York Yankees. During that time, his team won the World Series nine times.

Known for his tenacious competitiveness and phenomenal skill, 'The Yankee Clipper' summed up his heart with these words: 'I'm just a ballplayer with one ambition, and that is to give it all. I've got to help my ball club win. I've never played any other way'.[11]

Late in his illustrious career, when his aging body was wearing out, and he could only play with great pain, 'Joltin' Joe' was asked why he still insisted upon giving it his all, every game, every play, no matter what, even if the effort would have no impact on the outcome of a particular game. His reply? 'Because there's always some kid who may be seeing me for the first or last time. I owe him my best'.

Such an attitude grips me. It challenges me! It judges me! Can I sum up my heart so clearly? Can I say of my dedication to Christ and His Gospel: 'I'm just a Jesus-follower with one ambition, and that is to give it all. I've got to help the cause of Christ win. I've never lived any other way'? Can I say of my resolve to give my all for Christ, every moment, regardless of pain and discomfort: 'There's always some lost soul who may be seeing Christ in me for the first or last time. I owe him my best'?

Jonathan Edwards would understand Joe DiMaggio ... at least in a sense. His resolve 'to live with all my might, for all of my life', resonates with Dimaggio's, only for Edwards the stakes are infinitely higher, the rewards more glorious, the cost of lethargy so much greater.

The thing that gets me is that we applaud such resolve in a ballplayer. We make a hero of him and induct him into our Hall of Fame. But, let a Christian show such heart-attitude for Things Eternal, and we deem him:

A fanatic,

Unbalanced,

Legalistic,

Weird ...

Joltin' Joe knew he could never get a ball game back. We can never get back a meal with a friend, a talk over the garden fence with a neighbour, or an encounter with a lonesome soul on the bus. Every day we receive 1440 minutes from the Lord. We can waste them or use them well. Every week we receive 168 hours from Jesus. We can give our best with them or squander them. But we can never get them back.

Solomon, reflecting upon a life largely wasted, urges us:

Whatever your hand finds to do, do it with all your might. (Ecc. 6:10)

Resting in Jesus and His finished work for our sins (a good thing) is not to be confused with becoming lazy or half-hearted (a bad thing). The quaint slogan, 'Let Go and Let God', might look sweet on a coffee cup, but its questionable theology might put you to sleep when you need to be on high alert.

How about some biblical descriptions of discipleship:

Fight the Good Fight!

I make my body a slave ...

Make every effort ...

Pursue holiness!

Take up the cross and follow!

I die daily ...

Count it all joy when you experience trials ...

Spur one another on ...
Awake! You sleeper ...
The Love of Christ compels me!

It is hard to find a picture of DiMaggio in a baseball uniform without a smile on his face. Could it be that there is a direct link between being sold-out for something and joy? I think so! Could it be that the lot of the half-hearted is joylessness? I know so! Do you picture a lemon-faced Edwards, or a joy-filled, earnest, worshipping, delivered, focused, relieved, Heaven-bound, young life-grabber making this *Resolution*?

For Jonathan Edwards it is all or nothing, every day, for all of his days. Christ is worthy of nothing less. Joy demands nothing less. The 'team' deserves nothing less. The watching world needs nothing less.

I am greatly encouraged; in all our troubles my joy knows no bounds.
(2 Cor. 7:4)

For the joy that was set before him Jesus endured the cross, scorning its shame. (Heb. 12:1)

Jim Elliot (1927–1956) knew the joy of giving his all for Jesus.What an impact his brief life had ... and is having! Elliot prayed, '... flame is transient, often short lived ... make Thy Fuel, Flame of God.'[12] That is just what he received. Found dead in an Ecuadorean river with a spear in his back, his all-or-nothing life for Jesus not only resulted in an entire Amazonian people group coming to Christ, but in thousands of young people being motivated for missions (I was one of them!).

Jim, Joe, and Jon would have had a bang-up time together. They were cut from the same bolt of cloth. If ever I could find them sitting around a fire, passionately and joyfully talking about giving life their all, I would have to crash the party: 'Hey Jonny, Joey, and Jimmy, move over! Let me squeeze in! I need a dose of what you have!'

I want to be a happy member of that exclusive but inviting club: The Fellowship of the Whole-Hearted.

Will you join me?

Jesus replied: 'Love the Lord your God with all your heart and with all your soul and with all your mind ...' (Matt. 22:37)

Wherever you are, be all there! Live to the hilt every situation you believe to be the will of God.[13] (Jim Elliot)

Resolution 7

Resolved to never do anything which I would not do if I knew I had
but one hour left to live.

*You also must be ready because the Son of Man will come at an hour
when you do not expect him.* (Luke 12:40)

Dear Friends,

Before we write this *Resolution* off as 'impossible' or 'unreasonable',
let's take some time and consider the wisdom in it. It just might do
us (and those around us who are having to put up with us) a world
of *good*.

Part of our problem might be that we do not rejoice in the thought
of Heaven enough. Do we really believe that the Bible is right when it
tells us that to 'depart and be with Christ is better by far' (Phil. 1:23)?
If we can anticipate Heaven – which we cannot gain without dying
first – like a child anticipates Christmas morning, Jonathan's
Resolution suddenly makes obvious sense. How else can I think?

Do you ever ponder your final day? Students think about
graduation; businessmen dream of their retirement; little girls
joyfully imagine their wedding day. But when it comes to thinking
about, hoping for, living for, the sure-to-come day when we exchange
these 'Shadowlands' for God's solid Heaven, we, strangely, push those
thoughts away. But it is not morbid to consider, often, the brevity
of life, the nearness of death, and the wonders of Heaven. It is wise
to do so. We live better *in* time when we realize that soon we will
be *out* of time. In fact, the Jesus-followers who have lived the best,

most useful, lives have been those who have lived with their fast-approaching death in clear view.

Calvin Miller tells the story of a dying friend to demonstrate that living each day in the light of our last day delivers us from selfish, surface living.

> I met one of my best friends on the day she learned that she had less than six months to live. No life should be lived without one such friend. For only when the edges of life are clearly marked, does friendship celebrate all its gifts with understanding ...
>
> Her name was Anne, and while, by her own confession, her last months were far from morose, she spent her days 'sorting'. With Anne's short lifespan, we had time to contemplate and enjoy only the absolute essentials of our relationship. The dial of the clock's finality moved with hands so swift that things cheap and temporary held no fascination.
>
> Anne was physically beautiful. She had spent a great deal of her life maximizing her beauty with cosmetics. Her skin was ivory and warm. But things dermal and outward lose their importance when things visceral and inward go wrong. Down where creams and oils cannot penetrate, the body must sometimes reckon with strong judgments. Then the deep issues of life must hold sway over all things surface.[14]

'The deep issues of life' – these are the very things we tend to ignore. Like that sick goldfish you had when you were a kid, our culture sucks from the surface, afraid, unwilling, unable to go deep. But find almost anyone who is knowingly living their last days and you will find a person who has moved beyond surface to depth, beyond image to substance. Our eighteen-year-old Jonathan is advising us to live every day this way.

Living with the end in view produces power and perseverance in us. Seeing the finish line emboldens us to call out to God for power to run well.

Eric Liddell (1902–45) was a follower of Jesus. He was also a very fast runner. The 'Flying Scotsman' ran for Great Britain in the 1924 Olympics. Having refused to run the 100 meter heat on a Sunday, he opted to run the mid-week 400 instead. It was not his best event but he won the race. He set a new Olympic record.

When asked how he managed to win he revealed his simple strategy:

> I ran the first 200 as fast as I could, and then, with God's help, I ran the second 200 even faster.[15]

Friend! There is something about having the end in view that causes us to call out for God! There is something about knowing that you are rounding that last bend that focuses one's attention, spurs one on, and energizes one's efforts. Living with the end in sight encourages – forces – one to summon God's help. And God gives us His help!

Now, here is the thing: We *never know* when we are rounding that last bend! You might be rounding it today! I might be on the home stretch. You might be 18 or 85, but you never know when God's ordained days for you are up. Only God knows.

> *All the days ordained for me*
> *were written in your book*
> *before one of them came to be.*
> (Ps. 139:16)

So, either we:

1) Ignore death. Live carelessly, with no thought of tomorrow, of our death, of eternity ... only to die unprepared.

2) Fear death. Live a frightened life, hugging the shore, afraid to venture out lest we perish ... only to miss God's purposes for us.

3) Be ready for death. Recognizing our mortality and God's saving mercy, fix our eyes on the prize and live every day as though it could be our last – thereby discovering the freedom and joy of running this race with all our might.

Jonathan is wise beyond his years. I need to learn from this eighteen-year-old! Oh, to live *every day* with the conscious thought that soon, very soon, I shall be summoned by the King!

What a tonic for the tired!

What a boost for the bored!

What a rebuke to the restless!

What a jolt to the joyless!
What a warning for the worldly!
What a wonder for the weary!
Heaven! Being with Jesus! Soon!

Therefore, since we are surrounded by such a great cloud of witnesses, let us throw off everything that hinders and the sin that so easily entangles. And let us run with perseverance the race marked out for us, fixing our eyes on Jesus, the pioneer and perfecter of faith.
(Heb. 12:1–2)

When it comes time to die, make sure that all you have to do is die.[16]
(Jim Elliott)

Resolved 8

Resolved, in my speaking and in my doing, to always remember that there is no-one more a sinner than I, to always remember that I have the same weaknesses and failings as others, and, when I see *others'* sin, to be reminded of my own sins, and use the failings of another to lead me to confess my own sins.

Why do you look at the speck of sawdust in your brother's eye and pay no attention to the plank in your own eye? (Matt. 7:3)

Dear Friend in Jesus,

Running with Jonathan is, for me, like trying to keep up with Usain Bolt. 'Hey Jonny! Wait up!' I am not going to keep up with Jonathan stride for stride. But that does not mean that I cannot run the same race as well as *I* can and finish the course. It does not mean that I cannot learn from Jonathan's stride. The more I see Jon sprinting ahead, the more I need to remember that this whole adventure with Jesus is a *grace adventure*. Jesus has saved me and apprehended me because *He* is wonderful, not because I am! And He will give me all the power I need to run well.

Jonathan would be the first to say that this entire enterprise of following Jesus is a *Gospel* endeavour. It is all from God. The will to run is from God. The ability to run is from God. Grace is there when we stumble and fall. Some of us will run with a firm, strong stride. Some of us will limp our way along. Some of us will have to be carried. But for each one of us, it will be Jesus and His grace that enables us to start, to keep going, and to finish! I can imagine Jonny looking back over his shoulder at me – way back in his dust – having heard my faint, 'Wait up!' and shouting back, 'Don't look at me! Look at Jesus!' For it is Jesus, not Jonathan, who gives all strength and all joy for this race.

So, with gracious Jesus in full view, let's hit the track with Jonathan's next *Resolution*.

It is all about how we see and deal with our own sins.

How we view our own sin and failing says much about the true state of our souls. Many of us spend much of our time fussing over the sins of *others*, when what is needful is that we be diligent with our own hearts, and deal with our own sins.

Listen! We have a merciful God who is *always* ready to hear us when we confess and cleanse us when we cry to Him! So, you and I will do well to realize our sin and run to – not from – Jesus:

> *If we confess our sins, he is faithful and just and will forgive us our sins and purify us from all unrighteousness.* (1 John 1:9)

To view *myself* as 'the sinful one' is not morbid. It is reality. When I stop complaining to God about everyone else and instead humble myself before Him and deal with *my* sin, then my world actually changes. Do you remember the parable Jesus told of the two men who went to the temple? You can read the story in Luke 18. The 'good man' prayed, 'Lord, I thank you that I am better than others!' The 'bad man' simply beat his breast and – literally – prayed, 'God, remove your wrath from me *the* sinner!' *The* sinner! 'Lord! I am the problem! I thought it was my wife, or my kids, or the other person, but now I see that the problem is *me*!' Jesus said that *this* man – the 'bad man' – *not* the *other* man – the 'good man' – went home right with God.

What victory!

G. K. Chesterton (1874–1936) was a famous British author and Christian thinker. The story is told (it may be true, it may be an urban legend, but either way it bears truth) that *The London Times* newspaper asked numerous famous authors to write an essay answering the question:

What is wrong with the world?

Chesterton's essay was the shortest … and the most profound:

I am.[17]

What if, as Jonathan resolved to do, *I* get to grips with *my* own sins before God and give grace to others for theirs? What if, as urged by Jonathan, when I see another's sin, I go to the Lord over *my own* instead of 'tut tut-ing' over theirs? *My reaction* to the sins of others is often *more sinful* than their sin was in the first place.

Certainly, this is the 'speck vs. plank' issue that Jesus spoke of. Let's admit that we can feel a perverse pride over our brother's sin. We can gloat over his speck, all the while not seeing that our *attitude* toward his speck has become a log in our own eye! Fellowship is broken as our pride and self-deceit cause a barrier to be raised between us. How much better it is Insert: it isto use their sin as an occasion to examine our own hearts and lives!

This would be revolutionary, both in terms of my relationship with God and my relationship with others.

O Friend! Through the Gospel we have a merciful God and an open Heaven! Never be slow to repent and confess, for your cries will be heard, your sins will be cleansed, and your peace will be restored. Avoid like the plague seeing yourself as better, and others as the problem. You and I have jurisdiction over no hearts but our own.

Anything (including someone else's sin!) that brings me to the foot of the cross again, repenting, confessing, and being cleansed by the blood of Jesus, is a *good* thing.

In repentance and rest is your salvation … (Is. 30:15)

Love will flow from one to another, when each is prepared to be known as the repentant sinner he is at the Cross of Jesus.[18]
(Roy Hession)

Resolved 9

Resolved to think much on all occasions of my own dying, and of the common circumstances which attend death.

Show me, Lord, my life's end,
and the number of my days;
let me know how fleeting my life is.
(Ps. 39:4)

Dear Friends,

Some years ago, my eye caught the headline of a British newspaper: British Death Rate Declines. Really? I know what the well-meaning journalist was *trying* to say – simply that people in the UK were living longer.

But the death rate hadn't declined. It was, is, and shall forever be ... 100%.

In the olden days, followers of Jesus prepared themselves for their dying day. They contemplated the brevity of life as a normal part of their devotion to Jesus. Christians wrote and read books about death. Preachers preached about how to die well. Pastors considered it their duty to prepare their flock to meet God. The early Methodists were known for their 'good deaths'. A physician said to Charles Wesley, 'Most people die for fear of dying, but I never met with such people as yours. They are none of them afraid of death!'[19]

Refusing to contemplate your death will not make you live one minute longer. Considering your life's end will not make you live longer, but it will make you live – and die – better.

Jonathan Edwards was not morbid to 'think much on all occasions' of his dying. Neither was Richard Baxter, who disciplined himself to think on Heaven for thirty minutes each day. They lived in the light of Eternity. They kept an eye on Heaven. They did not love *this life* more than they loved the thought of being with Jesus, and they knew and understood that in order to be with Jesus, they would have to die. So, they diligently prepared to die well.

As a great piece of music builds toward its finale, or a sports event moves toward a goal and a prize, so the aim of a Christian must be to finish well. We need to see that it is *normal* and *needful* for a Christian to make all effort to do so.

As followers of Jesus, we look at death through the lens of the Gospel. As believers in Jesus, we must have neither a morbid fascination with death nor a fanciful denial of death. Death has been defeated through the death of Jesus and His victorious resurrection. John Owen, a Puritan, actually wrote a book entitled *The Death of Death in the Death of Christ!*[20] Death no longer has power over us, and the grave will not have the final say over us.

Considering our death makes us wise for life. Psalm 90:12 invites us to ask God to '[t]each us to number our days, that we may gain a heart of wisdom'. We gain focus. We stop wasting time and energy on useless things. We love better. We endure better. Remembering our approaching death actually causes us to treasure this transient life while at the same time holding it with loose hands. The ordinary becomes sacred. Fleeting moments become valuable. Gospel opportunities become treasured moments not to be wasted. Family meals, church services, days at the office, happy times, hardships, feasts, and fastings all take on new value and proper perspective when we keep death in view.

Remembering our impending death humbles us. And it is *always* good for us to be humbled. We are safe when we are low. *Nothing* is diminished when a Christian contemplates his death. Everything is enhanced.

But Jonathan does not stop at thinking 'much on all occasions' about his death. He thinks also of 'the common circumstances which attend death'. In other words, what is typical about one's dying day? How do people actually die? It is foolish and brazen for believers to think that we will get a free pass from the trials which accompany dying. We too must embrace the 'common circumstances'. We get sick. Our bodies begin to fail. We have racking pain. Or we are suddenly taken without notice. We go to sleep one night, not to awaken in the morning. An accident overtakes us. A virus steals in and with a cough we are gone. The doctor's office phones, and it is not good news. These are 'common occurrences'.

As a pastor, over the years, I have seen many people die. Some have been ready; some have not. Not all Christians die well. I make this observation regarding the 'common circumstances which attend death'. No matter how death comes upon us, it is foolhardy to believe that we can wait until we are dying to put anything right. Sometimes a believer is privileged to see their death approaching and 'put their house in order', but often people are too sick to think, in too much pain to repent, to correct relationships, or to do anything meaningful. Sometimes death comes in an unexpected instant. The common circumstances which attend death will prevent most of us from making last-minute repairs. We need to live every day with the accounts cleared, and the books balanced.

Now … Smile. I mean it. SMILE! We have a Saviour 'who has destroyed death and has brought life and immortality to light through the gospel' (2 Tim.1:10). We will benefit in every area of our lives (I mean that) if we think often of our last day. We do not need to walk in fear. We do not need to pretend or ignore. We agree with God that life is brief and uncertain, that Jesus has conquered death, that we have conquered with Him, and that the grave will not have the final say over us. So …

Prepare every day to die, and then get on and live for Jesus, the Gospel, and others!

We are Resurrection People!

My flesh and my heart may fail,
but God is the strength of my heart
and my portion forever.
(Ps. 73:26)

Soar we now where Christ has led, Alleluia!
Following our exalted Head, Alleluia!
Made like him, like him we rise, Alleluia!
Ours the cross, the grave, the skies, Alleluia!
(Charles Wesley)

Resolution 10

Resolved, when I feel pain, to think of the pains of martyrdom, and of hell.

At this they covered their ears and, yelling at the top of their voices, they all rushed at him, dragged him out of the city and began to stone him ... While they were stoning him, Stephen prayed, 'Lord Jesus, receive my spirit.' Then he fell on his knees and cried out, 'Lord, do not hold this sin against them.' When he had said this, he fell asleep.
(Acts 7:57–60)

So, he called to him, 'Father Abraham, have pity on me and send Lazarus to dip the tip of his finger in water and cool my tongue, because I am in agony in this fire.' (Luke 16:24)

Dear Friends,

In these days of relentless tragedy in the news, this *Resolution* is very timely: it is about perspective; it is about context; it is about thinking deeply. It is a simple, plain, understandable, and realistic statement. It has life-changing power.

When it came time for Jonathan Edwards to die, his was a most painful and horrible death. At the age of 54, with a wife and eleven children, a smallpox inoculation went wrong, and he contracted the dreaded disease. His death was excruciating. This *Resolution,* which we remember he would have read weekly for 35 years – some 1,800 times – must have been a strengthening elixir in his great hour of need.

Here is Jonathan's premise: Life has painful seasons; for some of us our lives are like a never-ending winter of pain; others know sunny days but storms loom. Pain is not polite. It does not form an orderly queue. It does not take a number. It does not wait its turn.

Here is Jonathan's strategy: While we must not make light of our pain, we can put pain in perspective. Many of us are experiencing profound pain. Indeed, our entire society – our world – is in a season of extraordinary pain. But Jonathan has wisdom for us here: My pain today is slight when placed alongside the pains that many have suffered, and are suffering, for Jesus' sake, and when compared to the pains that I deserve – but have been delivered from – in hell.

Consider the pain of our martyred sisters and brothers. Whenever Jonathan feels pain, he has resolved to consider it in the light of the myriad of brothers and sisters in Jesus who have been tortured and finally killed for their confession of Christ. He considers their separation from loved ones, their deprivations, their emotional and physical torture, their violent and vicious deaths.

The 20th century was the bloodiest century for Christians ever, with more dying for Christ in that century than in the previous nineteen together. The Gordon-Conwell Seminary Center for the Study of Global Christianity estimates that about 90,000 believers in Jesus are martyred every year. That is one every six minutes.[21]

Jonathan takes his cue straight from the Bible when, in his own suffering, he remembers those who have paid with their lives. He is not being fanatical here, but biblical, reflecting on the heroes of the faith in Hebrews and on Jesus, '*who endured such opposition from sinners*' against Himself. (11:35–38; 12:3, 4)

By putting his pain into this perspective, Jonathan is avoiding destructive self-pity. He is steeling himself against any ingress of bitterness or accusation toward God. He is drawing inspiration. While not making light of our present sufferings, considering our brothers and sisters imprisoned today in the cruellest of circumstances, and those who will die as we read this, is a great help for us. We are enabled to retain a sweet heart of faith and thanksgiving. Whether your pain be physical, relational, emotional, or financial, take his pastoral advice and apply it like a salve to your situation.

Elyse M. Fitzpatrick reminds us that the comforts of martyrs are

Gospel comforts. As the wonders of Christ crucified and risen sustain them in their trials, they surely will sustain us in ours.

When those early [and present day] Christians faced the chains and the beatings and felt the lick of the flame, the humiliation of the stripping, the mocking and the persecution, they didn't assuage their breaking hearts through a rehearsal of their personal accomplishments. They remembered that God became a man; He died and rose again; He is ruling as the ascended Lord, and He is also dwelling within – their only hope of glory. What do you need to remember today? The same thing: the incarnation, the resurrection, the ascension. Believe the Gospel ...[22]

And the pains of hell? Why should a Christian ever think of these? Considering these delivers us from the temptation to accuse God of being 'unfair' in regard to our pain. Let's admit it, we can sometimes be tempted to lift a hand toward God in protest that 'we deserve better'. Oh friends! Let us be careful here! What I *deserve* is hell and judgment. What I *get* is forgiveness of sins and Life Eternal!

He does not treat us as our sins deserve or repay us according to our iniquities. (Ps. 103:10)

Is God 'unfair'? You bet He is! If God were 'fair' to me, I would go to hell. He is *gracious*. He does *not* give me what I deserve. I need to remember the deserved pains of hell from which I have been saved – and the *un*deserved joys of Heaven which await me – when I am tempted to complain to God about my temporal pains. Doing so will deliver me from a bitter, accusing spirit, and bring a sweetness toward God into my present painful situation.

Oh, to have a well-instructed soul which learns to think and dwell upon solid truths! Solid truth will deliver solid comfort to our souls, even through the deepest trials.

Again, thank you, Jonathan.

I am not my own, but belong with body and soul, both in life and in death to my faithful Saviour, Jesus Christ.
(Heidelberg Catechism)[23]

Resolution 11

Resolved, as far as possible, when presented with something wonderful and puzzling about God and His ways, to not delay in opening my Bible and my heart to search and discover all that God has revealed to me about Himself.

The secret things belong to the Lord our God, but the things revealed belong to us and to our children forever. (Deut. 29:29)

Dear Friends,

We have been created to know God. Sin has been dealt with by Jesus, not simply so that we can 'go to Heaven', but so that we can *know God.* What makes Heaven heavenly is that that is where God is.

I can promise you that the greatest need in your life, the deepest desire of your heart (even if you do not know it), is to deepen your knowledge of God. The same is true for me.

Now God is not hiding; He discloses Himself. He *wants* to be known. He speaks to us through His creation. But more, He has spoken conclusively to us through Jesus Christ, and has given us the Bible as a faithful record of His self-disclosure. And the Bible will give up its treasures to anyone who is dissatisfied with surface things and dares to dig. Knowing God is not the reserve of pastors and PhDs. No! Anyone can, with an open Bible and the help of the Holy Spirit, know God truly and deeply. Not *exhaustively* – that would make us God – but just because we cannot know *everything* about God, does not mean we cannot know God *truly* and *sufficiently.* The problem is that we often do not want to. We are content with a dim knowledge of Him who has created us to be thrilled by Him. We end up fascinated by the frivolous and temporal and bored by the weighty and eternal.

Are you bored?

I am often spurred on in my pursuit of Jesus by the stories of those who were very far from bored in their life's endeavour.

George Washington Carver (1864–1943) was born into slavery. As a young black man in the Reconstruction South, life was stacked against him. Kidnapped, orphaned, unable to begin school until age twelve, he nevertheless had an insatiable curiosity for life. He loved to learn and eventually entered Iowa Agricultural College (now Iowa State University), where he achieved his Bachelor's and then his Master's in botany. These achievements for a man of colour in his day were testimony to his resolve in overcoming racial obstacles and to his sheer dedication to learning. Carver eventually taught at the Tuskegee Institute in Alabama. Faced with an agricultural crisis in the southern USA, through tireless research, he is credited with 'saving the South' by delivering it from the monocrop of cotton. He introduced the peanut as a cash crop and developed more than three hundred commercial uses for it, as well as hundreds more for soybeans and sweet potatoes.

George applied his mind to learning for the sake of others. He was offered huge salaries to leave the South and go and work for the likes of Thomas Edison and Henry Ford, but he declined, drawing a meagre $125 per month for more than forty years at Tuskegee. His calling was to discover; as a devoted follower of Jesus Christ, he said of his many discoveries, 'God gave them to me. How can I sell them to someone else?' His tombstone bears the words:

> He could have added fortune to fame, but caring for neither,
> he found happiness and honour in being helpful to the world.

George was provoked by mysteries and unanswered questions to a life of discovery. In the same way, Jonathan Edwards longed to discover all that he could of Christ and Christian Truth. Sadly, few today apply their minds to the diligent, fascinating study of Jesus, 'in whom are hidden all the treasures of wisdom and knowledge' (Col. 2:3).

We are satisfied with surface, elementary knowledge where the most important subject is concerned, while at the same time we apply all sorts of effort and diligence to lesser subjects, some important, some not. But Carver's brilliant observation, 'If you love it enough, anything will talk with you,'[24] applies to the Bible as surely as it did to his peanuts!

Believing that God talks with us truthfully, authoritatively, clearly, and sufficiently in the Bible, Edwards set out to discover all that he could about Him this side of Heaven. Jon was not content to shrug his shoulders and mumble, 'I dunno', to theological puzzles. He aimed to search the Scriptures, pray and ponder, study, and beat on the door of Truth until he had answers ... not to the 'secret things of God', but to those 'things revealed', to everything that God has given to us to know. Being determined to 'grow in the grace and knowledge of our Lord and Saviour Jesus Christ' (2 Pet. 3:18), his writings and his sermons became rich resources – carefully woven tapestries of biblical Truth and real experience. They were not removed from life, not the products of sheltered study, but the products of a life lived in the warp and woof of authentic discipleship.

Like Carver, Jonathan Edwards was useful because he applied himself to learning. How we need such men and women today! How the work of God cries out for hungry students of Truth who will resolve to solve! On our knees before God, let's ask Him to give us hearts to know Him in truth! In the end, we are as happy, holy, and useful as we want to be. There will never be an easier time to get serious with Jesus and Truth than right now.

I want to know Christ ... (Phil. 3:10)

Once you become aware that the main business that you are here for is to know God, most of life's problems fall into place of their own accord.[25] (J.I. Packer)

Resolution 12

Resolved, that if I take delight in the discovery of a wonder of God because it makes me think highly of myself, or if I hope that others will see my accomplishment and think much of me, I will waste no time in laying that discovery aside until I can enjoy it only to the Glory of God, the betterment of myself, and the blessing of others.

We all possess knowledge. But knowledge puffs up while love builds up.
(1 Cor. 8:1)

Dear Ones,

Remember Jonathan's last *Resolution* with me: that he will diligently and avidly seek after a true knowledge of God and His ways. But our young friend sees two deadly vipers hidden in the pathway of all discovery and knowledge: pride and vanity.

Pride: The tendency to think more highly of yourself than you ought.

Vanity: The desire to have others think more highly of you than they ought.

All true and genuine discovery of Jesus and His ways should humble the explorer. How can it not, when God is eternal, unchanging, holy, and awesome, while man is temporal, transient, sinful, and pitiful? And yet God gives us grace and means to discover *Him*. How can this do anything but humble us? I remember John Piper saying that no one goes to the Grand Canyon to boost *their own* self-esteem. No! The vista humbles the observer. How much more *must* the beholding of the ineffable God produce reverent awe in the worshipper!

A 20-year-old Charles Spurgeon reminded us that God 'is so deep, that all our pride is drowned in [His] infinity' and that, '... in ...

Christ there is a balm for every wound, a healing for every grief.'[26] Two things should happen when wonderful things about God are discovered: the proud should be reduced and broken and the humble should be lifted up and healed. But sadly, and more often than not, a third thing happens: the discoverer becomes proud and puffed up. He feels himself superior because of what he knows. Having – in the midst of his Bible reading – forgotten that he is nothing and that God is everything, he has begun to think that he is something special and that his learning has placed him above others. This is offensive to God, for, 'God opposes the proud' (James 4:6). When we stop and think about it, little else can be as offensive – and as *silly* – as pride in one's knowledge of God, the God who made Himself nothing to save miserable offenders, the God of Whom we would know *nothing at all* were He not gracious to show us Himself.

Now, Jonathan's *Resolution* requires him to know his own heart very well. It demands that we bring our hearts daily before the Lord, praying with the Psalmist:

> Lord ... you know me ... Search me, God, and know my heart; test me
> and know my anxious thoughts. See if there is any offensive way in me
> and lead me in the way everlasting. (Ps. 139:1, 23–24)

When Jon learns something wonderful about God, if he somehow feels himself superior or desires for others to see his advancement, he quickly employs a simple soul-defending strategy: He lays that discovery aside like one would lay aside a razor-sharp knife, until such a time as he can hold it rightly and employ it only for the Glory of God, for the proper good of himself, and the good of others. He will not allow his spiritual knowledge to be an occasion for showing off. He knows that pride is deadly – especially when cloaked in spirituality! It is destructive to one's own soul and to all others within range! It separates. It divides. It destroys peace. Pride is the very foundation of Satan's Kingdom, while humility is the bedrock of Christ's.

All sin, every war, each division is built upon that evil foundation of pride. And pride finds a home in 'religion' as certainly as it does in 'the world'. Indeed, entire churches and denominations have been founded upon ... *pride*! Pride often causes followers of Jesus to divide from other followers of Jesus. Being convinced that 'I am right' (and I might be) can lead me to no longer walk with a brother for whom Christ died. In that case, while my position might be right, my posture is certainly wrong. How the heart of Jesus must break! Pride leads one down an increasingly narrow path until there is no room for anyone to walk alongside ... including Jesus! Jonathan will have nothing of it. Neither must we. Any true encounter with God and the truth of God will lead one toward other believers – especially weaker ones, especially ones who might differ from you – in a humble desire to serve them and walk in meaningful fellowship with them.

True discovery, where Christ is concerned, brings joy and a humbling sense of how little one really knows. It should make one sweeter and easier to live with! Sometimes I need to examine myself and ask: What is making me cross? Why is that brother bugging me? Why am I losing my peace? Why am I discouraged? Have I not been noticed? Have I been passed over? Have I not been applauded? Has someone been preferred before me? Has my pride been aroused? Oh friends! May we seek God and His ways – but on our knees. And may every discovery, every step of growth, serve only to bring us to a new place of humble adoration of the wonders and goodness of our gracious God.

Nothing sets a person so much out of the devil's reach as humility.[27]
(Jonathan Edwards)

Resolution 13

Resolved to be eagerly seeking out those to whom I can be generous and charitable.

But when you give a banquet, invite the poor, the crippled, the lame, the blind, and you will be blessed. Although they cannot repay you, you will be repaid at the resurrection of the righteous. (Luke 14:13–14)

Dear Friends in Jesus,

What great Gospel days we are living in! What perfect times to reach our culture with the love of Jesus! These are *our days of opportunity.* We need to pray for, and receive, a spirit of abounding, lavish generosity that we might lead a revolution of Jesus-empowered love. Jonathan Edwards' *Resolutions* cannot be contained in the small world of private faith. They must spill over into the wide world of public action. A heart that is extravagant for Jesus must be a heart that is extravagant toward others.

The same year that Jonathan was born in Connecticut, 1703, John Wesley was born in Epworth, England. While the two never met, they would certainly have known of each other through their mutual friend, George Whitefield. Wesley was not a perfect man. But the grace of God in his life spilled over into extravagant giving to others. For him, holiness could not remain private. He maintained that here is no holiness that is not social holiness. Bearing in mind that he had no children to support and no heirs to care for, his life's record of generosity bears remarkable testimony to the holiness of his heart. Over the course of his lifetime, he generated tremendous wealth through the selling of books and writings. Yet the more he made, the more he gave. Zach Van Zant, in his article *The Radical Budget of John Wesley*, gives us the details:

> His first year at Oxford, his income was 30 pounds a year (enough for a comfortable living for a single individual). Through budgeting, he found that he could live on 28, and gave away 2. In his second year, his income doubled to 60 pounds, but he kept his expenses the same, and thus gave away 32 pounds (more than he kept for himself). This process continued, even as his income vastly grew.[28]

Eventually, John Wesley was giving away 98% of his income. This is what *Jesus does* when He gets a hold of a heart.

Has He gotten a hold of your heart?

Is He the sole owner of mine?

As our culture is gripped by a grave crisis, *we* need to be gripped by something greater: the grace of God. As others 'hunker down', it is time for us to 'break out'. We have a chance now to move against the spirit of our age. Our age has often been marked by selfish gain. A looming economic crisis is spreading a pandemic of fear. A spirit of 'looking out for number one' is infecting people far and wide. How the people of Jesus need to demonstrate the values of the coming Kingdom right now! There is a fascinating look at the overwhelming, grace-fuelled generosity of the early Christians in Acts 11:27–30: A famine is prophesied … for the entire Roman world. What is the response of the disciples? *'The disciples, as each one was able, decided to provide help for the brothers and sisters living in Judea.'*

Question: Who thinks like this? Answer: People who have become citizens of a New Kingdom, who have heard the words of Jesus:

> *Do not be afraid, little flock, for your Father has been pleased to give you the kingdom. Sell your possessions and give to the poor. Provide purses for yourselves that will not wear out, a treasure in heaven that will never fail, where no thief comes near and no moth destroys. For where your treasure is, there your heart will be also.* (Luke 12:32–34)

A spirit of radical, extravagant generosity finally boils down to how I view God (doesn't everything?). Do I really get that He has been wildly good to me? Do I really believe that He is my Portion, my

Treasure, my Enough? Do I truly trust that He is good and will always outgive me, whatever I give to others? (I am not trying to abuse this like the 'prosperity preachers' do, but it is true that I can never outgive God.)

Generosity results in something even greater than people getting blessed. It results in God being blessed. His Father-heart must be so warmed when the generosity He has poured into us is poured out of us to others. And all of this redounds in praise and thanksgiving back to the God who gave in the first place. The circle is completed: *'This service ... is overflowing in many expressions of thanks to God'* (2 Cor. 9:12).

Here is a plea to all happy citizens of a New Kingdom in these great days of Gospel opportunity: What if we – each and every one of us – deliberately and joyfully seek to simplify our lives so that we can give more freely to the cause of Jesus in our day? How about adopting a 'war-time' instead of a 'play-time' mentality to free up our (vast) resources for Kingdom-minded living and giving? Lord Jesus! Work this in us! Cause us to be so sure of your ever-generous disposition towards us that we will become increasingly extravagant givers in this age of greed and fear. Make us eager to seek out those in need, and ever eager to seek to meet those needs. And may this all result in You being blessed and praised in endless expressions of thanks to You.

And God is able to make all grace abound to you, [so]that always having all sufficiency in everything, you may have an abundance for every good deed. (2 Cor. 9:6–8)

A whole lot of what we call 'struggling' is simply delayed obedience.[29]
(Elizabeth Elliot)

Resolution 14

Resolved never to allow any feelings or actions of anger towards irrational beings.

Everyone should be quick to listen, slow to speak and slow to become angry, because human anger does not produce the righteousness that God desires. (Jas. 1:19–20)

Friends in Jesus,

Have you ever kicked your dog? How about screaming at your computer? Do you always respond sweetly, in a Jesus-loving way, to the distant voice in those telemarketing calls you receive? You don't slam the phone down, do you? A bit of road rage now and then? Does your spouse 'get your hackles up' when she 'just doesn't get it'?

The dog did not make me mad. He only gave occasion for the inner me – the *real* me – to come out. Your anger is not your phone's fault. You are responsible for your response. Your wife did not understand what you meant, but your sharp response says more about you than about her.

We might think Jonathan Edwards has gone too far. The popular taunt these days is to accuse him of overreach. But our young mentor is actually onto something here. He is taking us deep – to heart matters. Like a wise physician, he is looking for the tell-tale evidence of deadly disease.

By 'irrational beings' Jonathan simply means creatures who don't know better. In Jonathan's day, he probably thought of his horse. Today it might be the dog, your child in certain circumstances, the old lady who cannot back her car up straight, that snail-slow kid at the check-out counter. It could be your husband at times when he is out of his depth. (My wife once sent me to the cabinet to get her 'pink make-up.' At that point, *I* was certainly an 'irrational being' in need of mercy and not anger!) I think we can fairly expand the *Resolution* to include inanimate objects: phones, lawn mowers, computers – whatever gets the sharp end of our 'Why won't this stupid thing work?' exasperation. It will be helpful to stand back for a moment and remind ourselves of what God wants in our salvation. He is not just after outward obedience. He is wanting sons and daughters, not slaves. He wants to reproduce His character in us.

And consider His character as He displays it toward us, who, compared to Him, are all at times 'irrational beings'. He (thankfully) is never short-tempered, capricious, or irritable but, since His aim is transformation, not just reformation, He must deal with us at depth – at heart level. Jesus cares about things which often – at least for a while – remain unseen by others: things like peevishness, fault-finding, and unwarranted anger. Jesus said,

> *You have heard that it was said of those of old, you shalt not murder; and whoever murders shall be in danger of the judgment: But I say to you that whoever is angry with his brother without a cause shall be in danger of the judgment.* (Matt. 5:21–22, NKJV)

As a doctor is concerned with hidden cancer cells, not just with full-grown tumours, so Jesus sees the tell-tale trouble spots that perhaps no-one else sees: That golf club I threw, that irked response to my wife, that irritability, that little fit over the lost TV remote, me being bothered because the barista did not make the coffee to my liking ('Can't a person just get a decent cup of coffee around here?').

These things are *revealing*. And, left unchecked, if allowed to play out their natural course, left to grow and fester, they become destructive outward behaviour. They do not stay politely in their place. They break out. They grow. If unchecked, ungodly attitudes and angers can ruin lives and even generations. God sees the little things, the seemingly trifling attitudes and actions that we excuse and overlook. It is *not* that God is picky. It is not that He is impossible to please. It is that He is *loving*. He is *wise*. He is *thorough*. He really intends to get us through this dangerous life and safe into our Heavenly home. He really sees that the greatest dangers are not outward, but inward – right in our own hearts and in the secret places. The root of all this is sinful self-righteousness, wanting my own way, and, therefore, being annoyed at others for not bowing to me and my agenda.

God won't have it. And neither should we. God really intends to make us like Jesus. Entire transformation is His goal. It may not be yours, but it is His. We might be content with a little change in outward behaviour – giving up drunkenness or swearing. But God does not stop there. He will redo us all the way.

> ... *He who began a good work in you will carry it on to completion until the day of Christ Jesus.* (Phil. 1:6)

The make-over is to be complete. God will sweeten us all the way through. He will beautify to the core. I once knew a good and godly pastor who would regularly pray, 'Lord, when somebody kicks me, let them get honey all over their foot!' Invite God, the Holy Spirit, to bring a new sense of conviction to you regarding your attitudes, angers, and seemingly trifling irritations. Learn to abhor these as you would poison in the pot. And then, ask God to help you love the beauty and sweetness of a pure, love-filled heart. Be glad to be able to say as a physician would, 'It was bad ... but we caught it early'. Let us not settle for less than all that God has for us in saving us from sin and unto Christ-like holiness, for,

> *The unfading beauty of a gentle and quiet spirit ... is of great worth in God's sight.* (1 Pet. 3:4)

> A cup brimful of sweet water cannot spill even one drop of bitter water, however suddenly jolted.[30] (Amy Carmichael)

Resolution 15

Resolved never to do anything out of revenge.

Do not take revenge, my dear friends, but leave room for God's wrath, for it is written: 'It is mine to avenge; I will repay,' says the Lord. (Rom. 12:9)

Dear Friends in Jesus,

Cain, Samson, Jezebel, Absalom, Herodias, Haman, Saul, Joab. The stories of men and women whose lives were driven by – and ruined by – a desire to get even are almost too many to count in the Bible. They give warning to us that a vengeful spirit is a doomed spirit and that a desire to seek out one's own view of justice hews a path of destruction.

In exploring Jonathan Edwards' *Resolution* 'to never do anything out of revenge', we could write pages. But go for yourself and read some of the stories of the characters named above. See the ruin of revenge. Even if one's revenge is not literally expressed – as it was in Absalom's tragic life – it will fester and rot you from within until it ruins you and those around you, because bitterness and vengefulness are never found alone. They bear many children. They have a large family. Just look at their names!

Get rid of all bitterness, rage and anger, brawling and slander, along with every form of malice. (Eph. 4:31)

Rage! Anger! Brawling! Slander! Malice!

Consider with me:

Firstly: If I am going to live for Jesus, people will hurt me, misunderstand me, and take advantage of me. So be it. I have Jesus, and He understands. I will, by grace, seek a sweet spirit of forgiveness and refuse to nurse a vengeful heart. I will leave retribution to Him and 'as far as possible ... live at peace with everyone' (Rom. 12:18).

Then: If I am going to live a life that is effective for Jesus, if I am going to be useful to God, then I do not have the *time or energy* to have a bitter, vengeful heart. A vengeful spirit is a drain on everything good. It consumes thought time. (Have you ever spent time mulling over what you 'would say to so-and-so' if given the chance?) It ruins prayer time. It robs joy. It taxes strength. It side-tracks from good endeavours. If I want my life to count (and I do), then I do not have the perverse luxury of expending my energy and efforts in 'trying to get even' or daydreaming about giving some offender a 'piece of my mind'. I am a servant of Jesus! I have a Kingdom to proclaim and a Saviour to live for! I have all Heaven ahead of me. I can endure a bit of abuse along the way.

And also: seeking revenge is brazenly predicated upon the self-righteous thought that I occupy some moral high ground over another person. It cannot exist without the ridiculous notion that *I* have a clear understanding of all the facts, and *I* am in a position to justly punish. What foolishness!

Am I not a sinner too? Is there no speck (or beam!) in my eye as well? Have I not been forgiven by our Holy God of infinite crimes against His Highness? Do I not stand by grace alone? Do I have complete knowledge of another's heart and motives? Is not my own heart enough for me to deal with? Has not Jesus already died for that very sin my brother committed against me? Dare I hold against him what Jesus has atoned for? Must I not freely forgive him?

Consider Corrie ten Boom (1892–1983). How she suffered at the hands of the Nazis in Ravensbruck concentration camp! Her sister, Betsie, died in that camp. In 1947, she was preaching in Germany when she was approached by a man whom she recognized as one who had been a cruel Ravensbruck guard. That man extended a hand to her, asking her for her forgiveness:

I stood there with ... coldness clutching my heart. But forgiveness is not an emotion ... Forgiveness is an act of the will, and the will can function regardless of the temperature of the heart.

'Jesus, help me!' I prayed silently. 'I can lift my hand. I can do that much. You supply the feeling.'

And so woodenly, mechanically, I thrust my hand into the one stretched out to me. And as I did, an incredible thing took place. The current started in my shoulder, raced down my arm, sprang into our joined hands.

And then this healing warmth seemed to flood my whole being, bringing tears to my eyes. 'I forgive you, brother!' I cried. 'With all my heart!'[31]

You and I will probably never walk through the abuse and mistreatment that Corrie did, far less that Jesus did. And yet we learn that '[w]hen they hurled their insults at him, he did not retaliate; when he suffered, he made no threats. Instead, he entrusted himself to him who judges justly' (1 Pet. 2:23). God, and God alone, is able to rightly execute revenge. He alone occupies the office of Judge. He is righteous in all that He does, and is moved by the pure motives of His Glory, the security of His redeemed, and the good of all creation. My revenge will inevitably be tainted by sin and selfishness. God is infinitely more patient and measured than I. I will take a sledgehammer to a nut. God's vengeance will be exact and never provoke an apology from Him. We can therefore leave our case and cause with Him, release people from their debt to us for pain caused, walk in forgiveness and peace with all men and women, *and go live for Jesus!*

If we will serve Jesus and His Gospel, then we have not the strength or time for anything less than free hearts of love toward all.

Those who were able to forgive their former enemies were able also to return to the outside world and rebuild their lives, no matter what the physical scars. Those who nursed their bitterness remained invalids. It was as simple and as horrible as that.[32] (Corrie ten Boom)

Resolution 16

Resolved never to speak with a motive to dishonour anyone, and, if I speak negatively of anyone, to do so only if it is necessary for their genuine good.

The King will reply, 'Truly I tell you, whatever you did for one of the least of these brothers and sisters of mine, you did for me.' (Matt. 25:40)

Dear Friends,

Oh, to be delivered from every ounce of sourness, fault-finding, and tale-bearing: from a perverse delight in discovering – and then discussing – the faults and failures of another! Jesus takes that behaviour terribly personally. His razor-sharp teaching in Matthew 25, with the cutting edge being those words 'whatever you did [for others] you did for me', apply not just to good works of charity, but certainly as well to unkind words of gossip. He loves the people we are speaking unkindly about. Just think about that! How would you like it if someone was speaking in a cutting way about your dearest?

Christ died for that one – and their faults – whom we are delighting to criticise and to denigrate to others.

Personally, I need real help here. I confess to you and to all that I have broken Jesus' heart in this manner more times than can ever be counted. Oh, may His blood atone for my sins in this regard! That whisper, that 'tut-tut', those unkind words, that little bounce of glee over another's missteps are grievous sins that need to be confessed and cleansed by Jesus' blood.

The fact that my unkind words about another offend God is bad enough. But they also offend me, the offender. The one who shares the malicious morsel actually poisons his own soul in so doing. I cannot be walking intimately with Jesus and be breaking His heart at the same time. My *abiding* in Christ is interrupted, so my fruitfulness is diminished. Love, joy, peace, patience, kindness, goodness, gentleness, self-control, these precious fruits of God's Spirit, are stunted when I spoil my intimacy with my Saviour by my malicious attitude and speech.

But the poison spreads farther than God and myself. These unkind words do not stay put: they stray. What I whisper in the ear, what I say in private, if said from a motive to dishonour another, finds its way out. It is inevitable. Then fellowship is broken, people are hurt, secrecy becomes suspicion, teams are destroyed, the Gospel suffers, churches fracture.

But replace these bitter, sour words with sweetness: oh, to *abide* in Jesus and have His nature formed within us; oh, to have hearts that are so transformed by grace that we are overflowing with love for all; oh, to have a heart that is moved *only* by love for one another, that would not *dare* speak against one for whom Christ has suffered and died: that should be our goal. God gives us language to build up, not to tear down – to encourage, not to hurt.

The spiritual discipline of controlling one's words, of never speaking unkindly to or about anyone unless it is absolutely necessary for their well-being, is a major battle for each of us. But fighting it is not optional.

> Do not let any unwholesome talk come out of your mouths, but only what is helpful for building others up according to their needs, that it may benefit those who listen. And do not grieve the Holy Spirit of God, with whom you were sealed for the day of redemption. (Eph. 4:29–32)

Of course, sometimes we might have to share a painful word with or even about someone. Be careful here! Make sure that your heart is right before God before you venture a sound! Have you wept first? Has your heart broken first? Here are two preachers: Both find a need to speak a word of warning about some man's ministry. One is weeping as he speaks while the other is wagging his head and sounding off. Which is pleasing to Jesus? Which is helpful? I get terribly concerned when I find myself delighting in someone pointing out the faults of an aberrant preacher or politician. We dare not take delight in the faults of another. We should grieve, our hearts should break, and, if we *must* speak, we had better speak from a place of brokenness and sorrow, with no motive other than to bring help and healing.

Gossip, in Romans 1, is listed alongside murder, for it kills spiritual life, relationships, missions, families, and so much more. And it is as much a sin to receive it as to give it!

I spread gossip not just by speaking unkind words, but by receiving them as well. Here are three questions to ask a talebearer that will stop gossip in its tracks:

1) Why are you telling me this?
2) Does Bill know that you are telling me this?
3) If I go to discuss this with Bill, can I quote you as my source?

Beloved, may we seek all grace (for God will give it) to be so filled with the sweetness of Jesus that our words will ever and only be to build one another up. May it be that we never take delight in the faults of another. May we always and only bring honour to God as we speak well and humbly about those for whom Jesus died.

Lord Jesus! May your love conquer me in every way!

If anyone speaks, they should do so as one who speaks the very words
of God ... so that in all things God may be praised through Jesus Christ
(1 Pet. 4:11)

With the help of grace, the habit of saying kind words is very quickly formed, and when once formed, it is not speedily lost.[33]
(Fredrick W. Faber)

Resolution 17

Resolved that I will live as I will wish I had done when I come to die.

By the grace God has given me, I laid a foundation as a wise builder ...
But each one should build with care. (1 Cor. 3:10)

Dear Pilgrim,

Many years ago, I heard a statement from a preacher that arrested me. I think the preacher was Stephen Olford.[34] If my memory fails me as to who the preacher was, it does not fail me as to what the preacher said:

> You had better build a good life because you are going to spend eternity with it.

The story goes of a builder who was asked by a generous and kind man of means to build a fine house. The builder, not being given to diligence, cut many corners, hid many defects, and overall made a shoddy job of it.

'The owner will never know', he thought. Upon completion, the builder presented the house to the kind man as a 'job well done', only to have that generous man hand the keys right back to the shifty builder with the words, 'You did not know it, but you built this fine house for yourself, my friend, for I am giving it to you as a gift'.

This brief life is valuable, not only for its own sake, but because it spills over into the next.

Jonathan Edwards lived with an eye on Heaven. Even as a young man, he saw life as brief, and Eternity as near. How wise we will be to do the same! This *Resolution* carries with it both a *backward* glance and a *forward* gaze. Soon, our precious, fleeting sojourn on Earth will end. To then look back and see our lives as having been lived for Jesus and His Eternal Kingdom should be in our thoughts every day.

How many backward glances bring regret and tears?

May it not be so with you and with me! May we not be like the man who climbed to the top of the ladder only to find he had it leaning against the wrong wall! Heaven is ahead. Joy unspeakable awaits every redeemed soul. Feet-dragging-following is sure to produce regret at the end. No man or woman ever got to the end of their days and regretted being sold-out for Jesus.

I remember a story about the short life of William Borden (1887–1913). Six words were written in the back of his Bible, words that belong together. Perhaps you can write them not just in your Bible, but into your life's story:

No Retreats, No Reserves, No Regrets.

Grace frees us to choose Jesus over lesser things every day and those choices have eternal significance.

But what of the forward gaze? Ah, friend! There is no greater motive for an all-in following after Jesus than a bright hope of Heaven. Nothing steels the resolve like the knowledge that soon we will be with Jesus! What empowers simple believers to make otherwise impossible choices? What ennobles the soul to say 'yes' to God when it will cost one dearly to do so? What spurs on mission and service when ease and comfort beckon? What keeps a spouse faithful in the midst of a nearly impossible marriage? What strengthens one to praise and rejoice in the midst of agonizing illness with no happy ending in this life?

What is there like the hope of Heaven?

Living with a future hope is transformational. *Today* is transformed by my view of *tomorrow*. My view of the future shapes me right now. If I want to 'live as I will wish I had done when I come to die', then a bright view of the joy that is ahead is the best nourishment for me today. Think about it: Even Jesus, as He anticipated the cross, was motivated by Heaven:

> For the joy that was set before him he endured the cross, scorning its shame, and sat down at the right hand of the throne of God.
> (Heb. 12:2)

Do you see that? Jesus was enabled to do His Father's will – atone for our sins on the cross – because He focused on the *eternal joy* beyond the trial. Over and over, the Bible points us to future joy as a motive for present perseverance (see, for example, 2 Cor. 4:17; 1 Pet. 5:10; Rom. 3:3–5).

Jonathan, in a sermon entitled *The Portion of the Righteous,* presents a beautiful picture of the joy and happiness of Heaven. I want this picture to spur you and me toward 'no reserves, no retreats, no regrets' living.

He imagines Heaven as a boundless sea of happiness, into which each believer is cast. Seeing each believer as a vessel (jar), each will be filled to the brim with the happiness of God. But some believers, *because of their responses to grace in this life* will have greater capacity than others:

For all shall be perfectly happy; every one shall be perfectly satisfied. Every vessel that is cast into this ocean of happiness is full, though there are some vessels far larger than others.[35]

Why settle for a thimble-sized capacity for joy when God would want to fill a gallon? There is no shortage of happiness in Christ! Do you want to live as you 'will wish [you] had done when [you] come to die'? Then, certainly, live with regard to your backward glance. By grace, make choices that will finally leave no regret. But more, live with regard to your forward gaze. There is such glory ahead! May it be that the bright hope of Heaven fashions our today toward Jesus-shaped living tomorrow. Trust the One *'who is able to keep you from stumbling and to present you before his glorious presence without fault and with great joy'* (Jude 24–25).

Walk as if the next step would carry you across the threshold of Heaven.[36] (Jim Elliot)

Resolution 18

Resolved to live on my worst days as I already have determined to live on my best days, when my heart was most devout, when my mind best understood God's truths, and my spirit most longed for Heaven.

Has God forgotten to be merciful?
Has he in anger withheld his compassion?

Then I thought, 'To this I will appeal:
To the years when the Most High stretched out his right hand.
I will remember the deeds of the Lord;
yes, I will remember your miracles of long ago ...
(Ps. 77:9–11)

Dear Friends,

Praise God for His special times of grace and favour! Those seasons when the Bible seems to open itself, when prayer flows without hindrance, when the veil between earth and Heaven is paper thin, are all precious foretastes of a feast to come.

During such times we can make great spiritual progress. There are seasons when our heart's devotion is purest and our apprehension of eternal truth is clearest. At those times we can valiantly put off sin, change our course, and make momentous life decisions. These are times of grace, precious and powerful times that need to mark our journey with Jesus.

At those moments, truths about God – His nature and His ways – are taken hold of by the devout mind: understanding increases, Bible passages unlock and open up, great books are read, the brain works well and the heart warms in response to truth apprehended, the will makes great decisions, directions are set, and the stride lengthens.

But ... there are also dark days: Clouds roll in, prayer seems cold and formal. Old sins, long dormant, awaken and seem to overwhelm. Sickness racks the body. Sorrow is our portion. Perhaps we bury a loved one. Exclamation marks are replaced by question marks, the Bible seems a complicated book, the brain grows dull, the heart goes cold, the stride becomes a shuffle and the course ahead seems fraught with confusion and danger.

Jonathan's *Resolution* is ripe with practical pastoral wisdom (was he really only *eighteen*?). He recognizes the ups and downs of following Jesus. He understands the seasons of discipleship. And he determines that it is the progress he has made with Jesus when the wind is at his back, not the slog through the mud when the storm is in his face, that will define him. I have said many times before, but I need to say it again: What you think about when you think about Jesus Christ is the most important thing about you.[37] Theology – that is, your understanding of God – is all-important. Those things you have learned about the Lord on the sure days, the things you have seen clearly in the sunshine, the decisions you have made for Christ when you have most clearly grasped spiritual realities, *need to sustain you in the fog, the wind, the gales of life.*

Horatio Spafford (1828–1888) understood the importance of good theology, of things learned when in the light holding you fast when in the dark. A deep Christian and very successful businessman, most of his holdings were destroyed in the Chicago fire of 1871. This was shortly after his four-year-old son had died of scarlet fever. Believing it best to take his wife and four daughters (aged 11, 9, 5, and 2) on a trip to Europe, he sent the five ahead of himself on the steamer, Ville du Havre.

On 22 November 1873, that ship was struck by another in the mid-Atlantic. It sank in twelve minutes and all four dear daughters perished. Upon rescue, his wife Anna telegraphed him with the solemn words, 'Saved alone'. Spafford left at once for Ireland to join her. Mid-way across the Atlantic, the ship's captain called Horatio on deck as they approached the spot where his daughters had perished. At that very spot, he penned the words that became a great hymn of comfort to so many:

When peace, like a river, attendeth my way,
When sorrows like sea billows roll;
Whatever my lot, Thou hast taught me to say,
It is well, it is well with my soul ...

Though Satan should buffet, though trials should come,
Let this blest assurance control,
That Christ hath regarded my helpless estate,
And hath shed His own blood for my soul ...

For me, be it Christ, be it Christ hence to live:
If Jordan above me shall roll,
No pang shall be mine, for, in death as in life,
Thou wilt whisper Thy peace to my soul ...

But, Lord, 'tis for Thee, for Thy coming we wait.
The sky, not the grave, is our goal;
Oh, trump of the angel! Oh, voice of the Lord!
Blessed hope, blessed rest of my soul!

It is well with my soul,
It is well, it is well with my soul.

Do you see how theology matters? Do you see in this story that what Spafford *believed* about Jesus, what he *learned* in the light, *kept him in the dark*? If I waste my good days, trifling them away in all sorts of trivial pursuits, my spiritual poverty will be proven on my bad days. Conversely, if I 'make hay while the sun shines', my spiritual health will be evident when the storms hit (and they will hit).

Go to the ant, you sluggard;
consider its ways and be wise!
It stores its provisions in summer
and gathers its food at harvest.
(Prov. 6:5–9)

So, Jonathan's resolve to live out of the abundance of his fair-weather harvest in the foul-weather trial really is in no way optional. We have no choice but to follow his lead if we are to endure in faith until the end. Like Jonathan, we must hold tight to solid theology! And solid theology – what you know about God – keeps you when everything else falls away.

Blessed is the one ... whose delight is in the law of the Lord,
and who meditates on his law day and night.
That person is like a tree planted by streams of water, which yields its
fruit in season and whose leaf does not wither.
(Ps. 1:1–4)

His purposes will ripen fast,
unfolding ev'ry hour;
the bud may have a bitter taste,
but sweet will be the flow'r.
(William Cowper)

Resolution 19

Resolved never to do anything which I would be afraid to do if I expected it to be the very last hour before the trumpet sounded and Jesus returned.

Or, to put it in a positive light:

Resolved always to be doing what I would do if I knew that the trumpet was sounding and Jesus was returning within the hour.

Be dressed ready for service and keep your lamps burning, like servants waiting for their master to return from a wedding banquet ...
(Luke 12:35)

Therefore, my dear brothers and sisters, stand firm. Let nothing move you. Always give yourselves fully to the work of the Lord, because you know that your labour in the Lord is not in vain. (1 Cor.15:58)

Dear Friends,

How is this for a name and title: Anthony Ashley Cooper, 7th Earl of Shaftesbury, Baron Cooper of Pawlett, Baron Ashley of Wimborne St. Giles?

Anthony Ashley Cooper (1801–1885) was born into the British aristocracy. Raised by a cruel father and a social butterfly of a mother, he learned about Jesus and the Gospel from a family maid, Maria Millis (how wonderful is that!). She taught Anthony how to pray and trust Jesus and, in later life, Anthony, then the Seventh Earl of Shaftesbury, traced his life in Christ back to that dear household servant. As an ardent follower of Jesus, Anthony Cooper, the Seventh

Earl of Shaftesbury, served as a Member of Parliament for 50 years, beginning at the age of 25. During this time, Britain was in the midst of cataclysmic change as the Industrial Revolution rolled mercilessly forward. That revolution, coupled with a brutal class system of 'betters' and 'lessers', set the stage for an unimagined oppression of the poor, including of children and of the physically and mentally infirm.

Because Anthony was a Jesus-follower, he could not stand idly by. He laboured tirelessly for the rights of the voiceless. He used his gifts and position in life to transform his society. Through child labour laws, factory reform, prison reform, education for the poor, Bible publication, empathy for the 'insane' (he secured the passage through parliament of the Lunacy Act in 1845), he led the charge in bringing compassion and Christian values into what was otherwise a cruel and heartless culture.

He was known as 'The Poor Man's Earl' and, when he died in 1885, tens of thousands of London's poor lined the streets to pay respects to the man who had given his life on their behalf.

Anthony was motivated by an unusual love for Jesus, but especially by an unceasing moment-by-moment anticipating the return of Jesus. He lived on his tiptoes, like a kid at Christmas, expecting and hoping for Jesus to show up any minute. He wanted to be found busy about his Master's work when his Master returned. Hear him:

> I do not think that in the last 40 years I have lived one conscious hour that was not influenced by the thought of our Lord's return.

It was said that whenever he heard the clock strike, he raised his thoughts heavenward, considered the brevity of life, the imminent return of Jesus, and got to work.

Look again at Jonathan's *Resolution* at the top of this letter. It is a double-edged sword. When looked at one way it is a strong inducement *not* to do certain things. Looked at another way, it is a strong inducement *to do* certain things.

In the first way, recognizing that the King of Kings is at the door, makes sin look unattractive: Will I want to be doing this, or saying that, or thinking this thought, when Jesus turns up? Fear is *not* a bad motive! It might not be the *best* motive, but if it pulls me away from sinful behaviour, then so be it. For a follower of Jesus simply to think, 'I do not want Jesus to catch me doing this' is a good thing.

Whether we meet Jesus at His Second Coming or through death, He is at the door every moment and the desire not to be ashamed when He appears should jar us to reality when sin is wooing us:

And now, dear children, continue in him, so that when he appears, we may be confident and unashamed before him at his coming.
(1 John 2:28)

But there is another way to look at this *Resolution*. The hope of seeing Jesus soon, whether it be via His visible return or His calling us home, is a powerful inducement to *do* certain things. Soon, very soon, we will see our precious Lord and Saviour! Like a bride awaiting the return of her beloved, or a child excitedly expecting dad to appear at any moment, *love* for our Lord Jesus spurs us to joyful work as we watch for His appearing.

Christian history proves that those who have lived with an 'eye on the sky', ever watchful for Jesus' return, have been the most effective 'in time' for eternity. The taunt that we will be 'so heavenly minded that we will be of no earthly good' has proven itself to be false again and again. It is those most ready, most eager, most watchful for Jesus' appearing who labour most effectively. Witness Anthony Ashley Cooper as 'Exhibit A' of this fact!

Beloved! Live with 'an eye on the sky'. Learn to live with the conscious thought that soon – very soon – you will see Jesus.

What a tonic for the weary soul!

What an antidote for the poison of sin!

What a spur to the lazy labourer!

He who testifies to these things says, 'Yes, I am coming soon.'
Amen. Come, Lord Jesus. (Rev. 22:20–21)

Preach [and live] as if Jesus was crucified yesterday, rose from the dead today, and is returning tomorrow.[38] (Martin Luther)

Resolution 20

Resolved to practice diligence and moderation in my eating and drinking.

'I have the right to do anything,' you say – but not everything is beneficial. 'I have the right to do anything' – but I will not be mastered by anything. (1 Cor. 6:12)

Dear Friends,

I was surprised when I discovered that the great and godly evangelist, George Whitefield (1714–1770), kept slaves. Whitefield was a man who loved the Lord Jesus and his fellow man very deeply. His evangelistic efforts spanned racial boundaries, which was groundbreaking for his day. In most aspects, I count him a hero. Perhaps he was a 'kind' slave-owner. While that possibility might make the reality a little easier to take, it cannot erase the fact that slavery is evil and his keeping of slaves was wrong. Period. Why did he do this? How could he justify it? I cannot give an answer for George, but I think this blot on his otherwise exemplary life highlights the fact that we can be blind in certain areas of our lives, especially areas where the prevailing culture is likewise blind. It takes a remarkable work of grace to open eyes where everyone is blind and does not even know it (double blindness).

When I first learned this fact about Whitefield, I remember asking myself: To what are Christians in my culture blind? What are we justifying in our lives that Christians in other cultures and times would or do find shocking? What are the 'respectable sins' in my life that more consecrated Christians or a more consecrated conscience would disallow? The fact is that we, just like all Christians, at all times, in all cultures, have collective blind spots. We have areas where the surrounding culture has engulfed us not only as individuals, but as the Church of God.

Food and drink are such an area for us.

It is a strange and sorry fact that many of us in the evangelical Christian world speak out loudly and often against homosexuality, abortion, drunkenness, racism, etc., (and we should engage well with these conversations) between mouthfuls, fork in hand, while on our way back up to the 'all you can eat' bar. Once again, Jonny is timely and needs to be heard. Far from this *Resolution* being quaint, old fashioned, or outdated, it could not be more needful, relevant, and hard-hitting. Beware of thinking Edwards to be some miserable austere character who scarcely ever smiled. We dare not take the all-too-common way out by crying 'legalism' whenever we encounter a disciple who is more earnest than we. Our Western culture is food mad. It is as though we have gone crazy with our super-abundance. But are we called to a life of bread and water, or is that just as extreme as gluttony, but in the opposite direction? Let's begin with a brief 'theology of food'.

First, the easy-to-chew part: We affirm that God is a jubilant God who invented food, flavours, and taste buds. He creates and calls all things 'very good' (Gen. 1:31). We rejoice in the fact that the Bible refers not only to fasting, but to feasting many times and in many different contexts (see Ps. 36:8). Indeed, the coming Kingdom of God is marked by feasting (Luke 13:29). We affirm that we are to receive all things, including food, with thankful and worshipful hearts (1 Cor. 10:31).

Now, the hard-to-swallow part: We remember the concern of the Apostle Paul that a Christian is not to be mastered by anything (1 Cor. 6:12), food being the first thing Paul is referring to. We remember that it is possible to make a 'god' of your stomach (Phil. 3:19), and idolatry in any form is wicked and destructive. We hear the repeated warnings in the Bible against gluttony (Prov. 23:2) and remember that the Christian who chooses life over mere existence must view himself with the same attitude as an athlete who trains for a prize (1 Cor. 9:24). Finally, we are mindful that our Lord Jesus Himself tells us that fasting is to be a normal part of the Christian's life (Matt. 6:17), though, sadly, it is not common practice.

So what do we do with Edwards' *Resolution*? Let's first remember that Jon has chosen life over mere existence. He wants to live a life which both maximizes the Glory of God and his own joy. He wants to live at full stretch. He is not running aimlessly, but with purpose. His life can be likened to the disciplined life of an athlete. I have a casual acquaintance with an elite athlete. Every aspect of his life, right down to his eating, is devoted to his aspirations. He has '[r]esolved, to practice diligence and moderation in [his] eating and drinking'. And here is the thing: No one thinks him strange, legalistic, or austere. They admire him and understand that his resolve is a part of his determination to achieve his goals. Jonathan Edwards is running for a prize. He orders his life accordingly, right down to maintaining how and what he eats and drinks. He does not want to be sluggish. He does not want to love this life too much. He wants to sleep well, rise early, work hard.

This is not the passing fancy of a young zealot, but the considered decision of an earnest disciple. The best disciples have been measured, that is, careful, in all things, and it seems that *being measured in food and drink sets the pace in all other areas*. This fact is remarkable, but true. The overfed body tends towards spiritual laziness and becomes easy prey for sin and temptation. The temperate body maintains a vigilance that seems to help every other area of discipleship.

So, what are we going to do about this?

We need to see the deep relevance and wisdom of this *Resolution*, ask for grace to repent of our fork and spoon sin, and for wisdom and strength to begin to live like a disciple in this vital area of life. This is the wise, grace-way choice. It will lead towards brighter eyes, a sharper mind, a humble sprit, and a thankful attitude. It will help you run so as to win the prize. Go to Jesus over this. Tell Him that you are serious about discipleship. Tell Him that you really want to prize Him above all things. Tell Him that you want your life to count, and that you do not want to be lazy, sluggish, or a poor steward of your brief life. Ask Him for grace to be as disciplined as an athlete in every area of your life, especially concerning food and drink. Ask Him for the resolve to make hard choices so that you can make a difference.

God will give us all grace to bring this battle-ground area into submission to His Lordship. Jesus really will help you. He wants to. He is more concerned with your discipleship than you are!

So, whether you eat or drink or whatever you do, do it all for the glory of God. (1 Cor. 10:31)

Resolution 21

Resolved never to do something, which, if I saw someone else doing it, would lead me to despise him or to think poorly of him.

You, then, who teach others, do you not teach yourself? ... You who boast in the law, do you dishonour God by breaking the law?
(Rom. 2:21–23)

Dear Ones,

Some may be asking, in these days of tremendous social and cultural upheaval, why I am writing pastoral letters based upon the centuries-old *Resolutions* of a teenager's relentless pursuit of holiness? Can I not find a more culturally relevant theme? Should I not be addressing the riots in the streets? Race relations? Police reform? Political flaws? Surely, I should speak of social and structural injustices.

Here is my answer: While most certainly there is a need for Christians to deal with issues such as those named above, there is *nothing* more culturally relevant and transformational than personal holiness. Personal holiness is never private holiness. It spills over into the public arena. History demonstrates that the Christian who affects his or her culture the most is the Christian who has pursued holiness of heart and life the most. So, in these days of extreme social upheaval, I make no apology for our continued exploration of Jonathan's *Resolutions*. They could not be more timely.

The more diligent I am with my own heart, the more useful I will be in my Master's hands to effect changes so desperately needed in my world. History proves this in the lives of countless men and women whose deep rivers of personal holiness burst their banks in radical love for their neighbours. The problem with the world is *systemic sin,* and the answer for the world is the Gospel. And, as far as I am concerned, it has to begin with me – with my own heart and life.

We live in an age of finger pointing. Ours is a generation of blaming and accusing. Being assured of our own righteousness and everyone else's wickedness, we watch others' actions and quickly despise and think poorly of them. We focus on their speck, ignoring *our* plank. But Jonathan's *Resolution* won't allow us to hide in our self-righteous corner. The fact of the matter is that, to one degree or another, we do the very things we hate seeing others do. We have in us, at least in seed form if not sprouted and growing, the very wickedness we condemn in others.

For example, here comes a middle-aged, pick-up drivin', tobacco chewin', flag wavin', white guy in a baseball cap. In a moment I have him sized up. My subconscious has him pigeon-holed before he even opens his mouth. He must have a white sheet hanging in his closet, and a pistol somewhere under that belt-buckle. He is a prejudiced, narrow-minded bigot. I am glad I am not like him! Except, I am worse than him, for I have made my own savage heart judge and jury over him and am thereby every bit as prejudiced, narrow, and bigoted as I imagine him to be.

Or, here are angry youths demonstrating. Spewing violence, some are throwing bricks and breaking windows. From my sofa, I eat my nachos and silently curse them, forgetting that I spoke abusively to my wife earlier that day, slammed a door in anger, and have not spoken to my son in a week because I cannot abide his left-wing politics.

If only people were more like me. Except, I am as sinful and diseased as the next man, only my sin is hidden under a paper-thin veneer of social respectability.

Seeing things we despise in others must lead us to self-examination, not to self-justification. Imagine how this would change our culture if we all simply practiced this today! Remembering that God looks upon our hearts and knows them in depth, what must He think when He sees us despising in others what we put up with, or even applaud, in ourselves?

The unexamined heart will too easily excuse in itself what it decries in others:

He is hot-tempered. *I* am just passionate.
She is greedy. *I* am just appreciative of finer things.
He is lustful. *I* merely know beauty when I see it.
She is rude and offensive. *I* simply call things as I see them.
He is a glutton. *I* merely have a healthy appetite.
She covets. *I* admire.

How did Jesus put it?

For in the same way you judge others, you will be judged, and with the measure you use, it will be measured to you. Why do you look at the speck of sawdust in your brother's eye and pay no attention to the plank in your own eye? How can you say to your brother, 'Let me take the speck out of your eye,' when all the time there is a plank in your own eye? (Matt. 7:2–4)

The godly response to someone else's despicable behaviour is to search my own heart for evidence of the same. C. S. Lewis speaks of the first time that he, an educated, erudite Englishman, began to truly examine his heart. What he discovered horrified him: 'For the first time I examined myself with a seriously practical purpose. And there I found what appalled me: a zoo of lusts, a bedlam of ambitions, a nursery of fears, a harem of fondled hatreds. My name was legion.'[39]

True holiness of heart and life – what Jonathan is going hard after – will, without fail, result in not only personal, but social, transformation. To seek social change without going first for heart change will dress the wound lightly. The best thing I can do for my world is to become more like Jesus. The second-best thing I can do is to urge and encourage you to do the same. That is why we are 'hanging' with Jonathan. He is addressing causes, not symptoms.

May God enable me to have a single eye and a simple heart, desiring to please God, to do good to my fellow creatures, and testify [to] my gratitude to my adorable Redeemer.[40] (William Wilberforce)

Resolution 22

Resolved to seek, with all my might, to be as eternally happy as I possibly can be. By God's grace I will let nothing hinder me from pursuing eternal joy in Jesus. With all the power of my mind, body and will, I will battle for joy that will last in Heaven forever.

You make known to me the path of life; you will fill me with joy in your presence, with eternal pleasures at your right hand. (Ps. 16:11)

Dear Friends,

Jonathan Edwards' *Resolutions* relentlessly point us to eternity. Indeed, the Bible relentlessly points us to eternity. God motivates us during our brief journey here toward Jesus-glorifying living by constantly presenting to us the wonders of His Heaven. God speaks of pleasures and joys and rewards. He gives us word pictures of feasts and gardens, rivers and fruitful trees. We read of a glorious city whose citizens are countless redeemed people from every race and tongue. We hear of a wedding celebration, and of crowns and thrones. We are told that we will be in the very presence of the God of all Glory.

I fear we often view salvation in a very sterile way. We believe certain doctrines, then God is obliged to remove our sins, then we do not go to Hell when we die but go to Heaven where everything is OK forever.

It is a sort of business deal.

But I do not think that is what God has in mind at all. It is not a business deal. It is a song. It is a dance. It is a romance. It is a feast. It is a consummation. And it expands into eternity.

Now, as our young Jonathan wants to be as happy in Heaven as he possibly can be, this *Resolution* provokes a number of questions: Will we all be the same in Heaven? What does the Bible mean by *rewards*? Is it OK to want to be as happy as you can possibly be? Does what Christians do in this life affect their eternity?

First, we need to grasp the fact that the Bible unashamedly speaks of rewards in Heaven. Jesus Himself does. The word *reward* is found 27 times in the New Testament, half of those times it is found on the lips of Jesus:

> *Rejoice in that day [the day of your persecution] and leap for joy, because great is your reward in heaven.* (Luke 6:23)

> *Truly I tell you, anyone who gives you a cup of water in my name because you belong to the Messiah will certainly not lose their reward.* (Mark 9:41)

> *For the Son of Man is going to come in his Father's glory with his angels, and then he will reward each person according to what they have done.* (Matt. 16:27)

Now friends, let us not try to be more 'spiritual' than God! If God wants to motivate us with rewards, so be it. But let's be vitally clear about two things:

> 1) Do not confuse rewards with salvation. Salvation is by grace and not by works. We do not in any way merit salvation through our human works or efforts (Eph. 2:8–9).

> 2) Rewards involve nothing other than God Himself, not stuff. There is no pleasure apart from Him: 'I am your shield, your very great reward' (Gen. 15:1).

Let me speak to you for moment from my personal experience: There is a real sense in which I will be as happy into eternity as I want to be. There is never any shortage on God's side, nor any hesitancy with Him. Now, I know that my sins are forgiven by the wonder of the death of Jesus on the cross. I know that I am saved and safe forever. But I also know that I am called to a relationship with God, not just to a legal agreement. I know that I can squander my days or use them well. I can hunger after God or allow the junk of the world to spoil my desire for Him. I can be diligent with my heart or careless with it. I can waste grace or use grace. I can freely choose Jesus today as my Satisfier or seek satisfaction in the things around me.

I face these choices every day, and my response to these choices matters not only in time, but into eternity. The grave has no power to sanctify me. Is it not presumptuous to think that I will suddenly be after death what I had little desire to be during life? The choices I make here and now will ring into eternity. Jesus says:

Do not be afraid, little flock, for your Father has been pleased to give you the kingdom. Sell your possessions and give to the poor. Provide purses for yourselves that will not wear out, a treasure in heaven that will never fail, where no thief comes near and no moth destroys. For where your treasure is, there your heart will be also. (Luke 12:34)

Do you see Him telling us to *choose* to 'provide ... a treasure in Heaven that will never fail'? It is not only OK for me to want to be as happy as I can be, but it also honours God supremely when I pursue my happiness in Him. Jonathan wants treasure in heaven. He wants abundant joy in Jesus ... forever. He does not want to waste grace. He is thinking beyond the weekend (quite something for an eighteen-year-old!) and into forever.

Are you? Am I?

But by the grace of God, I am what I am, and his grace to me was not without effect. No, I worked harder than all of them—yet not I, but the grace of God that was with me ... Now there is in store for me the crown of righteousness, which the Lord, the righteous Judge, will award to me on that day—and not only to me, but also to all who have longed for his appearing. (1 Cor. 15:10; 2 Tim. 4:8)

He is no fool who gives what he cannot keep, to gain what he cannot lose.[41] (Jim Elliot)

Resolution 23

Resolved to venture out often, to do new and unexpected things for God's Glory, but always to examine the motive behind those deeds, and if, upon reflection, a deed was not done for the Glory of God, to repent and not repeat that deed.

Live as children of light (for the fruit of the light consists in all goodness, righteousness and truth) and find out what pleases the Lord.
(Eph. 5:8–10)

Dear Friends,

Most of us live our Christian lives on the defensive. Our goal is to not make too many mistakes. We define ourselves not so much by our purpose in Christ as by what we do not do. We do not smoke. We do not gamble. We avoid certain places and people.

We tend to hug the frigid shore of life, afraid to venture into the deep lest we capsize, failing to understand the wonders and freedom of a life lived under the grace of God. Fear of failure and fear of 'getting it wrong' freezes us.

Jonathan is taking exactly the opposite course. He is setting his compass for adventure. He is taking risks. He is pushing out from shore. Rather than choosing the safe option, he is daring to discover God's deeper purposes for his life. He realizes that when one lives under the banner of grace, one can risk, and even fail, and not be cast aside by the God who takes endless pleasure in His children.

Fear freezes. Grace frees us!

So, our young hero resolves to venture often into new areas with

Jesus, testing the water, stepping out on the ledge, cutting a new trail. Why not? Jesus is His Saviour! His grace is sufficient! His mercies are sure! Like a child learning to ride a bike, the father's smile and encouragements make the skinned knees worth it. God is pleased when we understand His redemptive love so fully that we dare the adventure of faith. God is grieved when we have such a miserly view of Him that we cower in the safe shallows of familiarity. Jonathan's advice is simple, faith-filled, grace-aware, and daring.

Go for it! Give it a try! Write that next chapter of your life! By all means, examine your heart along the way and if you find that your motives are self-glory, instead of God's Glory (perhaps that is why there is so little joy in the effort!), adjust your motives or leave the thing alone altogether. But don't quit living the adventure of faith!

Jesus encourages this strategy! Remember His story of the servants who were given money to invest (Matt. 25:14–30)? In that story, three different servants (us) were given money to invest for their master (talents and abilities to use for God's Kingdom purposes). Not all had the same amount of money to invest (not all of us have the same number of gifts from God to develop). But all were expected to get on with it (all of us are expected to take steps of faith and invest what we have in furthering God's Kingdom). You know the story: One man was so afraid of his master and so afraid of failure that he did nothing,

> Then the man who had received one bag of gold came. 'Master,' he said, 'I knew that you are a hard man, harvesting where you have not sown and gathering where you have not scattered seed. So, I was afraid and went out and hid your gold in the ground. See, here is what belongs to you.'
>
> His master replied, 'You wicked, lazy servant!'

Big point: God is not like the master in this parable. But some of us think He is! We view Him as a 'hard man' instead of a loving father, and we bury our gifts instead of risking them for our joy and His Glory. Yet because He is a loving, grace filled father and not a 'hard man', He would far rather us try and fail than sit stuck fast in inaction because of fear of failure.

Go on! Write that book! Explore that yet hidden talent! Visit that needy neighbour! Make that mission trip! Play that instrument and sing that song! Start that class! Pursue that ministry! Make that move! Yes, of course, keep watch over your intentions and motives, and if you find that your motives are suspect, change them, or change course. But don't become a wallflower when Jesus has asked you to start dancing with Him. Don't settle for being a shore-hugger when Jesus has called you to go deeper and let your nets down. Know, without a doubt that ...

... God is able to bless you abundantly, so that in all things at all times, having all that you need, you will abound in every good work.
(2 Cor. 9:8)

And that ...

God hath not given us the spirit of fear; but of power, and of love, and of a sound mind. (2 Tim. 1:7 KJV)

Where would the Kingdom be without those who have displayed a spirit of risky faith in the face of fear and discouragement? When, in 1786, an English shoemaker named William Carey told his church leaders he wanted to take Jesus' Gospel to the people of India, he was scolded, 'Young man sit down! When God pleases to convert the heathen, He will do it without your aid or mine!' He went anyway, telling his praying friends, 'You hold the rope and I will go down into the hole'. Way to go, William!

Way to go, Jonathan, for reminding me to get on and live the adventure!

For we are God's handiwork, created in Christ Jesus to do good works, which God prepared in advance for us to do. (Eph. 2:10)

You cannot swim for new horizons until you have courage to lose sight of the shore.[42] (William Faulkner)

Resolution 24

Resolved, whenever I commit an obvious sin, to explore it back to its
root cause, so that I can be wise against it, so as not to repeat the act,
and so to destroy the very origins of it.

Above all else, guard your heart, for everything you do flows from it.
(Prov. 4:23)

Dear Ones,

Sixty-thousand people were on their feet. It was the 1929 Rose
Bowl in Pasadena California. The University of California Golden
Bears were head-to-head with the Georgia Tech Yellow Jackets. The
game was being broadcast across the entire continent, a remarkable
feat for radio in that day. Roy Riegels, the stand-out California
linebacker, had just picked up a Georgia fumble. With the ball firmly
in his hands, he spun around and sprinted the length of the field
towards the end-zone. The crowd was cheering as the player was
running with all his might, sixty yards, towards the goal. Nobody
was going to catch him ... Not even his own team-mate Benny Lomm,
who was running behind him shouting at the top of his lungs ...

Something was wrong.

Was the crowd cheering or laughing?

Roy Riegels was running ... the wrong way. Benny Lomm finally
caught up with him and pulled him down just before the Georgia
Tech goal line. But it was too late. The mistake cost California two
vital points and they went on to lose that great game 8–7. Roy Riegels
has gone down in football history as 'Wrong Way Riegels'.

After the game, a chastened Riegels said, 'I was running toward the sidelines when I picked up the ball. I started to turn to my left toward Tech's goal. Somebody shoved me and I bounded right off into a tackler. In pivoting to get away from him, I completely lost my bearings ...

I surely thought I was going the right way'.[43]

Roy could tell you the exact second, and point to the exact spot, where he got it all wrong. You can actually see it on the ancient film footage. If he could have rolled back time, he would have gone to that spot and moment when he 'pivoted to get away from him' and turned the other way!'

Our young Jonathan is wanting to go to the root of his sin. He wants to trace the error of his ways back to the seminal issue, the vital moment, the pivotal decision and deal with things there. He is not interested in simply dressing a wound; he wants to deal with the deeper disease. Long before the affair hits the headlines, the telltale, deadly signs become evident: the wink, the word, the flirt. Even before these are the wandering thoughts and the careless imaginings. But even before these we find the dusty Bible, and the missed prayer time ... evidence of a vacant heart toward God and of idols taking up residence. True repentance goes deep and deals with problems at their source. It is surgical, not cosmetic. When sin is recognized, Edwards resolves to run it down and deal with it at source. I would not be surprised if he had been reading Psalm 139 when he wrote this Resolution:

> *Search me, God, and know my heart, test me and know my anxious*
> *thoughts. See if there is any offensive way in me and lead me in the way*
> *everlasting.* (Ps. 139:23–24)

Shallow repentance produces shallow results. It cannot deliver joy and peace and freedom. In reality, shallow repentance is no repentance. True repentance recognizes the wickedness of the seemingly innocent first step. The kind of repentance we are dealing with here asks searching questions of the soul:

Why am I irritable?
What is behind this lust?

> Why does that person bug me?
> Where did this attitude come from?
> When did I lose my peace?
> Whom am I truly serving?

The Bible is full of the sad stories of those who, being slack with their hearts, allowed little indiscretions to lead them to disasters: Lot, Samson, David, Saul, Judas. We could fill volumes with their miserable tales. I just this week finished reading *Moby Dick* (I am sure I was supposed to have read it in high school). In its essence the book is about a man who has been careless with his heart. Captain Ahab allows vengeance to take root and eventually to control all that he is and does. He fails to nip it early. Vengeance comes to define him. His drive to avenge himself results in his – and his crew's – destruction.

Good repenting goes back to these early steps and deals with the heart sins that caused them: the arrogance, the pride, the lust, the laziness, the greed, the envy, the carelessness, the anger (cf. Mark 7:21–32). Finally, it goes to the root of all sin and resulting joylessness, the pivoting of the heart away from God as its first – and final – treasure. It knows that the game may be ultimately lost on a wrong first step. Our young mentor has chosen true life over mere existence. He refuses permission to anything that will stand between himself, joy, Jesus, and Heaven. Therefore, when he sins, he is determined to find the origin of that sin, excise the tumour, cauterize the wound, and have done with it. Painful it may be, but such is the price if one's choice is Jesus above all. Jonathan knows that Godly sorrow brings repentance that leads to salvation and leaves no regret, but worldly sorrow brings death (2 Cor. 7:10). However difficult thorough, diligent repentance may be, failure to do so will, in the end, be infinitely more painful. That first step might well be the most important.

Just ask Roy.

> Be a consistent Christian, live above the world ... and underneath you shall be God's everlasting arms.[44] (George Whitefield)

Resolution 25

Resolved to search my heart often, looking for that one thing within that is causing me to question God's perfect and true love for me, and then to wage war against it.

This is how God showed his love among us: he sent his one and only Son into the world that we might live through him. (1 John 4:9)

Dear Friends,

Jonathan Edwards was just eighteen years old when he wrote the first thirty-four of his seventy *Resolutions*. He then, over the following year and a half, conceived the next thirty-six. Then he committed to appraise himself prayerfully by them once a week. As far as we know, he did this for the next thirty-five years until his untimely death in 1758. That means he would have prayerfully considered the above *Resolution* over one thousand eight hundred times.

Imagine with me this young man, soon to be a husband, then a father (of eleven children), then a middle-aged pastor, then an aging missionary to Native Americans on the harsh frontier, then a college president (the first president of what would become Princeton University), searching his heart every week for any telltale evidence of doubt regarding God's perfect and wonderful love for him! Then see him go to war against whatever it was that caused that doubt to rise. Imagine his continued victories as doubt-causing intruders were regularly discovered and exiled and Gospel assurance continually flooded in! Is it any wonder that Jonathan Edwards, in the midst of the trials and hardships of eighteenth-century frontier life, lived so remarkably well for Jesus?

Gospel assurance – being sure and certain that we are eternally loved by God through Jesus Christ, and that our sins are *gone* by virtue of His death on the cross – is the precious birthright of every child of God. Gospel assurance liberates us from our past, empowers us for our present, and secures us for our future. Jonathan does not want anything to diminish his assurance that God loves him with a perfect and true love.

Now we must understand that God's love is not proven through circumstances going well for us. God's love is proven through one thing and only one thing: that He sent His Son to suffer and die for us. Here *alone* is the infallible proof that God loves us. This is plainly stated in the Bible:

> But God **demonstrates** his own love for *us in this: while we were still sinners, Christ died for us.* (Rom. 5:6–8, emphasis mine)

Do you see that word *demonstrates*? It is a very important word where our assurance is concerned! It means 'to exhibit', 'to show', 'to prove'. This tells us that God has already presented the proof of His astounding love for us. It happened while we were still His *enemies*, on a hill outside of Jerusalem.

John says the same thing:

> This is how God showed his love among us: he sent his one and only Son into the world that we might live through him. This is love: not that we loved God, but that he loved us and sent his Son as an atoning sacrifice for our sins. (1 John 4:9,10 KJV)

This tells me that if I look anywhere else for *proof* that God loves me with a true and perfect love, I am looking in the wrong place. My search will lead to confusion and not to confidence. For instance, here is a dear saint, a precious follower of Jesus, and he is sick. He has prayed, but God has not healed him. Jesus has instead chosen to walk with him through a season of suffering. But our friend takes this unanswered prayer as evidence that God may not love him with a perfect and true love. Others have been healed! His assurance is jolted and his faith is wobbling. What is the problem? Simply that our friend has taken his eyes off the cross. He is looking in the wrong place for proof of God's love for him. Now not only is his body suffering, but his soul is in turmoil.

Or there is a sister in Christ. How she has prayed for her wayward child! Yet the battle for that child's soul has now lasted decades. Her friends' children are all following Jesus. Our sister is wondering about God's love. She is questioning God's goodness. She is now not only concerned for her child but is in her own crisis of faith! The problem is simple, but profound: she has misplaced her confidence. Instead of confiding totally in the finished work of Jesus, dying for her sins while she was still an enemy of God, she is looking at the battle for her wayward one and wondering about God's love for her.

Both these dear ones are sidelined from the battle ... just as Satan wants them to be.

But ah! Here is one who has just received that raise at work! He was not sure if God truly loved him, but now he has proof! He has confused his boss's smile with God's smile. What will then happen when his earthly boss frowns? A faith crisis is in his future, for his eyes are on the wrong thing. His testimony is not Gospel-centred, but circumstance-centred.

He, too, is therefore sidelined from the battle ... just as Satan wants him to be.

We know that God loves us because Jesus died for our sins.

Period.

Friend, do not let anything or anyone rob you of Gospel joy and assurance. Plant your faith-flag on Calvary's hill and there make your stand. If you find yourself doubting the perfect and true love of God for you, a little self-examination will most certainly reveal that your eyes have moved from the cross to something else. Put your hope back where it belongs, – root it in the long, high and deep love of Christ and what He has done for you on the cross (Eph. 3:17–19).

> Sometimes I go to God and say, "God, if Thou dost never answer another prayer while I live on this earth, I will still worship Thee as long as I live, and in the ages to come, for what Thou hast done already." (A.W. Tozer)[45]

Resolution 26

Resolved to rid myself of anything that lessens my assurance that I am saved, safe, and walking in love with Jesus.

I write these things to you who believe in the name of the Son of God so that you may know that you have eternal life. (1 John 5:13)

Dear Ones,

Assurance is the birthright of every precious child of God. By *assurance* I mean the simple confidence that one is safe in Jesus forever – the past forgiven, the future secure. Assurance is possible because our salvation is warranted by the blood of Jesus shed once on the Cross for our sins:

God made him who had no sin to be sin for us, so that in him we might become the righteousness of God. (2 Cor. 5:21)

Assurance brings with it the precious peace that comes from knowing that our sins have been conclusively dealt with by God. Assurance has nothing to do with our performance, but all to do with God's promise:

But when the kindness and love of God our Saviour appeared, he saved us, not because of righteous things we had done, but because of his mercy. He saved us through the washing of rebirth and renewal by the Holy Spirit, whom he poured out on us generously through Jesus Christ our Saviour, so that, having been justified by his grace, we might become heirs having the hope of eternal life. (Titus 3:4–7)

It empowers the believer to live valiantly for Christ in a hostile world. Assurance makes mopers into missionaries and turns worriers into warriors.

Our young Jonathan does not want *anything* to abate his assurance that he is saved and safe in Jesus. We saw previously that taking one's eyes off the Cross and onto one's performance is sure to affect one's confidence in the finished work of Christ. To look anywhere but to the atonement for our proof of God's love is sure to lead one away from security and assurance.

But there is another deadly enemy of assurance: flirting with sin.

Shallow repentance, carelessness with one's heart, loving what God hates, walking in disobedience, will all bring the child of God into desert lands. Being 'saved' has a 'to' as well as a 'from' aspect. We are not only saved *from* sin, but we are saved *to* holiness, *from* loving the world supremely *to* loving Jesus supremely. That is why old Paul said to young Timothy:

> *Flee the evil desires of youth and pursue righteousness, faith, love and peace, along with those who call on the Lord out of a pure heart.*
> (2 Tim. 2:22)

But when a child of God plays around with sin, sailing too close to the rocks, wondering 'How worldly can I be and still get to Heaven?', joy, peace, and assurance are chased off. The times in my life when I look to the sinful world for my satisfaction are the times when I am not able to rejoice in the wonders of my salvation. How can I, when I am loving the world that hates my Saviour? There is a civil war within me, between the 'old me' and the 'new me'.

I am not saying that God casts me off on those bad days when sin and temptation overwhelm me. Not in any way! But I am saying that when I am careless with my heart, *I know* that I am not walking in a manner consistent with who I am as a new person in Jesus. All the wonders of my salvation, including the assurance that I am saved and safe in Jesus forever, are *experientially* under threat when I cuddle, rather than crucify, sin.

When I kept silent, my bones wasted away
through my groaning all day long.
For day and night your hand was heavy on me;
my strength was sapped as in the heat of summer.
(Ps. 32:3–4)

There is nothing, *nothing*, more precious and necessary to a believer than his walk with Jesus. Salvation is not just some legal contract between God and me.

It is a relationship, a friendship, a romance.

Consider a marriage, a good marriage. Consider *my* marriage. I am officially and legally married to Tessa. That bond is permanent and secure. Good ... but not enough! It is the daily *relationship* that the legal bond enables and exists for. And that daily relationship is dependent upon me constantly guarding my heart and my mind, my actions and my words. I cannot ruin the legal bond. I can ruin the daily romance. In order for the friendship to flourish, there need to be many repentances, many earnest corrections, many humble apologies. There needs to be active pursuit. There needs to be diligent prioritizing. Otherwise, my *experiential* assurance is under threat. The joy evaporates and the happy acts of love become chores. Before long we are wondering, 'Where has the love gone?'

The assurance – experientially –has been knocked.

This is exactly what happens with our daily relationship with Jesus ... Our *justification before God* is a legal and secure declaration. But the point of it is to bring us into a *relationship with God,* and that relationship can be tarnished and dulled if not guarded and polished.

Friend, let nothing threaten your assurance! Let nothing inhibit your joy in Jesus! Treat sin as a cancer and do not let it abide in the slightest form – not because you are insecure in Christ, but because you know that you have been saved from sin – *for* Him. The dear, simple believer who *abides* – which implies many repentances and cleansings – is the believer who becomes a fruit-bearing, joy-filled, assured friend of Jesus.

Don't settle for anything less!

May our God strengthen your hearts so that you will be blameless and holy in the presence of our God and Father when our Lord Jesus comes with all his holy ones. (1 Thess. 3:13)

We weren't meant to be somebody – we were meant to know Somebody.[46] (John Piper)

Resolution 27

Resolved to never purposely neglect to do what I should do, unless somehow it be for the greater Glory of God, and to regularly examine my motives for not doing something.

For we are God's handiwork, created in Christ Jesus to do good works, which God prepared in advance for us to do. (Eph. 2:10)

Dear Friends in Jesus,

Oh, to be eager to do good!

As we have already noted, following Jesus is often felt to be a matter of *avoidance* – staying away from certain places and people and actions. Certainly, there is truth to this. But too often we followers of Jesus have allowed ourselves to be *defined* by what we do not do, where we do not go and whom we avoid. Can we flip this on its head? Can we make it our goal to be defined by our nearness to the One who healed the sick, fed the hungry, preached the good news of the Kingdom, and loved the lost?

God anointed Jesus of Nazareth with the Holy Ghost and with power: who went about doing good and healing all that were oppressed of the devil; for God was with him. (Acts 10:38)

God wants us to do good. He likes to see us walk in His will and excel in the gifts he has given us, and so, God is as concerned with the good that we fail to do as with the bad that we do. We have been redeemed *for* good works as surely as we have been saved *from* bad works. True saving faith, by which the helpless sinner looks to his merciful and sufficient Saviour, is evidenced not only by turning from sin, but equally by a new desire to do good.

Here is a joyous piece of news for you: God is easy to please. He is impossible to impress, but easy to please. He is not against us but for us, and He:

– Saves solely by His grace, and then
– Gifts and equips us to do good works, and then
– Prepares those works for us to do, and then
– Rewards us when we do those works!

What a God!

In light of this, to be lazy and faithless, to be a timewaster, or to fill our day with *our* agenda, to neglect the good that we can do out of a fear of failure or a simple lack of concern, is as offensive to our good and wonderful God as is obvious outward sin. We need to see that 'sins of *omission*' are just as grievous to God as 'sins of *commission*'.

Now to sharpen our focus: I am convinced that of all the 'good works' we can fail to do, the most grievous, the most obvious, the most hurtful to God and people is ...

Our Neglect to Tell Others about Jesus.

Is this not our greatest duty? If you had a vaccine against cancer, and kept it to yourself, would this not be a grievous crime? Here we have the greatest news for mankind. Here we have the cure for the broken and poisoned heart. Here we have a chance to make our wonderful Saviour famous and people happy, and we sit in silence.

Do you recall, in John's gospel, these words of Jesus?

Very truly I tell you, whoever believes in me will do the works I have been doing, and they will do even greater things than these, because I am going to the Father. (John 14:12)

Have you ever puzzled over Jesus' words when he tells us that we will do 'even greater things' than He did? How can we ever do 'greater things' than He did? Why, He raised the dead! How can *we* beat that?

Well, there is *one thing* that we can do that Jesus did very little of – and we can do it because He has returned to His Father and sent us His Holy Spirit – and that is *evangelism*. Jesus spent almost all of His ministry pouring Himself into a few people, and then tasked and empowered them – now *us* – to do what He did not do: take the Gospel to 'all creation' (Mark 16:15).

Could it be that the 'greater things' we are intended and enabled to do all involve loving our neighbours, crossing boundaries of unbelief, engaging our culture with the Gospel, and going near and far with the Good News of Jesus? I think so.

Could it be that our reluctance to do so is the greatest crime of the Church? I fear so.

Could the greatest injustice in the world be that millions have yet to hear of Jesus while Christians 'sit at ease in Zion' (Amos 6:1)? I know so.

We all speak freely about what we love. We cannot help but 'evangelize' about our favourite sports team and our kids. Our hearts are full to over-flowing about such things! Does our reluctance to speak freely about Jesus reveal a heart-love problem? If the greatest joy possible is to know Jesus, then certainly to help others know Jesus is that joy multiplied! It is a simple fact that the vast majority of people who turn to new life in Jesus do so *because a friend shared Jesus with them*, not because some hot evangelist came to town.

We can take a good Gospel lesson from the lepers in Samaria who came upon a feast in the middle of a famine. What evangelists they became!

> *Then they said to each other, 'What we're doing is not right. This is a day of good news and we are keeping it to ourselves.'* (2 Kings 7:9)

Friends, may we lift our hearts to God and repent of this great sin of omission: our reluctance and failure to share Jesus! All we need to be is beggars telling other beggars where we found bread ... *the* Bread of Life!

It need not be more complicated than that.

Lord Jesus! Forgive us deep, and then fill us up, and then fling us out!

Let us not glide through this world and then slip quietly into heaven, without having blown the trumpet loud and long for our Redeemer, Jesus Christ.[47] (C.T. Studd)

Resolution 28

Resolved to keep up the good habit of faithfully studying the Scriptures, so that I can clearly see myself growing in the knowledge of God's Truth.

But grow in the grace and knowledge of our Lord and Saviour Jesus Christ. To him be glory both now and forever! Amen. (2 Pet. 3:18)

Dear Friends,

The Bible is given that we might *know* God. It is not just given to satisfy curiosity or to fill us with a range of facts. To read it only intellectually is to miss the point. Jonathan wants to encourage us to reverent Bible reading – reading with an aim to *know God in truth*.

Christians do not hold séances to discover the unknown; they read the Bible to discover God! Wonder of wonders, we have a God who wants to be known! He is not hiding. He does not play games with us. He is *self-disclosing*. And we, being created in God's image, and being redeemed from sin by His grace and gifted with the indwelling Holy Spirit, have the capacity to know Him.

Now this is eternal life: that they know you, the only true God, and Jesus Christ, whom you have sent. (John 17:3)

We do not – we cannot – know God through our own intuition, or via our own efforts and searching. It is not as though we are brave explorers and God is some mythological land we are seeking to discover. It is *God* who is the explorer. *He* is the one who condescends. We are the hiding rebels. He has revealed Himself in all that is around us, for '*The heavens declare the Glory of God; the skies proclaim the work of His hands. Day after day they pour forth speech: night after night they reveal knowledge ...*' (Ps. 19:1–2).

This is what theologians call God's 'general revelation.' Through creation He has spoken, and speaks, to every human who has ever gazed upon a night sky or heard the sound of the wind rushing by.

But more, He has revealed Himself in Jesus Christ, the ultimate self-disclosure. As Charles Wesley said:

> Our God contracted to a span,
> Incomprehensibly made man.[48]

And then, He has given us a faithful record of this revelation of Himself in Jesus by overseeing and shepherding the writing of the Bible. You and I can reverently open our Bible and read – not just *about* God, but the very inspired revelation of God's heart to ours!

> *In the past God spoke to our ancestors through the prophets at many times and in various ways, but in these last days he has spoken to us by his Son, whom he appointed heir of all things, and through whom also he made the universe...* (Heb. 1:1)

This is what theologians call God's 'special revelation'. For, in Christ and through the Bible, God has displayed the wonders of His redeeming love. With the help of the Holy Spirit, every child of God, be she or he simple or educated, can understand their Bible and, in it, can discover God and His ways. It is *not* a book locked up and reserved for the doctors and cloistered few! William Tyndale (1494 –1536) laboured to give England a Bible in her own tongue, and was burned at the stake for doing so. Although he himself could speak seven languages and was fluent in Hebrew and Greek (the original languages of the Bible), he wanted the Bible in English for all. He famously said to the bishops of his day, 'If God spare my life, 'ere many years I will cause a boy who drives a plough to know more of the scriptures than you do.'[49]

But friend, does your Bible gather dust?

In your Bible God's heart is opened to you. How sad to leave it unread! How strange to have 'Bible believers' who cannot remember when they last read their Bibles or where they left them! But happy are those who – with hearts lifted to Heaven – read and learn of Jesus and His saving ways. Bible-reading Jesus-followers become happy, healthy, and useful. They become stable and solid amidst life's storms. They cease to be gullible and find themselves powerful in spiritual battle. The more they read, the more treasures they find in the rich mine of God's truth. They increasingly think God's thoughts as their minds are renewed. Their words become wise, and they become helpers to others. Indeed, Bibles that are falling apart are usually owned and read by people who aren't. Blessed are those who read their Bibles! Do you read yours? Will you? God the Father wants you to read all about His Son and God the Holy Spirit will help you.

I leave you with a quotation from one of my Bible-reading heroes:

I am a creature of a day, passing through life as an arrow through the air. I am a spirit come from God and returning to God: just hovering over the great gulf till, a few moments hence, I am no more seen: I drop into an unchangeable eternity!

I want to know one thing – the way to heaven: how to land safe on that happy shore. God himself has condescended to teach me the way. For this very end He came from heaven. He hath written it down in a book. O give me that book! At any price, give me the book of God! I have it: here is knowledge enough for me. Let me be *homo unius libri* [a man of one book]. Here then I am, far from the busy ways of men. I sit down alone; only God is here. In His presence I open, I read His book for this end, to find the way to heaven.[50]

(John Wesley)

Resolution 29

Resolved to not pray frivolous prayers and shallow confessions that I do not really mean and that I cannot offer in faith that God will accept and answer.

For the Lord your God is among you, a mighty God and terrible.
(Deut. 7:21 KJV)

Dear Friends,

There is a great difference between *familiarity* and *frivolity*. We are invited to be familiar with God. We dare not be frivolous with Him. We can be familiar because He is Abba, Father. We cannot be frivolous because He is holy and awesome and – in the old English sense – *terrible*.

I think we tend toward being a frivolous generation, and that is a dangerous thing. I want to be very careful here. I can easily overstate my case (Jonathan's case!) and misrepresent God as being stern and austere. I do not want to do that.

Let me take you back to my boyhood for a minute, for my earthly father very well represented our Heavenly Father. As a small child I could climb onto the lap of my father, always assured of a welcome. As a teen I often knew his embrace. I could be myself – with all my attendant flaws – in his presence. As a young man I could gain access to him anytime, when others could not, by phone or in person, with a big problem or just to talk. He was always ready to listen (he really was). He was ready and willing to fix whatever mess I had made.

But I dared not waste his time.
> I could not slouch in his presence.
>> I could not approach with a swagger,
>>> Nor answer him with a 'yeah'.

I had to knock first and take my hat off when I entered his office.

Respect.

He was both 'daddy' and 'sir' to me. And that was good.

I have said all this, giving you a peek into a sacred part of me, just to illustrate that our Heavenly Father, though Holy and 'terrible' (the modern word is 'awesome'), is One with whom we can be wonderfully familiar. Indeed, because of Jesus we can *'approach God's throne of grace with confidence, so that we may receive mercy and find grace to help us in our time of need'* (Heb. 4:16). But I have also said all this to try to illustrate that this wonderful warm Father is One with whom we cannot be flippant, frivolous, or foolish.

Think about some of your prayers and confessions: Do you sometimes forget that you are dealing with a *Holy* Father, and that there is an immeasurable distance between you as a sinner and Him as God? Do you sometimes 'say your prayers' but not really pray? Do you sometimes forget that your sins are *crimes* and *catastrophes,* and that your confessions should be dead earnest and not mere shoulder shrugs?

The Psalmist got it right:

> *But there is forgiveness with you, that you may be feared.*
> (Ps. 130:4 NKJV)

Take some time and ponder the difference between:

> *fervent* and *flippant,*
> *familiar* and *frivolous,*
> *boldness* and *brazenness.*

Ponder the wonder of being able to approach God anywhere, at any time, with anything, great or small, good or bad. But dwell as well on the gulf between you and God that has been bridged by Jesus.

Tremble at the wonder of it.

We are welcome into His throne room – but should we put our boots on His sofa?

He will listen to our simplest words – but should we check our phones in the middle of a conversation?

He does not require us to stand on ceremony – but should we yawn while He is speaking?

Do we forget with whom we are dealing when we engage in the miracle of prayer? Think about this: If our prayers and confessions are bland when they need to be bold, if they are formal when they ought to be fervent, if they are wandering when they should be wondering, if they drift off when they need to drive in, if, in short, we cannot take our prayers seriously, *why should God*?

Enough lecture.

Let me draw to a close with some encouragement toward simple, believing, fervent, familiar prayer and confession. The Bible is full of episodes and examples of believers who prayed simple but earnest prayers and gained the ear of God with them. May we be encouraged to do likewise.

– Childless Hannah: 'Hannah was praying in her heart, and her lips were moving but her voice was not heard' (1 Sam. 1:13).

– The sinful man at the temple: 'But the tax collector stood at a distance. He would not even look up to heaven, but beat his breast and said, "God, have mercy on me, a sinner"' (Luke 18:13).

– The blind man on the road: 'He called out, "Jesus, Son of David, have mercy on me!"' (Luke 18:38).

– Lazarus' family: 'So the sisters sent word to Jesus, "Lord, the one you love is ill"' (John 11:3).

– The dying thief: 'Then he said, "Jesus, remember me when you come into your kingdom"' (Luke 23:42).

These dear, simple, praying saints show us that we need not

be *eloquent,* but we must be *earnest* in our praying. They show us that God is blessed by the *boldness* of His children. God is not impressed by words, but His heart is opened to the desperate. We dare not waste His time with pagan babble, but we will never waste His time with a desire for simple fellowship or the presentation of a desperate genuine need.

Where God is concerned, better one good groan than a thousand empty words.

> You are before the Lord; let your words be few, but let your heart be fervent.[51] (Charles Spurgeon)

Resolution 30

Resolved to give my best every week to grow in the grace of God and to be brought to a new and higher place with Jesus than I was the week before.

Abide in me ... for without me you can do nothing.
(John 15:4–5 NKJV)

Dear Friends,

In the Christian life, you must go 'down' in order to go 'up'. It is as we humble ourselves before the Lord Jesus that we grow and become more like Jesus. Many of us complain of an 'up and down' experience in our Christian journey. You might want to try going 'down and up' instead! Our young Jonathan wants to grow in grace. He wants to live life on a higher plane. He wants to grow up. He wants to become more like Jesus.

Now at this point, I want to make an assumption about Jonathan Edwards. Remember that he was a young man of eighteen when he first presented this and sixty-nine other *Resolutions* to himself. I figure that he understood this *Resolution* differently as a mature man than as a young man. I am making this assumption from examining my own growth toward maturity as well as from understanding the stories of many others as they have grown in grace. I can imagine a young Jonathan *determined* to grow, climbing the mountain of spiritual advancement, striving to be more like Jesus. I have been in that place! Going *up*! And ... how weary we become when we think our growth is a matter of our grit! Now I imagine an older

Jonathan. He still wants to be more like Jesus. He still wants to grow in grace. But – he no longer is going up! He is going *down*. He has discovered that Jesus is always found in the low place. Jesus meets us in the low place.

The way *up* is to go *down* where becoming like Jesus is concerned!

Jonathan has learned the way of humility. He has discovered (what a relief!) that growing comes not by striving, but by abiding. We, too, learn this by tumbling down the mountain of our own effort, often landing with a 'thump'. Lo and behold – there we find Jesus! And *He* lifts us up!

> *Humble yourselves before the Lord, and he will lift you up.*
> (Jas. 4:10)

So, are we simply passive in all of this? How do we 'give our best' and yet not 'strive' in our own strength and efforts? First, let's agree that every genuine believer wants to grow in his knowledge of God. Every follower of Jesus wants to become more like Jesus. Every child of grace is weary of their sin, wishes to be rid of it, and wants to say with the Psalmist:

> *I waited patiently for the Lord; he turned to me and heard my cry. He lifted me out of the slimy pit, out of the mud and mire; he set my feet on a rock and gave me a firm place to stand.* (Ps. 40:1–3)

Some will strive with their own might to grow 'up' thinking that it is all up to them and that they can do it. Some will be so passive as to do nothing at all, thinking Jesus will work some magic over and in them. But between the extremes of *striving* and *being passive,* we have *abiding.* There is a vast difference between striving and abiding. And there is a great difference between abiding and doing nothing.

Striving says, 'I am determined to be a better Christian! And I can do it in my own strength! My own grit and determination will get me to a higher place! I am not like those lazy (so-called) Christians! I pray more! I read more! I am a go-getter for Jesus! I've got this!'

Passivity says, 'I don't have to do anything at all. I just let go and let God. I need make no effort. Why wrestle when I can nestle? God is faithful, so I don't have to be. I need not pray. I need not read. No matter what I do, Jesus will take care of everything'.

I cannot quite imagine young Jonathan as a passive follower, but I certainly can picture him as a striver. Both are extremes, and neither is a proper picture of abiding. Abiding says, 'My one great concern is to walk with Jesus. He will be faithful to me, but I need to respond to His grace. My growth in Christ is dependent upon His love and power working in me, but I must avail myself of all that He has for me even as a branch avails itself of the vine. It is not up to me but up to Him, but He must have all of me. My *job* is daily surrender.'

I said earlier that we 'go down' in order to 'go up'. What does *abiding* have to do with this? Very simply: Jesus is always in the low place. He dwells with sinners. You do not find Him hanging out with the self-assured and successful but with the underdogs. This truth is all over the New Testament.

It is when we learn to repent quickly (that is, going to the low place), hungrily feed on His Word like a starving man would a loaf of bread (that is, staying in the low place), and pray for grace and help to live the supernatural life of a Christian (that is, going to a lower place!) that we meet Jesus afresh. He is always there, for He is the friend of sinners! It is as you and I learn to dwell there that we actually 'abide' with Jesus, and *He* brings us 'up.'

Would you grow in grace? Would you become more like Jesus? Would you be brought to a higher place of grace?

There is only one way, and it is not by striving, and it is not by snoozing: Get low. Be ever ready to humble yourself with repentance. Be always wanting to learn of Him. Be constantly in a place of need. And there you will be sure to find a ready, able, and willing Jesus ...

And He will bring you up.

Humble yourselves, therefore, under God's mighty hand, that he may lift you up in due time. (1 Pet. 5:6)

When I try to change myself and patch myself up I can't do it ... But if I surrender myself to Him who made me, I experience miracles.[52]
(Corrie ten Boom)

Resolved 31

Resolved never to say anything against anyone unless the Golden Rule demands that I do so. And if I must, to do so only out of love to others, in a way that honours Christ, and with a sense of my own faults and failures. And, when I have said anything against anyone, to bring it to the judgment of this *Resolution.*

Let your conversation be always full of grace, seasoned with salt ...
(Col. 4:6)

Friends,

One of the key aspects of being divine image bearers is the ability to speak and communicate through words. God is a speaking God, and He has made us able to communicate our innermost thoughts outwardly through words. Sadly, in our present fallen state we often use this glorious 'god-like' ability in perverse and destructive ways. Throw in a real devil who comes to 'kill, steal and destroy' (John 10:10), and speech, which should be a mighty weapon for good (to build up), can become a weapon for evil (to tear down). James 3:9–10 warns us that:

> 'With the tongue we praise our Lord and Father, and with it we curse human beings, who have been made in God's likeness. Out of the same mouth come praise and cursing.' He urges us, 'My brothers and sisters, this should not be.'

And yet today, it seems that we fling barbed words this way and that with little or no thought of the damage they do, the offense they cause to God, and the judgment we bring upon ourselves. So much venom is found in speech these days and it is so easy to enter the fray. What if we feared God before we flung our fierce words? What if our words were filled with love instead of inflamed with self-righteous judgment? What if we remembered that others, those at whom we are aiming our arrows, are divine image bearers – those for whom Christ bled and died?

Jonathan's *Resolution* – never to speak against anyone unless the Golden Rule demands it – would be revolutionary if employed in our lives and in our culture. Perhaps you are one of the rare, sanctified souls who actually controls her tongue. If so, then you are a blessing to God and to all around you. But for many of us, our undisciplined tongues are instruments of hurt rather than healing:

> *They make their tongues as sharp as a serpent's:*
> *the poison of vipers is on their lips.*
> (Ps. 140:3)

Do we realize that we do the devil's work for him when we tear another down with our words? We fling his fiery darts for him with our tongues. Do we realize that God hears, and God's heart is offended? God loves the person towards whom we are shooting arrows! He cherishes them. He sent His Son to redeem them. He sings over them. He delights to do them good. He is sanctifying them. He is keeping them daily in His love. He has covenanted with them to never leave or lose them. He is preparing a place for them. He is endlessly patient with them. He wants them to be with Him in Paradise. And here we come, with destructive, impatient, judgmental words. Over there is a person for whom Jesus died and here I am filled with self-righteousness toward them, looking at them with a critical spirit, assuming evil of them, speaking poorly of them to others, and perhaps harshly to their face. We can break a person when we speak harsh, rash words to them. And, when we speak these venom-words to a third party and not directly to the person in question, we are gossiping. In so doing we are spreading a bad report, and sowing discord among people. And *God hates that*! In fact, Proverbs 6:16–19 states that God does not just hate the words that cause discord, but He hates the *heart* that speaks those words! As J.C. Ryle, the nineteenth century Bishop of Liverpool, said, 'When a [person's] tongue is generally wrong, it is absurd, no less than unscriptural, to say that [their] heart is right.'[53]

We sin against God when we speak against His beloved child. Lord Jesus! Have mercy on us! Yes, there are times when love demands that we speak against another. There are times when to be silent is a sin. But how we should tremble at such times!

> *Brothers and sisters, if someone is caught in a sin, you who live by the Spirit should restore that person gently. But watch yourselves, or you also may be tempted.* (Gal. 6:1)

To bring a difficult word to or about another should be done only after one brings that word to God first ... 'Lord. I must speak a word against one for whom You died. I tremble at the thought, Lord. They are precious to You, and I must remember this as I speak to them. Also, Lord, I have no righteousness of my own! I am as needy and sinful as they. Lord Jesus! Have mercy on me!' Let's go on the offensive here. Rather than just resolving not to say anything against another, let's make it our goal to actually be channels of grace to all through our speech. How transformational if we earnestly and deliberately believe the best about others, seeking to see them as God sees them, and using our words to *build up* rather than *tear down*! Let us move against the vitriolic spirit of our age. Remembering our own sinfulness and need of grace, let us seek grace to make our words sweet and life-giving to all who hear us!

> *Gracious words are a honeycomb, sweet to the soul and healing to the bones.* (Prov. 16:24)

> While I disparage the exercise of 'building one's self-esteem', I indulge in it every time I imagine myself free from the defects I perceive in someone else.[54] (Elisabeth Eliot)

Resolution 32

Resolved to be ever diligent to be faithful to whatever has been entrusted to me, that the Proverb, 'A faithful man who can find?' may in no way be true of me.

Whatever you do, work at it with all your heart, as working for the Lord, not for human masters. (Col. 3:23)

Dear Ones,

Jesus Christ is to be Lord of all or not Lord at all. Jesus is Lord over my cleaning of the toilet just as certainly as He is over my prayer life. We cannot reverently read our Bibles and then irreverently do a half job at work. Faithfulness is as important on Monday as it is on Sunday, in things public as in things private, for *everything* is sacred to the Christian, because *everything* is sacred to Jesus. Jesus sees no 'sacred / secular divide', and neither must we. For the follower of Jesus there is not the least aspect of existence, over which Jesus does not say, 'Mine!'[55]

It is a fact of Christian history that the eighteenth-century Methodists became, under the Lordship of Jesus, such good and faithful workers that some ended up being business owners and leaders in their communities as they applied the Kingship of Christ to every aspect of their lives. In this way, Christian virtue infiltrated and transformed an otherwise corrupt and rotten society. These simple but consecrated Christians truly became salt in their world. Of them the proverb was true:

Do you see someone skilled in their work?
They will serve before kings.
(Prov. 22:29)

This is *not* to say that every hard-working Jesus-follower is destined to become a boss, and experience 'success' in the workplace. It *is* to say that God will be honoured in the diligence of a Christian's entire life, and that that life will inevitably be a blessing to many.

If I am a Christian, I must be able to offer any and everything I do as an act of worship to the Lord. At the very same time, this life has become for me both insignificant, for it is passing away, and profoundly significant, for it is a gift from our gracious Father to be offered back to Him in true worship and reverence. If I cannot genuinely offer something to Jesus, then I should not do it, and if I can offer it to Jesus – be it reading my Bible or walking in the woods or preaching a sermon or cutting my grass or going to work – then it deserves my very best effort. Simple.

Oh, but these days! As Christian virtue disappears, so does common diligence and the goodness and the satisfaction of a job well done. Age-old Christian-forged values such as 'a man is as good as his word', or a handshake being as binding as a contract, are relics of a former day. Corruption, shoddiness, cutting corners, and showing up late for work are the trademarks of paganism and its corresponding culture, not of Christianity and the world the Bible shapes.

Ah, but, as our culture moves ever farther away from its biblical moorings, these are becoming the trademarks of our day.

For a person today to give their best at any and every endeavour – precisely because Jesus is their Lord – is a powerful witness in a 'post-Christian', corner-cutting culture. Conversely, a person who dares to name Jesus as Lord and yet does not give a fair day's work or his finest effort for his earthly boss, is dishonouring his Saviour and presents a tragic and poor witness to the watching world because a person's faith in Jesus is proven in the workplace as much – maybe even more so – as in the church pew.

Slaves [employees], obey your earthly masters [employers] in

*everything; and do it, not only when their eye is on you and to curry
their favour, but with sincerity of heart and reverence for the Lord.*
(Col. 3:22)

Jesus sees what people do not see. And He rewards! Perhaps an
earthly boss overlooks you. Know that Jesus does not. Keep giving
that earthly boss the best because Jesus will make it right. Likewise,
He knows when we time-out early, or cut that corner, or fake it.
He sees the *back* of the toilet that no one else sees, and when we
are faithful in the little things, Jesus knows it and will bring us into
greater things. Perhaps the recognition will not take place until
Heaven, and perhaps only Jesus will ever know, but that is enough
for the simple Jesus-follower:

> *His master replied, 'Well done, good and faithful servant! You have
> been faithful with a few things; I will put you in charge of many things.
> Come and share your master's happiness! (Matt. 25:23)*

Diligence matters in our worship and witness. Grace is not a license
for laziness. Grace is power for service. Grace is not God shrugging
His shoulders at our sloppy second best. Grace is God infusing us
with ability to do what we cannot naturally do. Grace is not God
excusing our half-heartedness. Grace is God empowering us for
whole-heartedness. Friends, these are great days for us to shine with
the light of Christ into a dark world! But we do it not just with a
Bible, but also with a shovel, or a mop, or a pen, or a truck, or a
computer, or a diaper.

The world is waiting for ME to give my best.

> 'No work of art is more important than the Christian's life, and every
> Christian is called to be an artist in this sense ... The Christian's life is
> to be a thing of truth and also a thing of beauty in the midst of a lost
> and despairing world.'[56] (Francis Schaeffer)

> There is not a square inch in the whole domain of our human
> existence over which Christ, who is Sovereign over all, does not cry
> 'Mine!'[57] (Abraham Kuyper)

Resolution 33

Resolved to be always active in making and preserving peace, unless love requires otherwise.

Peacemakers who sow in peace reap a harvest of righteousness.
(Jas. 3:18)

Dear Ones,

Never confuse peace with appeasement: ask Neville Chamberlain, the befuddled British Prime Minister who, in 1938, returned to Britain from Munich, having met with Hitler. 'We can work with him,' he pronounced – to the doom of Europe. A savvy Winston Churchill saw through Chamberlain's foolishness and, knowing that true peace can never come via appeasement of evil, armed Britain for war.

Jonathan's *Resolution* urges us to pursue peace, but not at all costs. Not at the cost of appeasement of sin and wrongdoing.

When Jesus was preparing His first disciples for His departure, He bequeathed to them, and to us, something which this world can never give us: peace. Peace with God, peace within, peace with others.

Peace I leave with you; my peace I give you. I do not give to you as the world gives. Do not let your hearts be troubled and do not be afraid.
(John 14:27)

Peace with God is the direct result of the atoning death of Jesus Christ. On the cross, God's beloved Son averted His Father's righteous wrath away from us by absorbing it for us. Through Jesus being a propitiation – a wrath bearer – we, who have fled *to* God *for* refuge *from* God (think about that! See Psalm 2:12.), are now standing in the grace of God and have peace with God. The biggest question in all the universe (no exaggeration), 'How can a sinner find peace with an offended God?' is answered through the crucified Man-God on a cross. As Romans says, *'we have been justified through faith, we have peace with God through our Lord Jesus Christ, through whom we have gained access by faith into this grace in which we now stand'* (Rom. 5:1–2). War is over. Conflict has ended. This is not a tenuous cease-fire. It is total reconciliation between God and the believing sinner.

Peace with God!

A direct blessing of peace with God is peace within. The turmoil within the heart of the believer can and must end as a result of peace with God having been established by Jesus. The thinking goes like this: if the biggest problem in my life – me being under the deserved wrath of an offended God – has been conclusively solved through Jesus and the Gospel, then my inner conflict born of guilt, shame, and regret – a lesser problem – must come to a peaceful resolution as I lay down all weapons of rebellion and surrender to Jesus. Hebrews 10:22–23 describes exactly how this cleansing of conscience results in inner peace.

But then – oh yes – it *must* follow that I have peace with others. Peace with God, peace within, peace with others. Now, we can talk easily about peace with people that we will never meet. We can go on about international peace and building bridges between nations. It can all sound very good and, of course, it has its necessary place. But I need to bring this home – literally *home,* to my wife, children, brothers and sisters in my church family, and people in my neighbourhood – real people who might think and look and vote differently than I. It makes little sense if a person jets around the world spreading 'peace' in distant lands if he despises his neighbour or cannot get along with his own wife. Relationships are where discipleship gets real.

Whoever claims to love God yet hates a brother or sister is a liar. For whoever does not love their brother and sister, whom they have seen, cannot love God, whom they have not seen. (1 John 4:20)

How do we promote peace toward those with whom we actually share life? How do we become not simply passive appeasers ('Chamberlains'), but active peacemakers and peace protectors ('Churchills')?

Before we see a simple, practical, profound key to peace-making and peacekeeping, let's notice the caveat in Jonathan's *Resolution*: *unless love requires otherwise.* There can be times when genuine love and concern for the greater good requires one to break the peace. Perhaps sin needs to be confronted and doing so will cause – at least in the short term – a war to break out. False peace is an enemy of true peace and a peacemaker does not want to preserve false peace. So how do we promote, make, and preserve true peace among our fellows? The answer is profoundly simple but living it out can sometimes be profoundly difficult: we make peace with those around us the same way that God has made peace with us – via the wonders of the Gospel. Never forgetting the wonders of mercy and grace that have been lavished upon us, we in turn live a lifestyle of lavishing grace upon others. This does not mean we are soft on sin. It does not mean we do not confront difficulties that need to be faced. Quite the opposite: armed with redemptive love, and the Good News of Jesus, we are bold to speak, refusing to dodge issues that we know will only lead to conflict and destroy peace (think Churchill vs. Chamberlain again).

But it also means that, as those who have received lavish grace from God, we cease to be critical and judgmental. We refuse to be peace-destroying faultfinders. We relentlessly pursue redemption because that is how God deals with us. We do not 'write people off' as the world does and settle for fracture and brokenness because God did not write us off and settle for fracture and brokenness. He came and made peace through the cross and so we work tirelessly to apply that cross-shaped peace to the real people all around us. We love the sinner in front of us, and battle for peace with him, because we love the One behind us who first made peace with us. We are the ambassadors of the glorious Heaven-sent Gospel of Peace. We start right where we live. We do not have the option not to.

> The true soldier fights not because he hates what is in front of him,
> but because he loves what is behind him.[58] (G.K. Chesterton)

Resolution 34

Resolved to speak the plain and pure truth, without exaggeration, at all times.

Lord, who may dwell in your sacred tent? Who may live on your holy mountain The one ... who speaks the truth from their heart whose tongue utters no slander ... and casts no slur on others ... (Ps. 15:1–3)

Dear Friends,

Where is truth these days? It is a rare commodity, more precious than gold! 'Buy the truth and do not sell it', advises the wise man (Prov. 23:23). In ancient Israel, Isaiah came with the sad proclamation, 'Truth has stumbled in the streets!' (Is. 59:14). It has in our day as well.

One politician says one thing; another claims the opposite. Products are advertised as 'the biggest', 'the newest', 'the fastest' and so on. So many voices were telling us 'the truth' about the recent pandemic. Who do we believe? Then, need I mention all the differing perspectives on racial tension, police issues, international calamities, and climate concerns. Into this stale and toxic atmosphere blows the fresh wind of a godly eighteen-year-old who has resolved 'to speak the plain and pure truth, without exaggeration, at all times'. Ah ... take a deep breath and let that feel good. I need to let it impact me personally. I can change a culture by letting God change me. I do not have to be infected by the viral spiral of lies, manipulation, and spin. I can – and must – resolve to be a man of simple truth. Let's step back and survey things from God's perspective for a minute.

Let's remember a few things about *God*. Oh, how we need to have God, not man, as our standard in these compromised times! Let us remember:

> That God is a God of Truth: *He is the Rock; his work is perfect: for all his ways are judgment: a God of truth and without injustice, righteous and upright is he.* (Deut. 32:4 NKJV)

> That God hates lying, lies, and ... lying lips (which are attached to people with lying hearts): *The Lord detests lying lips, but he delights in people who are trustworthy.* (Prov. 12:22)

> That God will punish all liars eternally: *All liars ... will be consigned to the fiery lake of burning sulphur.* (Rev. 21:8)

Consider how transformed our families, our business dealings, our political systems might be if, in every communication, we remembered that *God loves truth, hates lies and lying lips, and will punish all liars forever in hell.* Make *that* part of the oath of public office! But it is too easy to point to politicians and movie stars to find our lies and liars. It is more necessary that we look at ourselves. There are numerous ways in which genuine Christians fail to tell the simple, plain, unembellished truth.

One is through the use of sarcasm (and teasing). This is all too common amongst us followers of the One who only and always speaks truthfully, and we need to see it as an ungodly form of communication. Sarcasm actually conveys contempt toward the object. It is a cowardly way to tell someone that we have a problem with them. The Bible teaches us to speak honestly with those with whom we have a problem (Matt. 18:15). I have had a life-long habit of sarcasm, teasing, and poking fun. I have been convicted that God (and my wife) simply wants me to speak the truth. I have for many years now been trying to break a habit of communication which fails to honour God and others. Help me, Jesus!

Exaggeration and embellishment are other forms of sinful communication. To overstate a case is to lie. Oh my! Who does not do this? Our whole world of commerce seems to overstate, puff up, mislead, garnish, etc. The old trope of the horse-trader who oversells his animal or the buyer who coyly grumbles at the purchase to haggle down the price are examples of dishonesty:

> *'It's no good, it's no good!' says the buyer – then goes off and boasts about the purchase.* (Prov. 20:14)

Exaggeration is a culturally acceptable form of lying. But it is not acceptable to God! I have struggled with this sin (I am the biggest exaggerator in the whole history of the world), largely because it is so acceptable. But Jonathan's *Resolution* will not allow for it.

Flattery is an abuse of truth. Flattery praises another, but for ulterior and selfish motives. It is therefore dishonest. The Apostle Paul could say plainly, 'You know we never used flattery ...' (1 Thess. 2:5) and Job warned, '... if I were skilled in flattery, my Maker would soon take me away' (Job 32:22).

(Oh dear. This is all getting too close for comfort!)

Making excuses is another form of lying. Many of us do it all the time. We do it so much we do not even notice the sinister nature of it. 'I forgot', can be just an excuse. So can, 'I do not feel well', when the real truth is that we do not want to do something.

How about apologizing when we do not really mean it? 'Sorry I was late'. Likewise, 'I'll pray for you', 'I'll call you', 'Let's meet up sometime', 'Leave it to me', can be either meaningful statements or convenient ways just to get out of a conversation which amount to ... lies.

So, dare we resolve with our young hero 'to speak the plain and pure truth, without exaggeration, at all times'? But by all means let's accept this challenge with a sigh of relief! Being a person of simple truth makes life vastly easier. You don't need a good memory if you never have anything to cover up. Relationships are kept strong and steady when truthfulness binds them. May the Lord Jesus forgive us our lying ways and make us simple, truth-telling, guilt-free, non-manipulating, God-fearing, truth-loving followers of Him whose very words are Truth.

> One man who stopped lying could bring down a tyranny.[59]
> (Aleksandr Solzhenitsyn)

Resolution 35

Resolved, when I am not sure if I have done as the Lord willed in a situation, and my peace is therefore disturbed, to not just ignore it, but to take note of it, and to also pay attention to how the matter was resolved.

Let the peace of Christ rule in your hearts ... (Col. 3:15)

Dear Followers,

We are, and will be, as holy – and therefore as happy – as we want to be.

It is hard to overstate the value of a healthy and peaceful conscience. The best and most useful saints of old were men and women who were careful with their consciences, their inner selves, their hearts. They could feel the approach of sin. They could tell when they were 'out of sorts'. They were aware of times when they crossed boundaries and trespassed into forbidden territory, even in the secret places of their hearts. They walked closely with God and, therefore, could tell when they had fallen out of step with Him.

Many of us, by comparison, are a clumsy bunch. We run roughshod over our consciences, bruising and battering our hearts. Having 'asked Jesus into our hearts', therefore considering ourselves to have settled the matter of our eternal destiny, we carelessly get on with doing what we really like to do: pursuing our own agenda with little thought of God. The idea of:

- daily fellowshipping with God,
- being watchful over our hearts,

- keeping in step with the Holy Spirit,
- knowing the deep secret chambers of our hearts,
- feeling the loss of tender peace,
- sensing when sin has gained a foothold in us ...

... such things (which our Jesus-following grandparents took as basic to their spiritual well-being and walk with Jesus) we see as optional, advanced and perhaps even excessive.

Jonathan watches over his heart as a banker would his books or a gardener his flowers. I have known diligent gardeners. My wife is one. A successful gardener takes notes. They write things down: 'This worked. I'll do that again! This did not work. I won't do that again!' No one thinks them strange when the beautiful fruit is borne. But ah! That fruit was not borne by accident. It was the result of deliberate, diligent, decisive direction!

Knowing that his heart – his real self – has been purchased by the blood of Jesus to be God's sanctuary, he is careful to notice when sin has disturbed his peace. Rather than having to be yanked around like a recalcitrant mule (Ps. 32:8–9), Jonathan urges us to be instructed by our loving heavenly Father, who will use His own peace within us as a guide and check to our attitudes and actions. Roy Hession, in his remarkable book *The Calvary Road,* invites us to allow God's peace to act like a referee in our hearts:

> There is one simple but all-inclusive guide the Word of God gives to regulate our walk with Jesus and to make us to know when sin has come in. Colossians 3:15 says, 'Let the peace of God rule in your hearts'. Everything that disturbs the peace of God in our hearts is sin, no matter how small it is, and no matter how little like sin it may at first appear to be. This peace is to 'rule' our hearts, or (a more literal translation) 'be the referee' in our hearts. When the referee blows his whistle at a football match, the game has to stop, a foul has been committed. When we lose our peace, God's referee in our hearts has blown his whistle! Let us stop immediately, ask God to show us what is wrong, put ... the sin He shows us under the Blood of Jesus, and then peace will be restored ...[60]

Do you see the diligence in this *Resolution*? Jonathan tells us that when he loses his peace, rather than just shrugging it off, masking it over, or blaming it on another, he will actually 'take note of it'. He will write it down. He will journal it. He wants to be able to refer to the experience in the future. He will not forget the experience. His walk with his Saviour is of paramount importance to him, and therefore, if some action or attitude has diminished his peace, he wants to know it, understand it, and not allow it to gain a foothold in his life. Likewise, he wants to note how he resolved the matter. When did he first notice his peace had vanished? What did he do to restore his peace? What did repentance look like in that instance? What did he learn from not only the misstep, but from the recovery?

I need to be gripped by the motive and heart of this young man. I need to make his resolve mine. Desiring Christ above all, pursuing holiness of heart and life, wanting continued fellowship with Jesus, seeking first to be shaped into God's likeness *–is not fanaticism*! It is what I (we) have been redeemed for. Friend, will you be like a horse or a mule, uncontrollable and in need of a heavy hand? Or will you be one controlled in the heart by the gentle and wonderful peace of God? Will your walk with Jesus be so important to you that you will allow nothing to destroy your fellowship with your dear Saviour? Oh, let us learn to cultivate that listening heart, that tender conscience, that hears the referee's whistle!

Blessed are the single-hearted, for they shall enjoy much peace.[61]
(Amy Carmichael)

Resolution 36

Resolved never to speak against anybody, except I have some good
and necessary reason to do so.

*So, the people grumbled against Moses ... They grumbled in their tents
and did not obey the Lord.* (Ex.15:24; Ps. 106:25)

Dear Friends,

This is now the third time our young Jonathan has checked
himself in regard to speaking words against another. Why?

Is it that Jonathan, wanting to live rightly in a world gone wrong,
is aware of a particular proneness on his part to be critical of others –
especially when he takes his eyes off of Jesus? Could be.

Perhaps he, knowing that it offends God to speak against another
for whom Christ has died and whom Christ deeply loves, is aware
of and grieved by his own critical spirit. Being critical of others is
a particular danger for earnest Christians who care about truth,
witness, and lifestyle.

Notice that Jonathan is not saying that we must *never* speak against
another. His caveat is that there must be a good and necessary reason
to do so. Speaking against someone must be motivated by love. There
must be a true and genuine desire before God and people to bring
about a greater good.

Look with me at the Bible passages given at the top of this letter.
I have blended two passages into one because they refer to the same
event. Exodus 15 narrates the grumbling of Israel against Moses, and
Psalm 106 – written centuries later – gives an interesting commentary

on that grumbling. I could have cited many occasions in the story of the Exodus when Israel grumbled, because grumbling had become habitual for them. But Psalm 106 gives a vital insight: 'They grumbled in their tents ...' In other words, they sat around, in what they thought was private, and complained about Moses. And here is the stinger: *God heard them and judged them.* They no doubt were thinking that no one heard. 'We are in the privacy of our own tents,' they thought. But they had not factored *God* in! Major mistake!

> *So, He swore to them with an uplifted hand*
> *that He would make them fall in the desert.*
> (Ps. 106:26)

Yikes!

Clearly there are multiple reasons why Jonathan repeats and repeats this *Resolution*. To speak against another without just cause is a grievous, pernicious sin. The offense caused to God and the hurt caused to man is massive. I think that we today habitually speak against brothers and sisters in Christ. We find ourselves taking delight in the folly of others and we sometimes take perverse pleasure in re-telling the stories of others' failings and flaws. How God is grieved! Moreover, in our current cultural climate, venom flies between public figures at a furious pace and it is all too easy to enter in. Be careful lest you find yourself sucked into the swirling vortex – like refuse in a toilet – of fault-finding. It is one thing to speak your mind plainly and with a humble heart; it is another thing to speak hatefully and with a haughty heart against another ... even a politician. Remember that, while politicians are accountable to the voting public and should be held to account, they are made in God's image and Jesus loves them too.

So, I want to venture out on a limb for a moment in an effort to give real wisdom as to *how* and *when* it is right to speak against another.

I will begin with *how*, for the how to speak against another is very simple: with tears and in the conscious fear of God. If I can speak against another without a broken heart and being forgetful of the fact that God hears every word I speak (see Matt. 12:36), then I am part of the problem and not part of the solution.

As for the *when,* I am going to borrow wisdom from Bishop Augustine (354–430). This good and godly genius forged for us what has been called *The Just War Theory.* Augustine has given us guidelines for when it is right for a Christian to go to war, which I will attempt to adapt into a *Just Speaking-Against-Another Theory.* Ready?

When speaking against another, I must be certain that:

1) I have the *authority* to do so. My relationship to the person or the situation puts me in a position whereby I am not merely meddling or sticking my nose into someone else's business.

2) There is a *just cause* which compels me to speak. Something has happened, is happening, or might happen which will offend God or harm people if I do not speak.

3) I have the *right intention.* My desire is not just to 'be right' but to genuinely promote good and avert evil.

4) Speaking against another must be *a last resort.* I have prayed. I have approached the person first, if possible, and I see no other course of action but to speak.

With these four principles in mind, now my words must be:

1) *Proportional:* as few as possible and absolutely no more than needed to do good.

2) *Discriminating:* not scattered carelessly but spoken only to those who must hear them and to no others.

3) *Responsible: I* am responsible for the words I say including the pain they may cause to others.

Thank you, Bishop Augustine!

Perhaps you will pray these words with me:

Lord! I want my words to be sweet and healing! I do not want to be a grumbling, gossiping, fault-finding, part of the problem! I sanctify my tongue, as an expression of my heart, to You, Lord Jesus. 'Set a guard over my mouth, Lord; keep watch over the door of my lips. Do not let my heart be drawn to what is evil so that I take part in wicked deeds.' (Ps. 141:3–4)

May the Lord Jesus cause us to sanctify our words to His greater purposes.

Be careful what you say. Be careful how you say it. Be careful that you send the right message, that you send it to the right person, and that you do so with the right motive.[62] (Chuck Swindoll)

Resolution 37

Resolved, each night at bedtime, to take an account of my day, asking myself, 'In what ways did I fail to do God's will for my life today? What sins have I committed that I need to confess? In what ways have I done well, denying myself and living for Christ?' I also resolved to take such account weekly, monthly, and yearly.

We want each of you to show this same diligence to the very end, so that what you hope for may be fully realized. (Heb. 6:11)

Dear Friends in Jesus,

I have said it before and it is worth saying again: each of us will be as holy – and therefore as happy – as we want to be. There is no shortage of grace available on God's part. Every child of grace can know the joy and purpose that comes with being diligent over one's heart.

I like stories of men and women who give their best and, in return, become excellent in their endeavours. Golfer Gary Player was just such a person for me. Gary was born in South Africa in 1935 and his mother died when he was just eight years old. His father worked away in the gold mines. The family didn't have much. Little Gary (he was only 5'6") excelled in sports ... especially golf. Gary dedicated himself to becoming the best golfer he could be. He would go on to win more professional tournaments than any man in history ... 160! He and Vivienne, his wife of 63 years, raised their six children in a Christian home. To this day, his Gary Player Foundation has raised and given over $65 million to children's charities around the world.

Gary, otherwise known as 'Mr. Fitness,' is famous for many slogans and sayings but perhaps for none more (when referred to as 'lucky') than the response, 'The harder I practice, the luckier I get!'

No man, no woman, no person ever has achieved their potential without hard work and deliberate intention. Diligence! Focus! Purpose! Perseverance! So, we shift from a young golfer in South Africa to a young Jesus-follower in early America. The stakes for Jonathan Edwards are vastly higher than those for Gary Player, but the attitude and intention that we find in one are to be found in the other. Jonathan has a goal as sure as Gary does, but Jonathan's embraces both time and Eternity. Jonathan wants to be all that he can be for Jesus. He has already resolved to live with all of his might for Jesus, to waste not a day, to live with intention and purpose. And ... *he knows his goals will not be achieved by accident, by luck.*

We can look with envy upon those who have pressed in with Jesus. We can wish that we too had discovered Him in all the wonderful ways in which He has revealed Himself to them. We can dream that we had their peace, their power, their purity. But the fact is that they have run after God! They have yearned while we have yawned! They have worshipped while we have wandered! They have been diligent while we have been delinquent! Nothing happens without discipline and diligence. Diligence and discipline are *not* opposed to grace. Grace is not opposed to effort. Grace is not license for leisure, but power for purpose. Picture Jonathan at bedtime. His day is over. Like a careful accountant or an earnest shopkeeper, he takes stock. He goes over things. He considers, he tallies, he reckons. He leaves nothing to chance. His investigations are vital to the achieving of his goal. His goal is to be more like Jesus and to be useful in His hands. So, he asks himself vital questions:

- How did I do today as a Jesus-follower?
- Did I put myself to doing what Jesus had for me to do?
- In what ways did I shirk my duties?
- Were my attitudes and words and thoughts God-honouring?
- Did I live to please myself or my Saviour today?
- Did I say 'no' to self and 'yes' to Jesus today?
- Did I seek to serve or to be served?

– Did I employ the abundant grace of God for His Glory and my growth today?

What might I need to confess to my wonderful Lord before I close the books on this day? Such questions are not toilsome to a Jesus-follower who has a clear aim in view. They are helpful. Many (most?) of us end our days with a bleary-eyed TV show or by scrolling aimlessly through our phones. How might our spirits benefit from some earnest time of reflection with Jesus? Having observed people who excel in their passion, you cannot escape spotting their diligence. They track their progress. They go back over their weak points. It is the musician who practices her scales with the metronome ticking who becomes the virtuosa. Every person who has reached a goal has learned to chart and journal, to examine and adjust, saying 'yes' to what is truly important and 'no' to a thousand lesser rivals.

Israel's David, who knew what it was like to be careless with his spirit, learned the hard way to be careful over it. He prayed a prayer we can join in: *Search me, God, and know my heart; test me and know my anxious thoughts. See if there is any offensive way in me, and lead me in the way everlasting.* (Ps. 139:23–24)

I present to you a happy challenge: learn the skill of self-examination. Jonathan did. Jonathan became a spiritual giant. Don't leave your growth in Jesus to luck or happenstance. Ask Jesus to help you become diligent over your inner life the way (I am assuming) you are over your business and hobbies. Don't be afraid to ask yourself hard questions. Don't be slow to make adjustments. Be willing to say 'no' to the lesser so that you can say 'yes' to the greater. And remember: God is for you (2 Pet. 1:3–8)!

In a very real sense, a diligent person must learn to be neglectful. There are myriad clamouring and demanding temptations and lesser priorities a diligent person must strategically neglect.[63] (Jon Bloom)

Resolved 38

Resolved to never use the Lord's Day for my own entertainment, for foolish words or for foolish behaviour.

There remains, then, a Sabbath-rest for the people of God. (Heb. 4:9)

Dear Friends,

While I doubt that anyone will ever name a son 'Covid', there is one great redeeming quality this virus had for us: It forced us as individuals and as communities to *rest*. God has given us the *gift* of fifty-two days off a year and we, as a culture, have said, 'Thanks, but no thanks!' We go through our days frazzled and frayed. In 2 Chronicles, a disobedient and godless Israel has been hauled off into exile. And *finally*, the land is getting the 'Sabbath rest' it is due and desperately needs. (You can almost hear the sigh of relief.)

For Christians, the Sabbath – the Lord's Day, Sunday – is a powerful statement to God, to ourselves and to the watching world. When we stop to rest, re-create, revive, and revere, we say to God, 'We *treasure* You, Lord, above work and play. We *trust* your goodness as we come away from other things to draw near to You. We say something to ourselves. We say, 'We believe that time spent *apart* will keep us *together*. We are resting from our labours as a statement that we have entered the Rest of the Gospel. Jesus has delivered us from the labour of earning our salvation!' We say something to the watching world: 'We are citizens of another Kingdom, where we honour Jesus, who has given us Rest from our enemies and brought us into the peace and safety of salvation'.

Sabbath is God's appointed Rest, a time to *abide*, a rhythm in our lives, a Day to pause, pray, and ponder on the forgotten realities of another world. We receive it to our blessing; we reject it to our peril. But let's quickly dispense with the obvious extremes in regard to Sundays:

1) Legalism. A day to dread. One dare not laugh, or play. One dear old English saint was so against any form of ball game on a Sunday, he used to say, 'If it's round, its *wrong!*' Perhaps (and who am I to say?) Jonathan errs on this side.

2) License: Sunday is just an extension of Saturday. Get church over with (or, better yet, worship God on the golf course) and then work, indulge, watch sports, and shop-till-you-drop. Perhaps (and I say this from my own experience) you and I err on this side.

Can we agree that both are extremes?

Now, how can we best keep our Rest?

Firstly, we can remember the goodness of God and our own foolishness. I do not think it is possible to live a meaningful, joyful, and impactful Christian life without a meaningful, joyful, and impactful Sabbath. John the Revelator tells us, 'On the Lord's Day I was in the Spirit' (Rev. 1:10), not, 'On the Lord's Day I was in the shopping mall'. It is safe to conclude that there was a direct relation to where he was on that day, and what he received on that day. He had set apart time to meet with Jesus ... and, boy, did he! I seriously doubt that he would have had his encounter with Jesus at the local Stuff Mart.

Then, we need to earnestly apologize to God for mocking His design and gift. We have made a day that our grandparents reverently called 'The Lord's Day' into 'Our Day'. We *do* waste it in entertainment, worldly pursuit, and foolishness. Even if we squeeze church in, many of us exhaust ourselves with our agendas. Our bodies, our families, our friendships, and mostly *our souls* are suffering greatly for our foolish, arrogant disobedience.

The Sabbath was instituted right at the beginning – creation has Sabbath in it: Genesis 2:2–3. You will remember that after God redeemed Israel from Egypt, He enshrined it in the Ten

Commandments: Exodus 20:8. And then, many times, God promised blessings for Israel for keeping the Sabbath, and warned of consequences for playing fast and loose with it: Isaiah 58:14.

Eventually, the religious rulers of Israel ruined the Sabbath by making certain observances of it a demarcation of true spirituality. They forgot that it was a gift from God (52 days off a year!) and turned it into a burden:

> *Then Jesus asked them, 'Which is lawful on the Sabbath: to do good or to do evil, to save life or to kill?' But they remained silent. He looked around at them in anger and, deeply distressed at their stubborn hearts, said to the man, 'Stretch out your hand.' He stretched it out, and his hand was completely restored.* (Mark 3:4–6)

Jesus, God the Son, was angry and distressed at this misuse of the Sabbath! It was a gift from God to people, not a religious ritual that crushes people. He delivered the Sabbath from religious abuse but did not abolish it. He re-booted it:

> *Then he said to them, 'The Sabbath was made for man, not man for the Sabbath.'* (Mark 2:27)

Now get this: for Christians, the Sabbath is ... Jesus and His Gospel!

Jesus is our Sabbath. He is our Rest. Jesus, the One who saves us from the yoke of religion and sin, is the Sabbath Rest for the believer.

So, if we have Jesus, do we still need the day?

The *day* is still important because it points to the *Person* we treasure. We *do not* keep Sunday to justify ourselves before God, but we *should* keep Sunday as a testimony – to God, to ourselves, and to others – that we have found Rest in Jesus Christ. To keep Sunday without knowing Jesus is just old-fashioned legalistic religion. But to keep the day as a celebration that we have found the Reality to which it points is precious, powerful, rejuvenating, and joyful.

Let's not waste it!

I will leave you with a wonderful old Sunday Hymn to reflect on:

Dear Lord and Father of mankind,
forgive our foolish ways;

reclothe us in our rightful mind,
in purer lives thy service find,
in deeper reverence, praise.

Drop thy still dews of quietness,
till all our strivings cease;
take from our souls the strain and stress,
and let our ordered lives confess
the beauty of thy peace.
(John Greenleaf Whittier, 1807–1892)

Resolution 39

Resolved to never do anything that I question the lawfulness of, unless the prospect of not doing it appears to be equally unlawful.

Blessed is the one who does not condemn himself by what he approves.
(Rom. 14:22)

Dear Brothers and Sisters,

I want to follow Jesus with all my heart! But sometimes, in some situations, I do not know what to do!

Before we dive into this *Resolution*, I think we need to confirm ourselves in the profound freedom of life in Christ. There is the danger lurking in this *Resolution* for the unwary. If we are not keeping our eyes on Jesus and His finished work for our redemption, it can lead to over-introspection and an unhealthy fear of 'getting it wrong', which freezes rather than frees us.

Every believer lives under the banner of God's super-abundant grace. We need not hug the shore, forever afraid to venture out to the deep lest we somehow displease God and He washes His hands of us. I have known dear children of God who are so afraid of 'getting it wrong' that they never try anything at all! We need always to remember that Christians live in a state of grace and walk in the mercy and forgiveness of God. It is from that place of security that we leave the shallows and dare go to the depths. We can be sure that Jonathan does not want himself, or us, frozen in inaction through fear of making a mistake. He understands the grace of God too fully for that! His life of daring faith and full-on following is evidence of a free, not a frozen, spirit.

So, with a firm and joyful understanding of our security and freedom in Jesus, let's explore this *Resolution* – one which urges us toward caution, toward careful listening to the Holy Spirit's voice to our consciences. Just like every car needs *both* an accelerator *and* a brake, our conscience needs to act like a brake in our lives when the Holy Spirit prompts us to apply it! In the Christian life, there are matters of black and white – no need for discussion, no need even to pray about them! But there are grey areas. We might not want to admit that, but there are. There is wiggle room. There are points upon which Christians differ. There are things we need to wrestle over and seek God about. There are times when we move forward in faith, only to find that we are on thin ice and need to turn back.

In the Scripture at the top of this letter, the Apostle Paul is giving some guidance for just such times. The issue Paul was addressing was eating of certain foods. That may seem trivial and silly to us today, but in the Roman church, where Jewish Christians (and their endless food laws) and Gentile Christians (with their 'pass the ribs!' attitude) were learning to follow Jesus together, the issue was hot and serious. Paul's principle applies far beyond food. It is very simple: if I cannot move forward in faith, that is, engage in a particular activity with confidence that it is right to do so before the Lord, then if I proceed, I am sinning against my conscience. Jonathan's *Resolution* affirms that unless the weight upon one's conscience of *not* proceeding with an action is equal to – or greater than – that of proceeding, then it is wrong to proceed when one's Bible-instructed conscience is saying 'hit the brakes'.

There have been many times in Christian history when believers have had to make hard decisions and they were guided by this principle. A clear example was when Dietrich Bonhoeffer was faced with the evil of Adolph Hitler and his regime. The young pastor was a pacifist by conviction. He could not see room for violence in the life of a Christian, particularly in defence of the state. However, he finally saw that love demanded that Hitler be stopped. *Not* to do something was a clearer sin than to *do* something. So, his Bible-guided conscience led this pacifist to engage in a plot to kill Hitler, for which he was arrested in 1943 and hanged in 1945. Many Godly people down the ages have had to make such decisions – see the book of Daniel, chapter 6 – and we may find ourselves making them someday too. Consider the following all-too-relevant scenarios:

– A missionary must enter a closed country for mission work on a tourist visa because that is the only way in. OK?

– Should you allow your child and their same sex 'spouse' to share a room when they visit you?

– Do I give a homeless person money? Maybe they will only use it for alcohol, but what if they starve because I don't give?

– Should I attend a family event I don't approve of? If I go, I must consider the family effect. If I don't attend, it may cause a family fallout for a long time. Which is worse?

Such situations are real and increasingly pressing in upon us as our culture spins away from God, and the Church cannot and must not legislate every nuance of life. May the *Resolution* of a young disciple who lived in a saner age give us wisdom and courage to honour God and live boldly for Jesus in our world today. Let us '*[t]rust in the Lord with all [our] heart and lean not on [our] own understanding; in all [our] ways submit to Him and He will make [our] paths straight*' (Prov. 3:5–6).

Every day my conscience makes confession relying on the hope of Your mercy as more to be trusted than its own innocence.[64]
(Augustine of Hippo)

Resolution 40

Resolved to consider, at the close of each day, the habits of that day, especially in regard to my eating and drinking.

I have the right to do anything,' you say – but not everything is beneficial. 'I have the right to do anything' – but I will not be mastered by anything. (1 Cor. 6:12)

Dear Friends,

Jonathan! You have gone too far this time! We are happy for you to speak of the sins of others or of sin in the abstract. We are happy for you to talk about holiness in vague, undefined terms. But, now you have begun to meddle in our private world; now you are sticking your nose too far into our business; now you have touched a nerve; now you have offended one of our sacred *idols!*

There is a new 'super-spirituality' doing the rounds today that divides your spirit from your body. It wants to tell you that what you believe in your private heart about Jesus need not affect what you do with your body. Actually, this super-spirituality is not new. It invaded the first century church in a heresy called Gnosticism. Gnosticism taught – and teaches – that salvation is a secret inner thing, a private knowledge, that need not in any way affect your outward living. The Apostle John was speaking against Gnosticism when he wrote:

We know that we have come to know him if we keep his commands. Whoever says, 'I know him,' but does not do what he commands is a liar, and the truth is not in that person. But if anyone obeys his word, love for God is truly made complete in them. This is how we know

we are in him: whoever claims to live in him must live as Jesus did.
(1 John 2:3–6)

The modern Gnostic, super-spiritual Christian will recoil at this *Resolution*: What does what I do with my body have to do with what I feel in my soul? Moderation in food and drinking – taking stock of it every day? What does that have to do with discipleship?

In fact, bringing eating and drinking under the Lordship of Jesus Christ *is not advanced discipleship!* It is basic discipleship. Refusing to be mastered by anything, including – especially – food and drink is vital to learning to bring every aspect of our lives under the wonderful Lordship of Jesus.

OK. Let's make sure we have some balance here. Is this *Resolution* not moving us too far toward austerity and asceticism? Are we next going to be wearing burlap and sleeping on a bed of nails? Jonathan's legacy shows that he could rejoice and feast with the best of them.[65] His resolve to be diligent with what he put into his body must not be mistaken for crusty, grim, tasteless Christianity! God gave us taste buds. He invented flavours and textures and smells. Throughout the Bible, God invited Israel to stop all other distractions and *feast*. God is no killjoy; He is the source of all joy. But ... Satan's whole career is based around taking the good things God has given and enticing us to pervert them. He has done that with sex, work, creativity, and just about any and every good thing; food and drink are no different. We end up becoming enslaved to food. We harm our God-given bodies through food and drink abuse. We dull our senses, shorten our lives, and reduce our usefulness.

Tom Brady, the football player (for my UK friends, by 'football' I mean the American kind that you play with your hands), winner of *five* Super Bowls, widely called 'The Greatest of All Time' (the GOAT), is famous for his careful use of food. He has his own diet regime known as the TB12 Diet. His whole goal is to reach peak performance for the sake of throwing a ball. But! How dare Jonathan Edwards suggest to a follower of Jesus that they do *the very same thing!* Jonathan's goal is also 'peak performance', but for him this is all about Jesus and Eternal Kingdom and a crown that will last!

This *Resolution* is about stewardship of one of our most valuable resources, our bodies. Christians cannot, dare not, divide the physical life from the spiritual (1 Cor. 6:19–20). Friends, '[t]here is a time for everything, and a season for every activity under the heavens' (Ecc. 3:1). How wonderful is our God that He has given us wine to make us glad and food to feast upon! But we want to be at our best for Him, for His call, for His service. May we in joy, not in sorrow and servitude, bring every aspect of our lives under the Lordship of Jesus ... especially our food and drink habits. If Tom Brady can do it to win trophies that will tarnish, God will give us all grace to do so for trophies that will last forever! Remember that *[e]veryone who competes in the games goes into strict training. They do it to get a crown that will not last; but we do it to get a crown that will last forever* (1 Cor. 9:25).

No child of grace will ever reach the finish line and regretfully say, "Dang, I was too earnest for Jesus! I should have been more careless!"

> It is altogether fitting and proper that we should enjoy things made for us to enjoy. What is not at all fitting or proper is that we should set our hearts on them. Temporal things must be treated as temporal things – received, given thanks for, offered back, but enjoyed. They must not be treated like eternal things.[66] (Elizabeth Elliot)

Resolution 41

Resolved to ask myself at the end of every day, week, month and year, how I could possibly in any respect have done better.

Examine yourselves to see whether you are in the faith; test yourselves. Do you not realise that Christ Jesus is in you – unless, of course, you fail the test? (2 Cor. 13:5)

Dear Friends,

There is a big difference between self-examination and introspection. One is a good thing. One is a bad thing. One is healthy. One is not.

Should Christians examine their hearts, motives, actions, and intentions? Yes. Should followers of Jesus battle against indwelling sin, search their hearts, and repent often? Of course. Self-examination is vital to our growth in grace and to following Jesus well.

But ... there is a tendency among many of us to be forever looking inwards, ever scraping our insides, hunting for evidence of righteousness, ever looking for the vestiges of sin, in intense, navel-gazing introspection. This is not what God would have us do. As A.W. Tozer taught us, true faith is the gaze of the eyes of the soul away from itself and onto the God who saves. This means we need to avoid over-introspection. It is unhealthy and detrimental to our well-being in Jesus, and can lead to self-condemnation. The answer for a Christian is not found *within* but *without*. It is not *inside* but *outside*. I need to look to *Jesus* not to *myself*.

But if introspection is a bad thing, self-examination is a good and necessary thing. In the Scripture at the top of this letter, the Apostle

Paul urges us to examine ourselves with one aim in view: to see whether we are 'in the faith', so that we might discover and ensure that 'Jesus Christ is in [us]'. In other words, that within us is a living faith in Christ and not in ourselves, a faith which yields to the Word of God and the promptings of the Holy Spirit in our hearts.

Let's explore this *Resolution* through the lens of the Gospel. If we remove the lens of the Gospel and merely focus on the words 'wherein I could possibly have done better', we will inevitably default to introspection and end up either proud of ourselves or in despair. Everything must always be viewed through the Gospel!

So ... how does a Gospel-believing man or woman examine him or herself? Below I offer key questions to ask oneself daily, weekly, monthly, yearly. These questions are not just 'How am I doing?' questions, but – and the difference is vital – 'How am I doing *in Jesus*?' questions, which enable a proper self-examination that will help us to grow in grace. Neglecting self-examination will inhibit our growth in grace, allowing lies of the enemy to get in and sin to take root, proving harmful to both our joy and usefulness in Jesus' Kingdom.

Questions to ask myself at the close of a day and at other seasons of self-examination:

1) Have I looked away from myself today and to the God who saves, or have I been consumed by looking to myself for righteousness (1 Cor. 1:30)?

2) Have I looked at others, especially those nearest to me, through the Gospel, receiving them in Christ, giving and receiving forgiveness and grace, or have I merely looked with a critical, selfish eye (1 Cor. 5:16–17)?

3) In what ways have I chosen Christ today as my source of life and joy, and in what ways have I turned from Him and sought joy in things that cannot satisfy (Jer. 2:13; John 7:37–38)?

4) Have I sought grace to love my neighbour, including those who do not love me back? Have I reached out to serve others or have I merely pursued my own wants (Mark 9:35)?

5) Have I promoted the fame of Jesus and loved others by speaking the Gospel as God has granted openings or have I been silent and unloving, hiding my light under a basket (Matt. 5:14–15)?

6) Have I been open to the leading of God's Spirit, wanting to walk in His purposes for me, saying 'no' to self and 'yes' to Jesus, or have I selfishly pursued my own agenda (Eph. 2:10)?

7) Have I honoured Jesus in my inner thought life and in the secret place, or have I allowed sin to have its way in my unseen life, allowing lies of the enemy to overwhelm me (Ps. 19:14)?

8. Have I repented of any sin of commission or omission, received the cleansing blood and have I let go of regret (1 John 1:9)?

God wants us to do well! He is for us! By all means, examine yourself daily, weekly, often. Be deliberate about it. You will do well if you do. Perhaps the questions above will help you. If you have some other method, that is fine. But always do so through the Gospel, seeing Christ as your source and your sufficient supply. Avoid self-imploding introspection, thinking that somehow in your own sufficiency you can and will become the person God wants you to be. Look up and away to the God who saves, and then, in the light of His love and constant supply of grace, examine your heart and life.

It is a good practice to spend a few moments at the end of the day, perhaps as you lie down to sleep, and just go over your day in this way. Thank God for the blessings and obediences and repent and receive cleansing for the failings. Ask God for His perspective on your day and then receive God's peace.

Search me, God, and know my heart; test me and know my anxious thoughts. See if there is any offensive way in me, and lead me in the way everlasting. (Ps.139:23–24)

Do all the good you can, by all the means you can, in all the ways you can, in all the places you can, at all the times you can, to all the people you can, as long as ever you can.[67] (John Wesley)

Resolution 42

Resolved to frequently renew my dedication to the Lord, even as I was dedicated to Him at my baptism and was renewed when I was received into the fellowship of the church, and as I have renewed it today.

The fire on the altar must be kept burning; it must not go out. (Lev. 6:12)

Dear Friends,

The Lord knows what we need better than we do. He knows that our hearts quickly grow cold, that zeal abates, that desire dies down, that distractions overtake us. He knows that our memories fail us, that our resolve is often paper thin, and that the call of the world can deafen us to His voice. Before all else, we are called to Jesus. We are saved from sin to Him. But we are a fickle and fragile lot. We wander and wobble. The flame on the altar of our hearts sometimes burns dangerously low. We hear Jesus' call to take up the cross *daily* and follow Him, but we do not always heed. How wonderfully patient God is with us!

Jonathan is wise beyond his years. Recognizing the woefulness of his ways, he resolves to 'frequently renew his dedication to the Lord'. This does not mean he has to 'get saved' all over again. No, justification – the act whereby God declares us forgiven and right with Him through faith in Jesus – is a one-time, permanent pronouncement of God (phew!). But the working out of our salvation requires the frequent renewal of our consecration to Jesus.

In ancient days, God called Israel to Himself. They – of all peoples – were uniquely *His*. Knowing that they, like us, were fickle and failing, He gave them help in regularly renewing their dedication to Himself. Israel had a rhythm of feasts throughout the year. God instituted seven of them. Each one had a different emphasis in regard to their salvation history, each one provided opportunity for God's people – as individuals, families, and as a nation – to stop and think, to reflect and repent, and to rededicate themselves to their saving God. We are not obliged to keep these feasts today. Each one, in some way, looked not only back to Israel's saving history but forward to Jesus Christ; they are fulfilled in Jesus. But still today we need 'helps' in keeping us aflame for Jesus.

Many wonderful followers of Jesus throughout history have built seasons of reflection, repentance, and rededication into the rhythm of their lives. Advent, Lent, Christmas, Easter, and other days and seasons have been used well to keep the flame for Jesus burning for families and churches.

Of course, these can become mere formalities that hold no value and in fear of this many of us have dispensed with most of them. But is there a whiff of arrogance in our readiness to throw off things that helped our fathers follow Jesus? For generations, people have followed Jesus better than I have. Can I not learn from them? I have to confess to you that in my early Christian days, in my youthful zeal, I brazenly threw overboard almost anything that was more than five years old: I did not need the faith of my fathers! Had I to do it over again, I would root myself much more firmly in the wonders and ways of those who had already followed well before me:

Remember your leaders, who spoke the word of God to you. Consider the outcome of their way of life and imitate their faith. Jesus Christ is the same yesterday and today and forever. (Heb. 13:7–8)

We can (and I think should) stand on the shoulders of giants when we embrace the best of Christian history. We can affirm our faith and refresh our walk with Christ when we recite a creed *and mean it*. We can rededicate ourselves to Jesus when we *earnestly* pray the Lord's Prayer. We can do serious business with God when we sing a great hymn. We have, of course, kept Communion as a constant reminder of the Atonement and – hopefully – as a regular help in reflection, repentance, and rededication. Why not use a great, proven devotional to help you in your daily prayer life? Why not prayerfully read one of the great catechisms of our Faith? The Heidelberg Catechism,[68] for instance, dispenses ageless comfort in pithy answers to vital questions that are just as important today as they were in 1563 when they were written.

In our quest to stay authentic and fresh with Jesus, can I urge you to walk the paths that others have already walked? We do not have to reinvent what it means to live well for Jesus! The trails are forged; the way is very well marked! Here are a few great 'helps' that you might find to be a rich source to aid you in your devotion to Jesus:

- *My Utmost for His Highest* by Oswald Chambers,

- *Morning and Evening* by Charles Spurgeon,

- *The Valley of Vision: A Collection of Puritan Prayers and Devotions,*

- *If* by Amy Carmichael.

None of these are a substitute for your Bible, and there are many others that could be added to this brief list, but this is my plea – that we do not fall into the postmodern trap of believing that *we* are somehow the pinnacle of wisdom and that those who went before us have little to offer us. Let us humble ourselves and learn from those who have run well how to live lives truly dedicated to Jesus.

This is what the Lord says: 'Stand at the crossroads and look; ask for the ancient paths, ask where the good way is, and walk in it, and you will find rest for your souls' (Jer. 6:16).

Jesus, confirm my heart's desire
to work, and speak, and think for thee;
still let me guard the holy fire,
and still stir up the gift in me.
(Charles Wesley)

Resolution 43

Resolved, remembering my last *Resolution*, to aim to live all my days knowing that I am not my own, but that I wholly belong to God.

Do you not know that your bodies are temples of the Holy Spirit, who is in you, whom you have received from God? You are not your own; you were bought at a price. Therefore, honour God with your bodies.
(1 Cor. 6:19–20)

Dear Friends,

Purchased! No longer my own! The priceless and prized possession of Jesus Christ!

Settle the matter today, and remind yourself every day, that you are no longer your own. Jesus Christ, the Eternal Son of God, has purchased you for Himself with His own blood (Rev. 5:9). The sobering truth is we are not, nor have we ever been, sovereign lords over ourselves. We *want* to be – we *think* we are – but we are not. Once we were slaves to sin (see Rom. 6:17; John 8:34). Our will was bound and subject to our natures, which were sinful and themselves enslaved to Satan. But! As Romans 6:17–18 reminds us, having been set free from sin through the blood of Christ, we are now slaves to Jesus.

We are now bound to a wonderful Master! We find ourselves now owned by, and enslaved to, the One who made Himself nothing and took upon Himself the very nature of a slave (see Phil. 2:7). I am the servant of the One who did not come to be served, but to serve and to give His life as a ransom for me and for many (see Mark 10:45).

Here is wonderful Jesus, and *He* owns *me!*

So, whenever we speak of being under the Lordship of Jesus, of belonging to Him, of being bought and owned by Him, of giving up all rights to Him, of being ready – without complaint or protest – to do His bidding at all times, we need to remember:

1) The only thing we are free to decide is whose servant we will be, not whether or not we will be a servant.
2) That if we do not serve Jesus, we will serve sin, Satan, and self.
3) That Jesus is altogether wonderful and service to Him is sweet because He is sweet.
4) Slavery to sin leads to death. Slavery to Jesus leads to life.

It is when we forget these foundational truths and begin to think of ourselves as sovereign lords over ourselves that we fall right into the trap the evil one set for our ancient mother, Eve:

> *For God knows that when you eat from it your eyes will be opened, and you will be like God, knowing good and evil.* (Gen. 3:5)

The essence of sin is the desire to 'be like God,' that is, to be sovereign. But Jonathan makes the only *sane* choice! His reasoning is simple:

> I am not *autonomous.*
> I will be servant to *something.*
> I can serve sin, which leads to death, or Jesus, who brings life!
> I choose Jesus!

It is when I want to try to 'make a deal' with God that following Jesus becomes a joyless ball-and-chain. When I offer God part of myself, even most of myself, but hold back that special sweet thing for my own direction and delight, discipleship becomes an impossible chore. When, failing to see myself as totally His and with no rights of my own, I see God as somehow obliged to *my* agenda and wants, then I am surely headed to crash upon the rocky reefs of disillusionment and disappointment. But – there is the twist in the story!

> Surrender to Jesus brings ... *(drum roll)* ... Freedom!

Seeing yourself as 'not your own', reckoning yourself as 'wholly belonging to God', enslaving yourself to Jesus, *sets you free* from the tyranny of slavery to sin, Satan, and self. The Christian – being enslaved to Jesus, being the servant of all people – is in fact the freest man or woman you will ever meet. Sin is a terrible master. Satan is a tyrannical lord. Self is impossible to satisfy. But Jesus is wonderful. He commands, but then empowers. He directs, but first goes before. He is easy to please and delights in our efforts.

I have read so many biographies of men and women who have given up everything to be happily enslaved to Jesus. I have read of their sufferings and marvelled at the challenges they faced. But I have rarely – in fact, never – read of them complaining that service to Jesus has been a wrong choice. *He* has been a delightful and tender Master, and He has always given to *them* more than they give to *Him*.

Friends! When you find your peace abating and your joy deflating, check your heart. Chances are you are staging a – sure to fail – *coup d'état* against the Lordship of Jesus. Stop everything and repent of your holding back from your wonderful Saviour! We are not our own; we were bought with the blood of Jesus. We have been freed from slavery to death to become slaves to the Giver of Life. He has total rights over us, and whatever He chooses for us can and will only be for His Glory and our good. Total surrender leads to total peace and to true freedom.

Perhaps you will take a few minutes and earnestly pray John Wesley's Covenant Prayer. It exalts the Lordship of Jesus and binds the humble believer to His wonderful service:

I am no longer my own, but thine.
Put me to what thou wilt, rank me with whom thou wilt.
Put me to doing, put me to suffering.
Let me be employed for thee or laid aside for thee,
exalted for thee or brought low for thee.
Let me be full, let me be empty.
Let me have all things, let me have nothing.
I freely and heartily yield all things to thy pleasure and disposal.
And now, O glorious and blessed God, Father, Son and Holy Spirit,
thou art mine, and I am thine.
So be it.
And the covenant which I have made on earth,
let it be ratified in heaven. Amen.

Resolution 44

Resolved that I shall live for no other purpose than to know and glorify God, and that all that I do – even the small things – shall be motivated by nothing else besides living for Jesus.

For to me, to live is Christ ... (Phil. 1:21)

Dear Friends,

Is Jonathan Edwards a fanatic? Should we be worried about him? Has he become unbalanced? For an eighteen-year-old young man to say that he wants to 'live for no other purpose than to know and glorify God', and that he 'shall be motivated by nothing else besides living for Jesus', is this not a concern?

Jonathan!

What about finding a wife?
Don't you like sports?
How about your career goals?
Have any healthy hobbies?

Forgive me if I feel a need to defend my young hero. Perhaps he is sprinting out of the starting blocks, but, like a wise long-distance runner, our zealous follower will mature and settle into his stride as the years pass. But should his zeal abate? Should mine? Should yours? Should we begin well only to finish poorly, if at all? Should there not be a 'kick' to our stride as we round the last bend and see the finish ahead? Should we, like a dying fire, 'cool off' with the passing of time? Or rather, should we not find our hearts warming as we get closer to seeing Jesus, even as our excitement grows as we reach the journey's end and the long-desired destination is in view?

I would caution us against judging Jonathan's zeal by modern standards. We modern Western Christians are not the 'Gold Standard' for discipleship. Better to learn from one who ran well and finished his race – even if he sprinted too hard at the start – than from our sofas to criticize him too harshly. Jonathan's *Resolution* for all-out consecration of every aspect of his life to Jesus makes total sense and takes on beauty if we do one thing: dispense with the false and dangerous 'sacred/secular' divide in our lives. We have already talked about how insidious this can be and I will take the time to reiterate that we need to see *all* of life as a consecration of ourselves to Jesus, not just aspects of our lives. If we only see parts of our lives as 'religious' and the rest of our lives as 'regular', then we will forever be struggling with the impossible question, 'Am I *doing* enough spiritual stuff to satisfy God?'

The divide is a false divide because '*[t]he earth is the Lord's, and everything in it ...*' (Ps. 24:1). That means there is nothing outside of the Lordship of Jesus for a Christian. Reading my Bible is sacred, but so is cutting the grass. Praying is spiritual, but so is eating a meal with friends. A well-seasoned Jesus-follower sees everything she does as done before the Lord, unto the Lord, and as a worshipful expression of devotion to Jesus. If I cannot offer a thought or a word or a deed up to Jesus with a thankful, worshipping heart, then I should not do it. If I can, then I can proceed with freedom.

As a matter of fact, if one is reading their Bible when they should be helping with the dishes (as super-spiritual house guests have often done), then at that point, reading the Bible might be offensive to God. Rolling up your sleeves is a holy thing. Embracing your wife, swinging a bat, taking a nap, hiking a trail, going to work, are all expressions of worship for the understanding Christian. The resolve to 'live for no other purpose than to know and glorify God' need not drive one to a monastery. In fact, it is almost certainly better if it does not. The monk in his habit is not holier than the mother in her household. The priest in his parish is not necessarily closer to God than the boy with his ball.

The secularist sees the material, physical world as all that there is. The Christian sees the material world as an expression of the Eternal God, who made the seen world and called it 'good', but who also made an unseen world that transcends time. For the believer, all of life, both the 'hallelujah' and the 'ho-hum' are holy. Well-taught Christians have always understood this and have thus been enabled to offer up every part of their lives in worship, devotion, and freedom to God.

When salted with a bit of maturity, that is what Jonathan is saying in this *Resolution*. This is exactly what the Apostle Paul is presenting to the Philippians when he says, *'For me to live is Christ ...'* (1:21). A desire for total consecration to Jesus is not weird. It is wonderful. While I am at best a faltering follower of a Wonderful Saviour, I want to be "all in" for Jesus ... or at least I *want to want to be.*

Stop striving to make sure that the 'spiritual' section of your life is big enough to keep God happy. Instead, enter into the freedom of *enjoying* all of life as coming from the good hand of a generous God and offer your whole self back to Him in thankful worship. We are redeemed from sin so that all of our lives, and our deaths – whether they be gentle and timely or shocking and sudden – may be a sweet offering to God.

The *Westminster Shorter Catechism,* begins with an affirmation that is as glorious as it is alarming: Man's chief end is to glorify God and to enjoy Him forever.[69]

The crack of a ball on a cricket bat can be as sacred a sound as a church choir if offered to Jesus from worshipping hands.

And whatever you do, whether in word or deed, do it all in the name of the Lord Jesus, giving thanks to God the Father through him.
(Col. 3:17)

Till you can sing and rejoice and delight in God, as misers do in gold, and kings in sceptres, you will never enjoy the world.[70]
(Thomas Trahern)

Resolution 45

Resolved to surrender not only my actions, but my inner life – my emotions and the affections of my heart – to the Lord Jesus, to the end that joy and grief, pleasure and sorrow and all the circumstanes that bring them about, will together serve His greater purpose.

May these words of my mouth and this meditation of my heart be pleasing in your sight, Lord, my Rock and my Redeemer. (Ps. 19:14)

Friends in Jesus,

Ah, the inner life, the secret place – so often ignored, yet seen and cherished by God and as important as the visible outer life! Like an iceberg, or the deep foundation of a building, most of your life is not seen, except by God. What goes on in the secret place is as vital to who we are as what we do in public before people. God is concerned with our hearts. He is not a slave driver who is only interested in our outward productivity. We are not workers on an assembly line. To Him, we are children in a family, friends in a friendship, lovers in a marriage. Your boss may only care that you get your job done. He might not be the least bit concerned about your attitude, your motives, or your heart. Jesus is not like that. He loves us to the very depth of who we are. He wants to save us not just from sin's penalty but from sin's deep damages. He wants not merely to lop off the weed's flower but dig out the roots.

So, here is some *wonderful* news for you: the blood of Jesus, shed once on Calvary's cross, does *deep* work. Never be afraid to recognize pain and confess sin – including sins of thought and feeling – because

Jesus is always ready to cleanse. Our souls can be very sick and sinful. Greed, lust, envy, bitterness, irritability and wrath are all deep heart-sins that will erupt as surely as will a volcano. They offend God as surely as do outward acts. Left to themselves, they fester and seek a fissure through which they can vent themselves and will surely result in public pain and fractured friendships. But we have a Saviour! Look what His blood can do when we *draw near to God with a sincere heart and with the full assurance that faith brings, having our hearts sprinkled to cleanse us from a guilty conscience ...'* (Heb. 10:22).

Do you see those words *'cleanse us from a guilty conscience'?* That is *deep cleaning*. That is what Jesus can and wants to do. So, why would any of us hold back from bringing not just our obvious outward sins, but the hidden things of our hearts to Him? What joy and peace we can have when we learn to bring wayward ideas and impulses to our ready and willing Saviour! And it is not just our inner *sins* that we can bring to Jesus, but our inner sadness and grief that we can bring to Him. Why let pain simmer away in your soul until it cripples you when you can tell Jesus about it and ask Him to heal your heart? Circumstances outside of us deeply shape us on the inside. The old children's rhyme, 'Sticks and stones may break my bones, but words will never hurt me', simply is not true! Things from the outside *do* hurt on the inside and, if left undealt with, re-appear in some poisonous form on the outside again.

> But look at what Jesus has done: *Surely, he has borne our griefs, and carried our sorrows ...* (Is. 53:4 NKJV)

> So we can *[c]ast all [our] anxiety on him because he cares for[us].* (1 Pet. 5:7)

With Jesus being so wonderful and so ready to have us bring all of our *crud* to Him, why do we fail to do so? Sometimes we get a strange, even perverse comfort from old hurts, wayward thoughts, and tangled emotions. We hang on to our inner sins and brokenness like a toddler does a filthy and frayed old comfort blanket. But this dishonours God, and does damage to us and to those around us.

Don't look upon Jonathan's resolve to look after his inner life with all diligence as a burden. Don't respond with an 'ugh' but rather with a 'hooray'. Hooray! I have a place to go with my sadness, my lust, my envy, my wayward thoughts, my obsessions, my compulsions, my crud. If we did not have a wonderful Saviour whose blood cleanses and heals to our very depths, caring for our inner selves would just be another impossible task. But we *do* have a wonderful Saviour and, therefore, it is possible to be *free*. The key here is *not* to 'try harder' but to bring your sin and brokenness to Jesus, over and over, for He will forever receive you and you will never weary Him with your coming. He says: *Come to me, all you who are weary and burdened, and I will give you rest* (Matt. 11:28–30).

Many times, I have failed to fight the battle for my inner life. I have thought that as long as my outward conduct was passable, then all was 'OK'. But Jesus did not come so that I would be 'OK'. He came because He loves me and wants to redeem all of me. *Jesus* has battled for *my* joy and purity on the cross. Therefore, so should I. But remember: we do not battle in our own energies, but we battle by continually coming to Jesus. Let's learn to pray with the Psalmist: 'Search me, God, and know my heart; test me and know my anxious thoughts. See if there is any offensive way in me and lead me in the way everlasting' (Ps. 139: 23–24). Friend, you and I have a wonderful, wonderful Saviour. With your Bible open, go to Him continually. Bring your thoughts, your emotions, your *weirdness* to Him! He *will* receive you. He will never tire of you. He will cleanse you and strengthen you. Jesus is for you!

The one who calls you is faithful, and he will do it. (1 Thess. 5:23–24)

Sow a thought, reap an act.
Sow an act, reap a habit.
Sow a habit, reap a character.
Sow a character, reap a destiny.[71]
(Ralph Waldo Emerson)

Resolution 46

Resolved to carefully guard my attitude toward my parents, and toward all of my family. Resolved that my speech, my eyes, and my expressions will portray a good attitude of heart toward them.

Then He [Jesus] went down to Nazareth with them [His parents]and was obedient to them. (Luke 2:51)

Dear Friends,

Our young Jonathan sees clearly that following Jesus impacts every aspect of life. We cannot have 'compartments' that do not belong to Jesus!

I find it heartening to see an eighteenth-century young man concerned about his attitude toward his mom and dad. Apparently, this is not a modern problem! In fact, the Bible has so much to say about attitude toward parents that we must conclude that the problem is as old as human history. But the battle is raging today, perhaps hotter than ever. There is a disdain for authority in our day that is nowhere more evident than in the attitudes of children toward their parents (which then spills over into a wider disdain for God and all that is good). The Apostle Paul saw this day coming and warned of it when he said, 'People will be lovers of themselves, lovers of money, boastful, proud, abusive, *disobedient to their parents*, ungrateful, unholy' (2 Tim. 3:2, emphasis mine).

Yet the *command* to honour our parents comes with a beautiful promise, first given to Israel as a nation in Exodus 20:12, then reprised in the New Testament for Christians in every time and culture:

'Honour your father and mother' – *which is the first commandment with a promise* – *'so that it may go well with you and that you may enjoy long life on the earth.'* (Eph. 6:2–3)

It is *good* for us and for society if we honour our parents.

But Jonathan's *Resolution* embraces not just his parents; he includes his family too. Honouring our parents and loving our families is not optional if we are setting out to follow Jesus. Now, I must be careful here: we are *not* to idolize them. We are *not* to forsake Christ for them. Parents and families are *not* more important than others, and following Jesus demands that we be willing to leave them for the mission field (Mark 10:29). But our discipleship has to start with loving our neighbours; our parents, our spouses and our children are, in fact, our nearest neighbours.

For me to be Christ-like and sweet everywhere but home is offensive to God. To be charitable to those far away while I entertain a critical spirit toward those with whom I live is hypocrisy. I have to humble myself before Jesus over this. How easy it is to entertain a cynical or critical attitude at home, to roll the eye, to cut with the word. How deadly it is! How I need to pray about my attitudes and bring them under the lordship of Jesus! More often than not, our parents and our families get the worst of us, not the best of us. Yet can there be a more important place for the wonderful, sweet goodness that Jesus wants to produce in us to be manifested? Should my family not be the first port of call for my love and Christian expression? Again, are not my parents, my wife, and my children *my nearest neighbours*?

In Mark's Gospel, Jesus delivers a demonized man from Satan's power. He then gives him the toughest mission assignment of all:

Go home to your own people and tell them how much the Lord has done for you, and how he has had mercy on you. (Mark 5:19)

The man wanted to leave town and follow Christ wherever he went. Jesus' commission – to start with his family – is telling. For that man – or for me – or for you – to be off changing our world without first loving our families with the love of Jesus is never what

Jesus wants from us. Yes, again, we do not idolize our parents, our kids, our families, and yes, again, many of us will be called to leave them and go elsewhere for Jesus, but, again, grace *must* begin in the attitude of our hearts toward our nearest neighbours – our families.

This is tough but telling. It is almost always easier to have a good attitude toward 'farther' neighbours. "The problem must be with my parents (or wife, or kids). I can get along with everyone except them!" Ah, but you do not have to *live* with anyone except them! They jolt your pride and expose your selfishness like no-one else does, not because there is something wrong with them, but simply because you are around them so much. Believe me, your office mate, your gym buddy, your friends in the book club chew just as loudly and sneeze just as weirdly as your parents do ... you just do not have to put up with it. We are all bothersome, not just your parents or your husband. The ladies in the bridge club 'pass vapours' (a polite 19th century British term) just as surely as do the guys on the ball team. We all have gross habits. You just don't see (or hear, or smell) them in others like we do in our own family.

I need help! Lord Jesus! Forgive my sour attitude toward those closest to me! Give me sweetness in my heart that spills over in my actions, glances, and words!

This *is* the toughest assignment and my most telling school of discipleship. If I can follow Jesus at home – beginning with my parents, my spouse, my siblings, and my children – I can follow Jesus anywhere.

The father of a righteous child has great joy;
a man who fathers a wise son rejoices in him.
May your father and mother rejoice;
may she who gave you birth be joyful!
(Prov. 23:24–25)

The light that shines farthest shines brightest nearest home.[72]
(C.T Studd)

Resolution 47

Resolved to seek to cultivate a sweet, benevolent, contented, serving spirit, and to say 'no' to whatever might threaten the growth of such a spirit. Resolved to examine myself weekly in this regard.

... the unfading beauty of a gentle and quiet spirit, which is of great worth in God's sight. (1 Pet. 3:4)

Beloved in Christ,

The cultivation of a sweet and godly spirit is a deliberate work. God will produce it in us, but we must cooperate. To cooperate well, we need to understand the distinction between *Justification* and *Sanctification*. Here is a brief theology lesson for us all. (Humour me if you already know this!)

Justification is the glorious work whereby God pardons our sin and graces us with His righteousness *solely by the merits of Jesus and his death and resurrection.* We contribute nothing to our justification except our need and we receive our justification by faith alone. It is instantaneous and complete the moment we believe in the Gospel.

Sanctification is the glorious work within us whereby we grow in Christlikeness. Whereas in justification we contribute nothing but simply receive, in sanctification we cooperate with God. It is a process which is not complete until we die and are glorified in Jesus' presence. Some Christians grow to be more like Jesus than others because they are more diligent than others. Jonathan's *Resolutions* deal largely with sanctification, that is, with growing in Christlikeness. Jonathan is earnest in his desire to cultivate a disposition that reflects the very nature of Jesus.

Stop and think about this desire with me for a minute. This is *not* harsh legalism! Why wouldn't he want to be more like Jesus? Why wouldn't you? Why wouldn't I? The best thing I can do for myself, for my family, and for my generation, is to become more like Jesus. If His nature can be increasingly formed within me, what a blessing that will be to myself and to all who come into the orbit of my life! Growing in Christlikeness isn't a burden. It's a blessing! The key to it is given to us by Jesus Himself in John's Gospel. I'll use the King James Version because it employs the wonderful word 'abide', which means 'to stay with' or 'to live with'.

> *Abide in me, and I in you. As the branch cannot bear fruit of itself, unless it abides in the vine; no more can you, unless you abide in me. I am the vine, you are the branches: He that abides in me, and I in him, bears much fruit ...* (John 15:4–5; 7–8 NKJV)

The picture Jesus gives is of a vine, a branch, and fruit. It is a beautiful image. The vine has life in it. The branch remains or abides in the vine, and fruit is the natural consequence. The vine does not 'try' to bear the fruit. It is inevitable. The *life* of the vine produces fruit in the attached branch. Our job in all of this is to abide – to remain, to stay with, to stick to Jesus. If I choose sin, I will not remain in Jesus. I will be like a branch that withers. You see in Jonathan's *Resolution* that he will be careful to say 'no' to whatever might threaten the growth of a Jesus-like spirit within him. Please do not see this as a chore! It is a wonderful wonder that we can be transformed into the image of Jesus by abiding with Him. I am not 'Exhibit A' of what it means to be a Jesus-like Christian but I have had the privilege, for four decades, of watching my wife be continually transformed into Christ's likeness, and it has been a beautiful thing to behold. I have seen *four* things which I want to share with you:

1) She has, day by day, prioritized some time to be alone with Jesus, wearing Bibles out and reading good books that have nourished her inner life. She has done this because she sees the beauty of Jesus and she wants to be like Him.

2) She has been careful not to allow bad attitudes, bitterness, or unforgiveness to gain a foothold in her spirit. She consistently takes her thoughts and attitudes captive and makes them obedient to Christ (2 Cor. 10:5).

3) In a world where appearance is valued above character, I have watched my wife cultivate the true beauty of 'a gentle and quiet spirit' (1 Pet. 3:3–4). She is pretty too, but that isn't what is important to her!

4) And where many constantly clamour for more, my wife has cultivated contentment believing that the Bible tells the truth when it says that '... godliness with contentment is great gain' (1 Tim. 6:6).

I have seen her grow increasingly into the likeness of Jesus. She bears much fruit. How many have been blessed to be in her presence! If you make abiding with Jesus the non-negotiable priority of your life, He will pour His Life into you, transforming you to be more like Him, and His wonderful fruit will be the inevitable result. *He* guarantees it. May

God ... fill you with the knowledge of his will through all the wisdom and understanding that the Spirit gives, so that you may live a life worthy of the Lord and please him in every way: bearing fruit in every good work, [and] growing in the knowledge of God (Col. 1:9–10).

The branch of the vine does not worry, and toil, and rush here to seek for sunshine, and there to find rain. No; it rests in union and communion with the vine; and at the right time, and in the right way, is the right fruit found on it. Let us so abide in the Lord Jesus.[73]
(Hudson Taylor)

Resolution 48

Resolved to never assume that all is well with my soul, but to diligently and earnestly keep vigilance over myself, being sure, at any and all times, that all my trust is in Jesus, and that I am not allowing sin to take root. In this way I shall be ready both to live for Christ and to die in Christ.

Examine yourselves to see whether you are in the faith; test yourselves. Do you not realize that Christ Jesus is in you—unless, of course, you fail the test? (2 Cor. 13:5)

Dear Friends in Christ,

John Bunyan (the humble tinker – maker of pots and pans) wrote over *sixty* books. Perhaps his theology can be summed up in one great sentence: 'God justifies us by bestowing on us, not by expecting from us'.[74] Those are his wonderful words and it is of utmost importance that we understand this and do not take a breath without remembering it. We are not made right before our Holy God through anything we do or offer. Neither effort nor energy, neither emotion nor exuberance, neither education nor exactness, make us right before God. As is so often the case, the poet says it better than the theologian:

> Not the labours of my hands
> can fulfil thy law's demands;
> could my zeal no respite know,
> could my tears forever flow,
> all for sin could not atone;
> thou must save, and thou alone.
> (Augustus Toplady)

But this is not to say we should be passive. This is not to say that we become complacent. A true work of God awakens us and makes us alive to God. We become concerned for things that we used to ignore. Things that were once of no importance to us become matters of great importance.

One such matter is the health and well-being of our souls. Where we once ignored and abused them, we now realize the eternal value of our unseen selves and begin to exercise diligent care over them. A child of grace knows that Jesus has placed His caring hands upon him. He knows that he is saved and safe forever. But he is *alive* and *aware* where he once was *dead* and *dulled*. He is careful over his life in a new way.

Assurance and *assuming* are not to be confused! A Jesus-follower has a wonderful *assurance* that He belongs totally and forever to Jesus. But that does not cause him to *assume* that all is as it should be with his heart and that he need not exercise care over it. Trusting in Jesus wholly and totally for my safety and salvation does not mean that I have nothing to do.

Hence, Jonathan's resolve to diligently and earnestly keep vigilance over himself at all times does not in any way mean that he is striving in his own strength to be saved. It does not mean that he is ignoring the Gospel and thinking that he can and must establish his own righteousness before God. It does not mean that he thinks he will lose his salvation if, in a given moment, his zeal abates or sin grabs him.

Rather, it means that he constantly orients his soul to his Lord: that he will be careful moment by moment to look to Christ and not to himself for his justification and his security. It means that he will preach the Gospel daily – hourly – constantly – to himself, applying the wonders of Jesus as mediator, sin-bearer, intercessor, and advocate to his own sin-plagued life. It means that he will ensure that Christ is Lord of his attitudes and relationships. It means that he will live daily ready to die, knowing that at any moment his Saviour may summon him home.

Keeping careful watch over one's soul is not optional if one expects to live well and die well – and not all Christians do either well!

Here are five simple but searching questions a careful Christian should ask himself often if he is to cultivate a healthy, sweet, Jesus-like, ready-to-live and ready-to-die inner life:

1) Am I looking *away from myself* and to my Saviour Jesus for my hope, salvation, joy, and righteousness, or am I somehow believing that I can establish my own righteousness apart from Christ? (1 Cor. 1:30)

2) As I invite God the Holy Spirit to search my heart, is He putting His finger on any sin that is lurking? If so, am I quickly taking it to Jesus in confession and repentance, knowing that He is ever willing to receive me and cleanse me? (Ps. 139:23–24)

3) Am I walking in sweetness and forgiveness towards my brothers and sisters, or am I allowing roots of bitterness to worm their ways into my heart? (1 John 1:7)

4) Am I asking and trusting Jesus to empower me every day, every moment, to deny self and love Him and others, to say 'yes' to God and 'no' to Satan, or am I believing that I can live a Christ-honouring life in my own strength? (Phil. 4:13; John 15:5)

5) Am I living every day realizing that very soon, indeed, at any moment, my life on earth will end and I will be summoned to give my account to God, or am I foolishly forgetting the fragility of my mortal frame? (James 4:14)

May we learn to be diligent over our souls, to the honour of Jesus who purchased them, to the blessing of ourselves who must spend eternity with them, and to the good of others who must bear the burden or blessing of them (Is. 61:10).

As I began with John Bunyan, let me finish with words from the thinking tinker:

It is sad to see how the most of men neglect their precious souls ... when, in the meanwhile, their bodies are well provided for, their estates much regarded, and the things of this present life are highly prized, as if the darling was of less value than a clod of earth; an immortal soul, than a perishing body; a precious Saviour, than unsatisfying creatures.[75]

Resolution 49

Resolved that, with reference to my previous *Resolution*, it shall never be that when I come to die, I will realize that I have been careless with my life.

If anyone builds on this foundation using gold, silver, costly stones, wood, hay or straw, their work will be shown for what it is, because the Day will bring it to light. It will be revealed with fire, and the fire will test the quality of each person's work. If what has been built survives, the builder will receive a reward. If it is burned up, the builder will suffer loss, but yet will be saved – even though only as one escaping through the flames. (1 Cor. 3:12–15)

Friends,

There are numerous ways to be careless with one's life.

One is to ignore eternity and your soul altogether, forgetting that there is more to 'you' than meets the eye, and more to life than these brief years. In so doing, you see yourself as nothing other than a 'higher animal'. Christ and the Gospel are foolishness to you. This is the tragic, 'materialist' position of many in today's world.

Another deadly way to be careless is to ostensibly believe in Jesus and His Gospel but not take faith beyond mere outward appearance and conformity to a group. This is the position of the 'nominalist'.

Then, Jesus warns us, one can be seemingly very spiritual and even be deep into ministry, but in fact have no saving knowledge of God. Yikes! It is all too easy to attempt to substitute a full religious calendar for a humble walk with God, but God is not interested in our busyness and is unimpressed by our boasts of demons driven out and miracles performed. He has heard every sermon ever preached – and neither yours nor mine are going to impress Him when what He wants is that we simply walk with Him.

But I do not think that Jonathan is concerned with missing Heaven when he resolves not to be careless with his life. There is clear evidence in the Bible that it is possible – easy – to be a genuine believer, one who truly knows Jesus as Saviour and friend, and yet not to really understand that *this life* – our earthly journey – is valuable and should not be wasted. For a Christian to waste the grace given for each earthly day is a tragedy not only for himself, but for the cause of Christ in this world. For a Christian to yawn or fuss his way through the gift of each and every day in this present realm is surely to offend the loving heart of his good and wonderful God. Jonathan does not want to get to the end of his earthly journey and realize that he blew his chance to relish his precious days on earth. (How many days have *we* wasted with sin, fear, irritability, laziness, or selfishness?)

The sad little book of Ecclesiastes tells the story of a man's (probably Solomon's) regret for wasting his earthly days in vanity.

So, I hated life ... All of it is meaningless, a chasing after the wind.
(Ecc. 2:17)

His summary is one you do not want to repeat: Neither do I!

Time affects *eternity. This life* affects *the next life.* It seems that it is possible for a blood-bought child of grace to squander much of his inheritance and leave himself, though saved and safe, comparatively impoverished. In the Scripture at the top of this *Resolution*, the Apostle Paul is using a word picture to depict two kinds of people, the lives they live, and the eternal results of the lives they live.

Clearly *both* are saved from a deserved Hell, but they are not equal in their undeserved Heaven.

In Paul's word picture the fire is a picture of a judgment that all believers will go through. It is not a judgment to decide our eternal destiny; that has already been determined as we have been graciously delivered from wrath. But it is a judgment upon our works, our ways, our lives, our efforts. Some of us take the grace of God and apply ourselves to growth and usefulness; some are comparatively careless and therefore stunted in our growth and usefulness. Jesus spoke many times of *rewards* for believers. Clearly, salvation is free and by grace through faith alone. So, what can He mean? I think we have to deduce that we are not all the same in Heaven. This life affects Eternity! Hear the words of Jesus:

> *Rejoice in that day and leap for joy, because great is your reward in heaven.* (Luke 6:23)

> *But love your enemies, do good to them, and lend to them without expecting to get anything back. Then your reward will be great ...* (Luke 6:35)

Jesus is telling us that some will invest more into their eternity than others through the choices and moves they make today.

How is your 'Eternity Portfolio' looking?

I might be wrong, but I think the difference will be our eternal capacity for joy. Jonathan, as we have already seen,[76] proposed that the differing states of believers in Heaven might be likened to vessels (jars) with different capacities for joy – each one plunged into the sea of God's eternal happiness, and therefore each one full to the brim, but some being bigger, some smaller, than others, and, that capacity having been determined in *this* life, by one's response to grace and desire to know and honour Christ.

I do not want to waste *this life* and I do not want to have poor choices in the present spill over into my eternity. We will live well if we live with an eye constantly on Heaven! We will be most useful, joyful, and full *here and now* if we seek to be ready to be all that we can be in Jesus *there and then*.

> *Teach us to number our days, that we may gain a heart of wisdom.* (Ps. 90:12)

> The Christian ideal has not been tried and found wanting; it has been found difficult and left untried.[77] (G.K. Chesterton)

Resolution 50

Resolved to live and act in such a way that, upon my coming to Heaven, I will see that I lived my earthly life well and wisely.

He regarded disgrace for the sake of Christ as of greater value than the treasures of Egypt because he was looking ahead to his reward.
(Heb. 11:26)

He will wipe every tear from their eyes. (Rev. 21:4)

Dear Friends in Jesus,

I want you to do some thinking with me. I cannot be 'dogmatic' about what I am about to propose. I might be wrong, but I might be right (and I think I am).

I trust that every follower of Jesus is looking for that day when Jesus will open wide His grace-filled arms and greet us with a joyous, 'Well done, my good and faithful servant! Come and enter into my joy!' I know that is God's heart for us. What a reward that will be for every battle-weary believer!

But, I think it is possible for a Christian to have some regrets – at least for a while – in Heaven.

Hear me out before you slam the book shut!

Jesus uses the motive of future reward (a warm 'Well done' will be plenty of reward for me!) to motivate us in discipleship today. There are about a dozen times in the Gospels when Jesus speaks of rewards for believers. Clearly Jesus wants us to learn to make decisions with more than just the weekend in view. He wants us to think and act in the light of eternity and of being with Him forever. There is a *continuity* between our life on earth and our life in God's Heaven. This is made clear in Paul's letter to the troubled, worldly, eternity-forgetting church in Corinth:

> *So will it be with the resurrection of the dead. The body that is sown is perishable, it is raised imperishable; it is sown in dishonour, it is raised in glory; it is sown in weakness, it is raised in power; it is sown a natural body, it is raised a spiritual body.* (1 Cor. 15:43–44)

It is reasonable and right to infer that if there is continuity of our physical selves, from perishable to imperishable, that there will likewise be continuity of our mental selves, of our spiritual selves, and of our emotional selves. Everything will be enhanced, not diminished. Who we are here will have a continuance, but in a glorified manner, into eternity. (Likewise, it is reasonable to infer that the wicked will know a continuity as well but expressed in enhanced rebellion, agony, and, finally, the torture of regret.)

So, will we be able to look back upon our lives here? Is there any biblical evidence for such a thought? And if so, might a saved and safe person in any way look back with any regrets? Might there be any room, even for a short season, for tears in Heaven?

There is some evidence in the Bible that after we die and at least while we await the final renewal of all things (as promised in Revelation 21), that there will be a remembrance and awareness of our brief earthly sojourn. For instance, clearly the redeemed multitude gathered before the throne of God in Revelation 6 are fully aware of what happened and is happening on earth as they await God to avenge their blood.

It is interesting to me that it is not until the final consummation of all things and the glorious appearing of 'a new Heaven and a new earth' in Revelation 21, that God finally wipes away every tear (v.4). Could it be that, for a season, before the final presentation of the Kingdom in all its fulness, the redeemed who are living in the wonderful presence of their wonderful Lord still experience some degree of sorrow relating to this present life? Why else would Jesus have to wipe away tears in Heaven?

For a season, and to a degree, even in the Paradise of God, there might be room for regret amongst the redeemed.

Jonathan does not want to get to Heaven and then wish he had lived differently while on earth. Neither do you. He is not doubting his salvation. He is not striving to gain Heaven by his own merits. But he is realizing that he has *one* life, and that this earthly sojourn continues beyond death and into eternity.

Jonathan's resolve to enter Heaven with no regrets *will only make him live better now.* How can it not? Do we not all regularly experience the power of anticipation to transform the present? If I know that what I do today will enhance or diminish my joy tomorrow, then my today is transformed. My choices are changed, my direction is determined, my attitude is adjusted, my stride is strengthened by anticipations of future happiness or sadness resulting from today's decisions. Without question, those Christians who have lived best while on earth have been those who have lived each day with an eye on Heaven. C.S Lewis put it well:

> If you read history, you will find that the Christians who did most for the present world were precisely those who thought most of the next. It is since Christians have largely ceased to think of the other world that they have become so ineffective in this [world]…[78]

Lord teach me to live with a wonderful anticipation of future – falling into your grace-filled arms and so much more – always in view!

Look, I am coming soon! My reward is with me. (Rev. 22:12)

Aim at Heaven and you will get earth 'thrown in': aim at earth and you will get neither.[79] (C.S. Lewis)

Resolution 51

Resolved, by God's grace and not wanting at the last to discover that I was a false follower, to prove my faith genuine in how I live and act in every way and at all times.

But someone will say, 'You have faith; I have deeds.' Show me your faith without deeds, and I will show you my faith by my deeds. You believe that there is one God. Good! Even the demons believe that – and shudder. You foolish person, do you want evidence that faith without deeds is useless? (James 2:18–20)

Dear Friends,

That glorious pillar of our Faith, that bedrock of scriptural Christianity, that wondrous truth that has kept millions of believers sane and secure – that is, justification by grace through faith alone – does not imply that how I *live*, how I *act*, what I *do* is now of no importance since I have faith in Jesus.

It is a caricature of something great to suggest that receiving the Gospel by faith alone absolves me from any responsibility for how I then live, for what I *do,* and what I *do not do*. The best followers of Jesus over the years of Christian history have been those whose faith has been proven by their works. Let's be clear on this: for them, works were never a substitute for faith in the finished work of Jesus on the cross. But equally, faith was never allowed to exist in a vacuum, free of works. Faith produced works and, thereby, proved itself as genuine. Faith in Jesus followed from and existed through a deep inner work of God's Holy Spirit that moved and motivated them to labour and love in new and often supernatural ways.

Yes, the poet said well:

> I cannot work my soul to save,
> For that my God alone has done.
> But I will work like any slave
> For the love of God's dear Son.[80]

Faith is a living thing that produces acts of faithfulness. It keeps us *from* doing certain things and moves us *to* do certain things. Young Jonathan understood this from the earliest days of his journey with Jesus. I actually softened up the tone of this *Resolution* as it originally said:

> Resolved, that I will act so, in every respect, as I think I shall wish I had done, if I should at last be damned.

No! He is not getting morbid and negative in this *Resolution*. But he is being healthy and realistic. Even though fully assured of one's safety and security in Jesus, there needs to be a bit of a tremble in the heart of every true believer. You might want to call it *reverence*. Assurance – that wonderful inner witness, based upon the promises of God in the Bible – that one is saved and safe forever with Jesus, is the birthright of every believer. But alongside it should exist a moment-by-moment realization: 'I dare not take this salvation for granted. I dare not play fast and loose with God's grace'. The psalmist said it well:

> *Serve the Lord with fear [reverence] and rejoice with trembling.*
> (Ps. 2:11 NKJV)

Jonathan imagines a horrific future scene in order to move him to faithfulness in all he does today. Imagining this scene does not mean he thinks he can lose his salvation, or that somehow Jesus cannot keep him. But it does mean he sees the clear and present danger that he can be a false follower, and that only his deeds can prove his faith genuine. He imagines what John Bunyan's Pilgrim had nightmarishly imagined a hundred years before him:

'Then I saw that there was a way to Hell, even from the gates
of Heaven'.[81]

He imagines getting to the end of his life only to find his assumptions
were false and his assurance was misplaced. Such thinking moved
Jonathan Edwards (and John Bunyan) to avoid assumption, arrogance,
and carelessness in his profession of faith in Jesus. John Wesley called
false following 'antinomianism', that is, lawlessness. Bonhoeffer
called it, 'cheap grace'. The Apostle James called it 'dead' faith.

So ... take a moment and dare to imagine getting to the end of
your life, all along having been confident of your eternal safety,
only to find that there is indeed a gate to Hell adjacent to the gate
of Heaven ... and it has swung wide for you. Imagine discovering
that your repentances were shallow, that your motives were self-
serving, that your life was, in fact, in orbit around yourself, and
that your profession of Christ was little more than an opinion and a
feeling or two.

Read some of Jesus' parables and you will find a recurring theme
that we tend to view ourselves as better, more 'spiritual', than we
really are:

*Once the owner of the house gets up and closes the door, you will
stand outside knocking and pleading, 'Sir, open the door for us.'*

But he will answer, 'I don't know you or where you come from.'

*Then you will say, 'We ate and drank with you, and you taught in our
streets.'*

But he will reply, 'I don't know you ...' (Luke 13:25–27)

It seems the day will come when everyone will want to be known
as Jesus' friend. It seems that Jesus is warning that such friendship
needs to begin today. It seems that it is dangerously easy to assume
oneself to be 'OK with God' because, 'We ate and drank with you,
and you taught in our streets'.

No one will ever get to the end of their earthly pilgrimage and say,
'I was too diligent with my soul!'

But many will say 'Open the door for us!'

May it not be so with you, or with me.

> Cheap grace is the grace we bestow on ourselves. Cheap grace is the preaching of forgiveness without requiring repentance, baptism without church discipline, communion without confession ... Cheap grace is grace without discipleship, grace without the cross, grace without Jesus Christ, living and incarnate. (Dietrich Bonhoeffer)

Resolution 52

Resolved, as I often hear old people say that they would live their lives differently if given the chance, that I, by God's grace, may live as I can imagine I will wish I had done, should I live to one day be an old man.

But whatever were gains to me I now consider loss for the sake of Christ. What is more, I consider everything a loss because of the surpassing worth of knowing Christ Jesus ... I want to know Christ – yes, to know the power of his resurrection and participation in his sufferings, becoming like him in his death, and so, somehow, attaining to the resurrection from the dead. (Phil. 3:7–11)

Dear Friends,

Perhaps the most popular tourist attraction in Cairo is the gilded burial treasure of the young King Tutankhamun. While his embalmed body lies entombed in the Valley of the Kings, the gold that was buried with him has been removed to the Museum of Egyptian Antiquities for all to see. Fabulously wealthy, his life still speaks as a testimony of the 'best' this present, visible life has to offer ... and of its final emptiness.

While a flood of the intrigued and envious make their way to the Cairo Museum, a mere trickle finds their way to the inconspicuous grave of another young man buried in Cairo. A son of the Kingdom-yet-to-come, William Borden (1887–1913) had no earthly treasure with which to be buried, for he had given his fabulous wealth away. Captivated by Christ, he, like many other subjects of this coming Kingdom, 'regarded disgrace for the sake of Christ as of greater value than the treasures of Egypt, because he was looking ahead to his reward' (Heb. 11:26).

Borden, a millionaire by age eighteen, gave his wealth away and, upon graduating from Yale, headed for the mission field, treasuring the eternal well-being of a certain Chinese Muslim tribe above his own earthly comfort. While studying Arabic in Cairo he contracted meningitis and died at age 25. His death sent a shockwave throughout the Christian world of his day, but his brief life motivated many to likewise 'consider everything a loss because of the surpassing worth of knowing Christ Jesus'.

His gravestone bears a single sentence epitaph:

> Apart from Christ, there is no explanation for such a life.

In his Bible, six simple words were written which summed up his values:

No Reserves
   No Retreats
      No Regrets.

William Borden was a soul mate to our Jonathan – just born 150 years later. He, too, lived his brief days in light of Eternity and made decisions every day in light of his last day.

Compare William's life to the young Tutankhamun's, who very well might have breathed his last in the same spirit of regret as another king, Solomon, who, 'having it all', could only survey his vanity and confess: *I hated life ...* (Ecc. 2:17).

Getting to the end of one's earthly journey regret-free will not happen by accident. It requires one great goal: the Glory of God over self. Then come many crisis moments of redirection, and thousands of little daily choices and adjustments to keep one on course. But until we understand the heart God has for us, we will never get far in the Christian life. God is not a killjoy; He is the universal source of all true joy. He alone possesses infinite joy, and He is ready and willing to give it liberally away. The problem is that we seek fullness apart from the One who alone can give it. We seek joy in the back-alleys, pleasure in the tenement slums, hidden away from Him whose heart longs to meet ours with His very own Life. Jesus makes plain to us the heart and mind of the Eternal God regarding our good, profit, and pleasure:

I have told you this so that my joy may be in you and that your joy may be complete. (John 15:11)

I have come that they may have life, and have it to the full. (John 10:10)

But there is a cost! Jesus tells us that His Kingdom is like a valuable pearl for which a merchant will *gladly give up everything else*! His life-long search is over, for he has found the ultimate treasure (Matt. 13:45). Jesus warns that loving anything or anyone above Him makes joy-giving, God-glorifying discipleship impossible (Matt. 10:37).

Jonathan Edwards is aiming for the stars. He is not an austere ascetic. He is not a mystic trying to extinguish all desire. No! He is refusing all lesser desires because he is choosing the highest desire. He is not content with anything less than living for the highest purpose of all: the Glory of God – a life lived to know, love, and enjoy his Creator. Jonny, like William, knows why he has been made. He has been made for nothing less than to give pleasure to God and to receive pleasure from God. Do we see this? The pursuit of a life which gives Glory to God and the pursuit of one's own *highest* good, profit, and pleasure, are not mutually exclusive goals.

Call it Life vs. life.

Far from simply having a 'passing religious phase' in their lives, these two, William and Jonathan, were bent on living for Jesus and Joy for all their days and into forever, no matter the cost. Edwards and Borden both knew that God Almighty had apprehended them for nothing less than fullness in Himself.

And it isn't just the passionate young who perceive this: let me leave you with a power-packed quote, from a proven, old war-horse – British journalist Malcomb Muggeridge:

I can say that I never knew what joy was like until I gave up pursuing happiness, or cared to live until I chose to die. For these two discoveries I am beholden to Jesus. [82]

Resolution 53

Resolved, on my good days, when I am in the best frame of mind, to never miss an opportunity to draw closer to Jesus, to trust Him in new ways, to embark on new adventures in following Him, and to make fresh consecration of myself to Him. In so doing I will confirm my assurance in Christ Jesus as my Redeemer and that I am eternally safe in Him.

Go to the ant ... consider its ways and be wise ... it stores its provisions in summer and gathers its food at harvest. (Prov. 6:6–8)

If you stumble in safe country, how will you manage in the thickets by the Jordan? (Jer. 12:5)

Dear Friend in Jesus,

Like the ant, the wisest followers of Jesus have learned to capitalize on the good times, knowing that lean times are never far away, and sure to come.

Let's be realistic: There will be days when Heaven seems far off, times when God seems silent. There will be days when obedience is hard – and disobedience is easy.

There are sure to be storm clouds brewing. Some days will be sunny. Many will not.

Charles Wesley said it well:

Hide me, O my Saviour, hide,
till the storm of life is past;
safe into the haven guide,
O receive my soul at last!

We had better brace ourselves.

Here is Jonathan's counsel: we had better take advantage of every good day, every sweet season, every day of health and strength to store up, to build up, to prepare to venture out in faith. We will do well to press into Jesus on the good days. Habits of consecration learned when the wind is at our back will serve us when the gale is blowing straight in our face. Spiritual disciplines need to be learned before the tough phone call comes. Friendship with Jesus needs to be cultivated *before* tragedy comes knocking on our door. While it is true that tough times are unique seasons of grace in which God can do deep work in our lives, we dare not waste the sunny times when we have the strength and sanity to 'grow in the grace and knowledge' (1 Pet. 3:18) of our wonderful Saviour. It will not always be easy to get up early and pray, so do it now. You will not always have time to read your Bible, so read it today. You might not have the capacity one day to read great books of faith, or to spend days seeking God, so take the chance while you have it.

When the young Hudson Taylor, preparing for a life of service in China, was still living in the comparative ease of London, he took that time to learn the spiritual and life disciplines that he figured he would need if he was to survive in the harsh frontier of inland China. The faith lessons he learned 'in the safe county' served him well 'in the thickets' of the mission field. Indeed, years into his life's work, having suffered trials beyond his strength, it was from the deep well of Christ, dug in his stronger days that he was able to say: 'I am so weak that I cannot read my Bible ... even pray, I can only lie still in God's arms like a little child, and trust.'

Somewhere on our shelves at home is my wife's 'pre-marriage and children' Bible. Every page is worn. Every margin is written in. Line after line is highlighted. Its yellowed pages speak of a young woman taking advantage of the (comparatively) easy years to prepare herself for the rigours of what would turn out to be a large family, a busy ministry, and a (nearly) impossible husband. It has not been by accident that she has continued steadfast in Jesus and useful in her Master's hands through countless trials and challenges.

We find ourselves living in such emotionally fragile days. We are a generation of quitters. Our feelings are easily hurt and our feathers quickly ruffled. Many of us have had so much leisure and pleasure that we cannot endure even brief periods of trial, let alone long seasons of hardship. We have failed to make good of the sunshine in anticipation of the storm-clouds. We would do well to go to the ant and learn a lesson or two. We would learn to 'store provisions in summer' before the sure onset of winter. It is hard to strike out on some new adventure of faith and service when tribulation is unending and the waves are overwhelming. Better to lift your sails and hoist your anchor when the wind is favourable than to spend the fair-weather days loitering about the harbour only to find yourself unprepared for the adventure God has for you somewhere over the horizon:

Remember your Creator
in the days of your youth,
before the days of trouble come
and the years approach when you will say,
'I find no pleasure in them.' (Eccl. 12:1)

Friend, the Lord Jesus will give you all grace to know Him deeply and truthfully. He will give you all strength for the storms which are sure to come. Take advantage of every good year, day, moment. Receive every sweet season, every calm moment as a chance to pray, read, repent, venture out, and learn of Jesus. Teach your children to know the Lord in the days of their youth, knowing that trials await them when the Lord will be all they have.

There will never be an easier time for you to get real with God and earnest with His Son than today.

The Lord is good to those who wait for Him, to the soul who seeks Him. It is good that one should hope and wait quietly for the salvation of the Lord.

It is good for a man to bear the yoke in his youth.
(Lam. 3:25–27 NKJV)

Whatever is your best time in the day, give that to Communion with God.[83] (Hudson Taylor)

Resolution 54

Resolved, whenever I hear of or see something praiseworthy in another person to seek to imitate it in my life.

Remember your leaders, who spoke the word of God to you. Consider the outcome of their way of life and imitate their faith. (Heb. 13:7)

Walk with the wise and become wise,
for a companion of fools suffers harm.
(Prov. 13:20)

Dear Friends in Jesus,

Envy: a bad thing.

Admiration: a good thing.

Envy is to want what someone else has. The dictionary defines envy as: Desire to have a quality, possession, or other desirable attribute belonging to (someone else).

Admiration might also involve wanting what someone else has, but there is no bitterness attached to it. The dictionary defines admiration as: Respect and warm approval.

Everyone is better than me at *something* and I can learn from them if I am ready and willing. You know when you see something praiseworthy in another person and respond with envy in your heart. It feels terrible. I remember reading a godly author – I think it was Roy Hession – who astutely pointed out that jealousy (envy) is the only sin that *never* feels good. All other sins have seasons of pleasure, but envy is never any fun. Proverbs 14:30 warns us that 'Envy rots the bones'. But it can be a wonderful thing to admire a godly trait in another and desire it in yourself. The Bible counsels us to observe others, to see noble things in their lives, and to desire them. See how Paul urges his friends to imitate good role-models in, for example, 2 Thessalonians 3:9, Hebrews 6:12 and 1 Corinthians 11:1.

It is a beautiful thing to see young Jonathan wanting to find in himself the godliness that is evident in others. Rather than envying them, he admires them. In a life-giving way he desires in himself what he sees as life-giving and God-glorifying in another. Indeed, if envy 'rots the bones', admiration inspires the heart. It *feels good*.

Now the *caveat*. It is good to admire and desire what is good in others ... but we dare not fool ourselves. The Lord may no doubt be doing a good work in another's life, and admirable traits may be evident, but even the finest saints have 'feet of clay'. We finally look to Jesus for what is good and beautiful. We want to be like *Him*. All people, even the most admirable, are flawed and if we move from admiration to idolatry, we are sure to be disappointed and hurt. We should desire what we see in another only to the extent that what we see in them is a Jesus-like trait. That being said, it is spiritually healthy to seek out the wise and those who have walked well and long with Jesus, and to want to be like them. The Bible tells many stories of men and women who grabbed onto the coat tails of someone 'godlier' than they were, and hung on:

– I think of Elisha all but demanding of Elijah a double portion of [his] spirit (2 Kings 2:9). Envy? No. He saw something of God in his mentor that he admired and desired.

– Joshua attached himself to Moses. (Deut. 31ff)

– Ruth saw something admirable in broken Naomi (Ruth 1:16).

– Timothy pursued Paul who was pursuing Jesus. (2 Tim. 2:2; 3:10).

– Mary, when told of the child within her, went to stay with the godly Elizabeth for three months. (Luke 1:39–45)

I wish I could have been a fly on the wall as these older people mentored the younger ones.

A noble and good spirit is teachable, receptive, and, rather than reacting in jealousy ('Why does *he* get picked to be a (fill in the blank) and not *me*?'), runs up alongside and says, 'I want what you have! I like what I see! I am ready to learn!'

I want to venture farther with this. *Every Christian, no, wait, every person* has something admirable about them that I can discover if I am humble enough to see it, and that I can seek to imitate, if I am hungry enough to want it. All Christians (even ones that bug me) in some wonderful way have a knowledge and experience of Jesus and the Gospel that I know nothing of in my experience and life. Rather than envy them or write them off, I need to ask, 'Lord Jesus, show me what they know about You that I have yet to discover, and begin to form that within me'. But admirable traits are not the sole reserve of Christians! God's common grace and goodness are at work in every person's life (Matt. 5:45) and, if I will look, I will see admirable things in not-yet-believers that I should want to find in me. As I write this, a new book, *Talking to GOATS*, has just landed on my doorstep (*GOATS = Greatest of All Time*). It is far from a 'Christian' book. But I can learn much from it. In it, author and sports-caster Jim Gray tells the stories of greats in their respective fields. I want to *learn* from them. I want to be *inspired*. I want to *imitate the good*. What do these 'people of this world' know that this 'person of the light' (*cf.* Luke 16:8) needs to learn?

Do you want to become a well-rounded, mature, fully useful follower of Jesus? Do you want to function in your gifting and grow into areas yet uncharted in your life? Then learn to run with those who are running well. *Everybody* is really good at *something*. Every person has in them something you can desire and endeavour to imitate in your life.

Refuse envy and embrace admiration and see what God might birth and grow in your life.

Finally, brothers and sisters, whatever is true, whatever is noble, whatever is right, whatever is pure, whatever is lovely, whatever is admirable – if anything is excellent or praiseworthy – think about such things. (Phil. 4:8)

People should remain two things throughout their lifetimes: Curious and teachable.[84] (Roger Ebert)

Resolution 55

Resolved, to aim to live and to act as I would if I had seen the wonders of Heaven and the torments of Hell.

The rich man ... died and was buried. In Hades, where he was in torment, he looked up and saw Abraham far away, with Lazarus by his side. So, he called to him, 'Father Abraham, have pity on me and send Lazarus to dip the tip of his finger in water and cool my tongue, because I am in agony in this fire.' (Luke 16:22–24)

He will wipe every tear from their eyes. There will be no more death or mourning or crying or pain, for the old order of things has passed away. (Rev. 21:4)

Friends,

It will do us well to live every day with an eye on eternity. Saints of old did this as a matter of habit, as a spiritual discipline. They lived well in *time* because they were conscious of *eternity*.

Hear John Wesley:

> I am a creature of a day, passing through life as an arrow through the air. I am a spirit come from God and returning to God: just hovering over the great gulf; till, a few moments hence, I am no more seen; I drop into an unchangeable eternity! I want to know one thing – the way to heaven; how to land safe on that happy shore.[85]

John Bunyan wrote an entire book on eternity entitled *Visions of Heaven and Hell*.

Richard Baxter wrote 800,000 words on eternity in his book *The Saints' Everlasting Rest*.

Charles Spurgeon preached endless sermons on the theme of eternity.

Such preoccupations seem almost quaint today. But perhaps their 'eternal' perspective caused the believers of old to be healthier, more robust, than does our 'time-bound' perspective. The strange fact is that in ignoring eternity, we end up making a mess of time, too. In thinking too little of Heaven and Hell we think too much of this brief life and, in so doing, we ruin it.

Jonathan is resolved to live today as if he has already seen both the wonders of Heaven and the torments of Hell. Let me ask you, how might such a resolve affect you? Do you live with an eye on eternity? Do you live as though you have a soul? Are you remembering that you are built to last? How often do you allow the joys of Heaven and the sorrows of Hell to persuade you away from sin and self and toward Jesus and godliness?

When we read our Bibles, particularly the Gospels, we are confronted with Eternity. Jesus spoke often on Heaven and Hell. He often spoke in very graphic terms. When speaking about Eternity perhaps He was speaking literally; perhaps He was using metaphor (word pictures to explain the unexplainable). We cannot be sure, and we do not need to argue the point. Either way, Jesus was loving us enough to speak persuasively to us about realities unseen.

Jesus doesn't only reference hell, he describes it in great detail. He says it is a place of eternal torment (Luke 16:23), of unquenchable fire (Mark 9:43), where the worm does not die (Mark 9:48), where people will gnash their teeth in anguish and regret (Matt. 13:24), and from which there is no return, even to warn loved ones (Luke 16:19–31). He calls hell a place of 'outer darkness' (Matt. 25:30), comparing it to 'Gehenna' (Matt. 10:28), which was a trash dump outside the walls of Jerusalem where rubbish was burned and maggots abounded. Jesus talks about hell more than he talks about heaven and describes it more vividly. There's no denying that Jesus knew, believed, and warned about the absolute reality of hell.[86]

Why did Jesus do this? Could it be that He wanted us to live today as though we had already seen the torments of Eternity – separated from God and all that is good? Could it be that He wanted us to see the end result of a life of selfish choices and forgetfulness of God?

But Jesus spoke much about Heaven! Take courage! If Hell has no exit, there is a way to avoid it and a sure door to Heaven! Jesus spoke of Heaven as His 'Father's house' (John 14:2), with a place prepared especially for us. He called it 'paradise' (Luke 23:43). He taught that it is a tangible place where we can make secure eternal investments (Luke 18:22). It is a place of comfort (Luke 16:22), joy (Luke 16:7), and reward (Luke 6:23). It is 'home'. It is worthy of the costliest repentance (Matt. 18:8). According to Jesus, Heaven, wonderful Heaven, is worth more than the entire world. In fact, to gain the world but to lose one's soul and God's Heaven is an immeasurable loss (Matt. 16:26). Most wonderfully, Heaven is where Jesus is in His eternal Glory with His Father and the Holy Spirit, *and He wants us there* (John 17:24)!

We have a Saviour who has purchased us from Hell to Heaven.

Living today in anticipation of the unspeakable glories to come is transformational. Nothing severs the cord of sin and temptation, nothing is a balm for the wounded heart, nothing adds strength to the stride and zeal to the labour like a glimpse of the wonders of Heaven.

Richard Baxter taught himself to contemplate Eternity for thirty minutes every day. We would do well if we could muster a minute.

The benefits would be out of this world.

Eye has not seen, nor ear heard, nor have entered into the heart of man, the things which God has prepared for those who love him.
(1 Cor. 2:9 NKJV)

Once more consider, there is nothing, but heaven, worth setting our hearts upon.[87] (Richard Baxter)

Resolution 56

Resolved never to give up the fight against my own heart sins, nor to go easy on them, no matter how long the battle rages or how many times I fail and have to start again.

If God is for us, who can be against us? ... No, in all these things we are more than conquerors through him who loved us. (Rom. 8:31, 37)

Friends,

In 1983, upon the advice of the godly, aged evangelist Leonard Ravenhill, I purchased a copy of *The Christian in Complete Armour* by the English pastor William Gurnall (1616–1679). The book is a 1,200 page commentary on just eleven verses of the Bible, Ephesians 6:10–20. Have a look at its subtitle:

> A treatise of the saint's war against the Devil, wherein a discovery is made of that grand enemy of God and his people, in his policies, power, seat of his empire, wickedness, and chief design he hath against the saints: a magazine opened, from whence the Christian is furnished with spiritual arms for the battle, helped on with his armour, and taught the use of his weapon; together with the happy issue of the whole war.[88]

I think we can be sure that the book is not destined for the *New York Times* Best-Sellers List.

But I think it might be on *God's* Best-Sellers List.[89]

In those pages Gurnall describes the holy war that believers are engaged in and sets out the do-or-die strategy for victory. The very first directive he offers, is this:

> The Christian is to proclaim and prosecute an irreconcilable war against his bosom sins.

Ah! How good we are at 'proclaiming and prosecuting irreconcilable war' against other people's sins! We can go against our wife's sins with a vengeance! We can be relentless against the sins of our political opponents and bothersome neighbours ...

But! the only heart I have jurisdiction over is my own!

I wonder if Edwards had a well-worn copy of Gurnall on his shelf (mine is held together with duct-tape), for it seems that Jonathan and William were cut from the same bolt of cloth, both being resolute in going after their own heart-sins. I want to have some useful fun here; in commenting on Jon, I want to paraphrase Bill. That way we will get the best of two great men and, just to top it off, I might throw in some Augustine of Hippo, too.

From Gurnall:

> It is our nearest and dearest sins which we now must war against. What courage it requires to go after your own sin! Especially the deep, darling ones! Think of when God came to Abraham and said, 'Take your son, your only son, whom you love – Isaac – and sacrifice him as a burnt offering on a mountain that I will show you' (Gen. 22:2). So, God comes to you and to me and says, 'Take your lust, your dearest lust, which has at times given such pleasure and laughter, lay your hands upon it and offer it, and delay not!' And! Our lust will not lie so still on the altar as did Isaac! No! It will wriggle and writhe and roar, doing all it can to break you with its passionate cries.
>
> Or it will reason with you: 'I am just a little sin. Spare me. I will not kill your soul! You can have me *and* your Jesus. I will not mind. You can keep me and your ministry. I promise to stay in secret, to be polite, to stay away from the sight and hearing of others.' All the while sin pleads, it knows – and we need to know – that secret sins do not stay hidden; that lusts reprieved will one day get their full pardon ... The most valiant warriors of the world have proven to be cowards when dealing with their own hearts![90]

And here is Augustine on the same topic: he confessed that his will, being enslaved, had made a chain for him, and bound him. So, he prayed, 'Lord, make me pure, but not yet!' For he feared God would answer his prayer too soon. Sin was ever whispering, 'Can you part with me? ... You cannot live without me!' But then!

> There appeared unto me the beautiful dignity of Purity. She was serene – where sin was like a tossing sea. She was gay and honest, alluring me to come and not doubt. She stretched forth to receive and embrace me, her holy hands full of multitudes of good examples of those who had said 'no' to sin and 'yes' to holiness ... And she smiled on me and with persuasive words said: '... Why stand in your own strength and in so doing not stand against sin? Cast yourself upon Him. Fear not! He will not withdraw Himself that you should fail and fall. Cast yourself fearlessly upon Him and He will receive you and will heal you ... Stop your ears against [your] ... wicked, earthly sins. Kill them. They tell you of delights but they lie. Delight is found only in the way of God.'[91]

There will never be a better day than today to declare war upon your heart sins. Christ's blood has atoned and all Heaven will come to your aid. You will find an ever-gracious God enabling you by His Spirit and providing His very own Son as your Advocate. Take courage! You may fail a thousand times, but Jesus will never give up on you.

Fight the good fight of the faith. Take hold of the eternal life to which you were called ... (1 Tim. 6:12)

Sin is the dare of God's justice, the rape of His mercy, the jeer of His patience, the slight of His power, and the contempt of His love.[92]
(John Bunyan)

Resolution 57

Resolved, rather than give way to fear of bad things that might happen or adversities that may come my way, that I will seek instead to make certain that I am doing my duty to God and others and battling for holiness of heart and life. Then I know that I can simply trust God's providence and accept His ordering of my life as good and best.

Now I want you to know, brothers and sisters, that what has happened to me has actually served to advance the gospel. (Phil. 1:12)

Friends,

What a timely *Resolution*! There is a spirit of fear roaming about these days that seems to have taken many captive. Our culture is seeking iron-clad guarantees that we will be safe at all times. We are in danger of making safety an idol. And idols *never* deliver what they promise, and *always* demand more and more from their devotees.

Jonathan lived in an age of ever-present danger and death. Few made it to old age (Jonathan would die at 54, and Sarah, his wife, at 48). A growling appendix could be lethal. There was no health service to rely upon. There were no paramedics to show up, no hospitals, no anaesthetic. Vaccines were few and as dangerous as the illnesses they were designed to prevent (Jonathan actually died of a small-pox vaccine gone wrong). Indeed, there were endless threats to life that today have been all but eliminated by advances in science, medicine, and safety protocols.

But the death rate is still 100% and there are *no* guarantees of safety. In fact, Jesus Himself guarantees *danger and adversity* for everyone who follows Him:

> *I have told you these things, so that in me you may have peace. In this world you will have trouble. But take heart! I have overcome the world!* (John 16:33)

I wonder what Jonathan would make of us moderns. We are insured to the hilt, vaccinated to the brim, and medicated to the max. We have a pill or a procedure for almost everything. We are buckled and belted, helmeted and pillowed in almost every way possible ... Yet we are perhaps the most fearful generation ever. Having moved away from God and toward anything and everything else, we have become prey to a spirit of fear that threatens to totally redefine 'normal' life.

But ... do we *love this life* too much?

And ... do we *trust God* too little?

Jonathan – living in a world fraught with dangers – has a simple and powerful strategy for living above fear. Here it is: He is going to pursue Jesus, serve others, and run after holiness of heart and life; then he is going to leave his well-being up to the providential care of his loving and good Heavenly Father. This strategy is not fool-hardy or brash. It is freeing and empowering. This is how Christians are supposed to live.

A.W. Tozer was right when he said that, in the end, every issue of life is theological – it all boils down to how we view God. God is *good*. The Christian is to make it his consuming passion to know Him, love others, and hate sin – especially his own. If we are doing that, we can then rest in God's overseeing care for us. We can say with the Apostle Paul, '*If we live, we live for the Lord; and if we die, we die for the Lord. So, whether we live or die, we belong to the Lord*' (Rom. 14:8). The Psalmist has wisdom for us too. In Psalm 112 he observes that the '*man who fears the Lord*' (that is, the man who regards God above all things) '*has no fear of bad news*' (v.7).

Notice the Psalmist does not say that the man who fears the Lord *will never get* bad news. He says he will not be held captive to the *fear* of bad news. And why? Or better, how? How can he live free from fear? He tells us: '*(His) heart is steadfast, trusting in the Lord*' (v.8).

He knows God and God's character, and that is enough for him. His heart is held fast by a clear view of God.

If you want to see Jonathan's strategy lived out before your eyes, go watch the film *Hacksaw Ridge*. It is a true story. Desmond Doss, a committed Christian and conscientious objector, serves as a medic in the battle of Okinawa. Refusing fear, and defying safety, he relentlessly commits his way to his good God and Saviour as he perseveres under hours of hostile fire, rescuing 75 wounded marines off the field of battle. It was his knowledge of God that allowed him not to love his life more than he loved others and to live bravely in the midst of incredible danger. In doing so, Desmond Doss became the only conscientious objector to ever win the Medal of Honour.

Warning! Once we give way to fear and bow at the false altar of safety, discipleship and purposeful living will be all but impossible. Jesus warns us against loving our lives in this world too dearly. By all means, take reasonable measures. Buckle your seat belt. Take the medicine. God is not calling us to be foolish and cavalier. But guard yourself.

The spirit of the age is begging you to preserve yourself in this world at all costs, and Jesus is calling you to lose yourself for His Kingdom and for others. We cannot do both. Which voice are we going to listen to and obey?

> *Anyone who loves their life will lose it, while anyone who hates their life in this world will keep it for eternal life.* (John 12:25)

> 'The real purpose of this training,' Mr. Dinnen told me, 'is to teach our students that they can trust God to do what He has said He would do ... They cannot be effective if they are afraid or if they doubt that God really means what He says in His Word. So here we teach not so much ideas as trusting.'[93] (Brother Andrew)

Resolution 58

Resolved, when engaging with others in conversation, to refuse a proud, argumentative, easily angered spirit and to exhibit instead a loving, cheerful and gracious spirit.

Let your conversation be always full of grace, seasoned with salt, so that you may know how to answer everyone. (Col. 4:6)

Let your gentleness be evident to all. The Lord is near. (Phil. 4:5)

Dear Friends,

The desire to 'be right' is a wicked desire. It is fuelled by pride and selfish ambition. It causes conflicts, produces pain, and fractures friendships. The quarrel in the kitchen is no different in essence from the fight on the frontlines. For sure, the battlefields of the World Wars broke God's heart, but so do the battlefields of the breakfast table, the Waffle Wars. Whether it is an army on the march to war or a strutting brother ready to risk a friendship for the sake of 'giving a piece of his mind', the same scripture holds true:

For where you have envy and selfish ambition, there you find disorder and every evil practice. (Jas. 3:16)

Our world is living in a time of barbarism. The desire to shout another down, the willingness to walk away from an argument having 'wiped the floor' with our opponent, the readiness to 'give as good as we get', is all straight from the pit. The common courtesy of listening, understanding, and replying kindly has given way to making sure we get our point across even at the risk of a relationship.

In the midst of this, the Christian is called to a higher standard. He follows the One who, when 'they hurled their insults at him ... did not retaliate; when he suffered ... made no threats. Instead, he entrusted himself to him who judges justly' (1 Pet. 2:23). Our Lord and Master is the One of whom it was foretold:

> *He will not shout or cry out, or raise his voice in the streets. A bruised reed he will not break, and a smouldering wick he will not snuff out.*
> (Is. 42:2–3)

While we live in a world that loves to shout and break the bruised reed, we are subjects of another world. Jesus was misunderstood, misrepresented, and misjudged. He did not retaliate. He entrusted all things to His Father, and that was enough for Him.

We are called to be like *Him,* not like our culture.

What a freedom it is not to have to be right all the time! Hooray! What a relief it is not to have to always have the final word! Phew! What a peace and joy it is to be misunderstood and just give it to Jesus and walk in peace with our brothers! The Bible speaks of a peace that surpasses all understanding (Phil. 4:7), but we also have a peace that surpasses all *mis*understanding!

We have been taught to 'win at all costs' but the Bible actually teaches that it 'is to one's honour to avoid strife' because only a 'fool is quick to quarrel' (Prov. 20:3). Many times, I have walked away from a hot conversation, bloodied sword in hand, congratulating myself for my deadly duelling skills, when in fact I have either:

1) made a total fool of myself or
2) wounded my brother for whom Christ died.

Paul had to admonish the worldly, carnal, babyish Corinthians with the simple but penetrating question:

> *Why not rather be wronged?* (1 Cor. 6:7)

There is a great peace in cultivating an *unoffendable spirit.* An old Cornish farmer once said these wise words to me, ''Tis as much a sin to *take* offense as it is to *give* offense!' There is great spiritual value in praying for a sweet spirit. To ask Jesus regularly to fill me with sweetness and tenderness toward others, especially those with whom I disagree, is actually vital spiritual warfare. In addition to my Cornish farmer friend cited above, I also used to pray regularly with an old-time Arkansas Pentecostal Preacher (you bet I did!) whose words I quoted in Resolution 14, but will reprise because they are so good! That dear man used to pray every week 'Oooo Lord! When someone kicks me, let them get honey all over their foot!'

Oh, for a sweet, unoffendable, Jesus-protected spirit that does not strive and argue and wrangle with others! If I am going to be *useful* to Jesus, I simply do not have the time to embroil myself in trying to prove my point, be the expert (again), or be right – unless it is truly a *Gospel issue*. Indeed, for any lesser issue, I must not. So, Paul commanded Timothy:

> And the Lord's servant must not be quarrelsome but must be kind to everyone, able to teach, not resentful. (2 Tim. 2:24)

And Peter commands us all:

> Always be prepared to give an answer to everyone who asks you to give the reason for the hope that you have. But do this with gentleness and respect. (1 Pet. 3:15–16)

Believers in Jesus! We need to rise above the spirit of the age.

Jonathan resolves not merely *not* to fall into the cesspit of argument; he actually wants his words to be life-giving. He desires that his speech 'exhibit instead a loving, cheerful and gracious spirit'. He wants people to leave his presence edified, built up, blessed, refreshed ...

Jesus will help us. We do not have to do anything in the Christian life in our own strength, including this. As we increasingly surrender ourselves unto Him, He will work His sanctifying grace in us. I would be surprised if Jonathan read much of St. Francis of Assisi. But I would not be surprised if he read, and prayed, this timeless prayer of the humble 12th century Italian:

Lord, make me an instrument of your peace.
Where there is hatred, let me bring love.
Where there is offence, let me bring pardon.
Where there is discord, let me bring union.
Where there is error, let me bring truth.
Where there is doubt, let me bring faith.
Where there is despair, let me bring hope.
Where there is darkness, let me bring your light.
Where there is sadness, let me bring joy.
(Giovanni di Pietro di Bernardone,
aka, Francis of Assisi, 1181–1226)

Resolution 59

Resolved, when I am feeling irked, when my attitude is bad, when I am aware of emotions of anger or feelings of ill nature, to act in exactly the opposite manner to my feelings. Even if it seems that it will be to my disadvantage not to act according to my negative feelings, it is always best to obey God and act in a gracious manner, not only when I feel like doing so.

For the grace of God has appeared that ... teaches us to say 'No' to ungodliness and worldly passions, and to live self-controlled, upright and godly lives in this present age ... (Titus 2:11–12)

Friends,

If I waited until I 'felt like it', I would rarely get up early to read my Bible and pray, often ignore my wife's needs and just think of myself, *and never* go to the gym.

The popular thought these days is that the *will* must follow the *feelings*. People think that *emotions* should determine actions. If I do not feel like doing something, then I need not do it. In a culture that is collapsing inwards, being 'true to myself' (often code for 'doing what I feel like doing') has become the supreme virtue.

Older Christians knew nothing of this way of thinking. To them, almost across the board, the will was to lead the way and the emotions were told to fall in step. The will was subject to the Word (which informed the intellect), and the 'affections' (feelings) were expected to comply – without arguing. This does not mean that our feelings, our affections, our emotions are not important! But it does mean that they cannot rule us. We do not wait on our feelings before we go forward. We obey God's Word and tell our feelings to get in line. Actions precede attitudes. Feelings and attitudes are to be *subject* to, never *sovereign* over, the will which is itself subject to Jesus and His Word. A godly person who taught me this was Henry Scougal (1650–1678) in his remarkable book *The Life of God in the Soul of Man*. I had the privilege of re-writing that wonderful book a couple years ago, and here is my rendition of Henry's vital teaching:

> If we are having trouble getting our inner life changed, then we can begin with our outer life. I know that many say that without the heart, the actions are hypocritical, but that is not always the case. The heart can actually follow the actions. It can engage once the actions are engaged. In other words, there may be times when we do our duty, regardless of our hearts, and we find the heart follows the will …We can give God our best whether we feel like it or not … External actions can have value in moving you toward a warm heart … It is always good and right to do what we can, knowing that God will have mercy on us and help us with even our weak efforts.[94]

Like Henry's advice, Jonathan's *Resolution* is strange to our modern way of thinking. But it is actually refreshing and brings hope with it. He is telling us that we need not be held captive to miserable attitudes, bitter feelings, sour emotions, and cold hearts. Jonathan instructs us that it is *always* the best path to act in a gracious manner, and this is exactly what Jesus teaches us to do!

> *If you love those who love you, what reward will you get? Are not even the tax collectors doing that?* (Matt. 5:46–48)

Clearly, Jesus is teaching us here to rise above our feelings and emotions and act according to the grace that we have received from our Heavenly Father. We need to get over the notion – because it is erroneous – that our feelings and moods set the direction for our wills to follow. No! Listen to Paul on this:

> *We demolish arguments and every pretension that sets itself up against the knowledge of God, and we take captive every thought to make it obedient to Christ.* (2 Cor. 10:5)

A few years ago, I became very deeply convicted that my irritability was a sin. Giving in to morose moods and sour attitudes was dishonouring to the God who saved me and promised to pour His Joy into me (John 15:11). I had allowed Satan to build a stronghold in my life by failing to battle for joy and by caving in to the mood of the moment. All the while, Christ Jesus had been giving me all grace to deny self (which includes self-pity, self-hatred, self-seeking ...). 'Going into my cave', brooding, thinking the worst of others, responding irritably, using sarcasm, fault-finding, holding grudges, being irked, are all grace-denying ways of worshipping at the throne of myself. What a painful – then blessed – revelation it was to see all this! Dismantling this stronghold is proving to be a long, if vital, work. But I have no choice if I am to be a faithful follower of the One whose *divine power has given [me] everything [I] need for a godly life through [my] knowledge of him who called [me] by his own glory and goodness'* (2 Pet. 1:3).

Jonathan's advice is revolutionary in today's world: Forget yourself and *go do the opposite to how you feel.* This is *not* hypocritical. It is spiritual warfare. It is *willing* instead of *wallowing.*

I think I can honestly say that whenever I have acted out of anger, moved by irked, judgmental, irritated, or lazy feelings, *I have never been glad that I have done so the next day.* Why? *'Because human anger [or irritability, or laziness, or moodiness, or bad attitude] does not produce the righteousness that God desires'* (Jas. 1:20).

Lord Jesus, help me to deny myself, get off the throne, stop feeling entitled, quit following my moods, and man up!

Better a patient person than a warrior, one with self-control than one who takes a city. (Prov. 16:32)

Refuse self-pity. Refuse it absolutely. It is a deadly thing with power to destroy you.[95] (Elizabeth Elliot)

Resolution 60

Resolved, whenever I begin to lose my peace within, when my heart is the least bit uneasy, or whenever my outward behaviour begins to be inconsistent with being a follower of Jesus, that I will waste no time in subjecting myself to a strict examination.

Why, my soul, are you downcast? Why so disturbed within me? Put your hope in God, for I will yet praise him, my Saviour and my God.
(Ps. 42:11)

Dear Friends,

Roy Hession alarmed me with these words: 'Everything that disturbs the peace of God in our hearts is sin, no matter how small it is, and no matter how little like sin it may at first appear to be.'[96]

Remember what Jonathan is teaching us: diligence is not anti-grace. Being careful with your heart is not legalism. It is a proper response to being delivered from the ruin of sin. Jonathan Edwards did not believe that he was saved by works. He knew he could not perform his way into Heaven. He fully understood that salvation was totally a free gift of God's grace that could never be earned or deserved. But he did not cheapen the Gospel. He knew he was saved from sin to holiness. He knew that grace was not license for laziness but power for purpose. He knew that it was easier to head sin off at the pass than it was to watch it whizz by and then try to chase after it, lasso it, and wrestle it to the ground. He knew sin unchecked could run wild.

Look at this *Resolution* carefully. Jonathan does not want to give a head start to destructive thoughts or behaviour. Come with me to Joshua 7, to the secret (or so he thought) sin of a careless man named Achan:

> Achan replied, 'It is true! I have sinned against the Lord, the God of Israel. This is what I have done: when I saw in the plunder a beautiful robe from Babylonia, two hundred shekels of silver and a bar of gold weighing fifty shekels, I coveted them and took them. They are hidden in the ground inside my tent, with the silver underneath. (vss. 20–21)

Do you see a progression here? If you remember the story, Israel went up against Jericho and won a resounding victory by the grace and goodness of God. But! They were clearly commanded to touch *none* of the pagan artifacts of that city. Achan acted secretly, stealing some of their articles of devotion. But, ah! Sin never stays secret! You can trace its origin, but rarely predict its destination. How foolish was Achan! How wise he would have been if he had examined his own heart and wasted no time in redirecting his course!

Hear Achan's own words:

This is what I have done:

1) I saw. No crime yet! Achan! Check your heart! Look away now! Listen to your inner unease! Your behaviour is soon to be inconsistent with your beliefs. Get out of there!

2) I coveted. Crime is now being committed at heart level! God sees the heart. But there is still time to flee. Sin is starting to gallop. Get out of the way! Repent *now*.

3) I took. Now we have gone from eyes to heart to hands. Achan! You have suppressed your conscience! Sin *never* stays put. You must slay it, or it will slay you. At this point ... he still could have put those trinkets back and run away!

4) I hid. Secrecy. Dishonesty. Cover up. Lying. Can't sleep. Can't eat. Can't look you in the eye. 'What's up with Achan?' Sin has a grip on Achan's soul.

If you know the story, you will know that Achan's sin affected not only Achan, not only his family, but all Israel. You may know sin's origin, but rarely can you imagine its final impact.

Better not give it any ground.

Better search it out at source like the psalmist does in Psalm 42. '*Why are you downcast, soul?*' He knows there must be a reason for his loss of joy. He knows he needs to find out why his peace has left, why – in Roy Hessian's metaphor – God's referee has blown the whistle in his heart. Whatever the reason, the remedy is *Godward*. 'Put your hope in God!' Get back on track with Jehovah. Whether it is attitude or action, the answer is *always* to move toward God, never to step away and into the shadows. Here, in the Bible, we find a God who, when offended, invites us to approach. Imagine that! The Bible tells us of a *welcoming* God, a *willing* God.

We do not have to stumble from crisis to crisis. We do not have to leave a trail of tears behind us. We do not have to have a life that forever seems to resemble a demolition project more than a building site. The life of a Jesus-follower is a life of many little corrections, numerous repentances, countless trips to the cross, not a few tears, all followed by renewed joy and vigour as sin is cleansed, attitudes are changed, relationships are restored, and peace is refreshed. We must never be hesitant to allow God to lead us in a strict examination if it helps us to discover sin, repent of it before a gracious Jesus, and know the cleansing that His atoning blood continually gives.

And the peace of God, which transcends all understanding, will guard
your hearts and your minds in Christ Jesus. (Phil. 4:7)

When we lose our peace, God's referee in our hearts has blown his whistle! Let us stop immediately, ask God to show us what is wrong, put by faith the sin He shows us under the Blood of Jesus, and then peace will be restored, and we shall go on our way with our cups running over.[97] (Roy Hession)

Resolution 61

Resolved to rise above laziness. Whether laziness is tempting me to let my mind wander away from being fixed upon God and His grace or inciting me toward apathetic neglect of my duties, I realize it is always best to keep my mind on the Lord and my hands to my calling.

We do not want you to become lazy, but to imitate those who through faith and patience inherit what has been promised. (Heb. 6:11–12)

Dear Friends,

Goodness, it is hard to imagine Jonathan Edwards struggling to overcome apathy! My first thought upon wrestling with this *Resolution* is simply: If Jonathan has an issue with laziness, where on earth does that leave the rest of us?

The fact of the matter is, none of us are machines. Jonathan Edwards was not a machine. The Lord Jesus knows this. We can all lapse into apathy and the temptation is there to yawn our way through an hour or a day, or an entire season of life. But before we explore the problem and excise the root cause, I think we need to draw a sharp line between laziness and legitimate rest, for we have an enemy who will always lead us to extremes. Anything to ruin us. As the old saying goes: If Satan cannot rock us to sleep, he will ride us to death. Either will do. Both will render us useless, and that is his sinister goal.

So first, a look at rest and re-creation. We need look no farther than Jesus Himself for the model and the balance. Here is the One who was able to say of Himself: *Very truly I tell you, the Son can do nothing by himself; he can do only what he sees his Father doing, because whatever the Father does the Son also does* (John 15:19). He lived and breathed His Father's will. I think we are on safe ground to say that Jesus did not succumb to laziness on the one hand or drivenness on the other. He worked hard (go read Mark 1!) and He took time off. In the middle of a very busy stretch, he says: *'Come ... apart into a desert place, and rest a while', for there were many coming and going, and they had no leisure so much as to eat* (Mark 6:31 KJV). Jesus will have us "come apart", lest we come apart!

Also, Jesus kept the Sabbath as a day of rest. (Remember that quaint old gift from our loving Heavenly Father?).[98] Rest, including Sabbath, would have been part of the rhythm of His God-guided life. And He invites us into His rest: *Come to me, all you who are weary and burdened, and I will give you rest* (Matt. 11:28–30).

Now on to laziness. We need to see laziness as sin but we need to see it against the background of a wonderful Saviour who invites us to His rest and to a life rhythmed by work and repose.

Laziness *is* a sin: it is wasting a treasure. Jesus addressed laziness directly in His story of the servant who buried his master's treasure in the ground rather than investing it. He called that servant 'wicked and lazy' (Matt. 25:26). Sloth is seen in Catholicism as one of the Seven Deadly Sins. Our word derives from the Latin (*acedia*) via the Middle English (*acciditties*) and means 'to not care'. It is interesting that we have named a ponderously slow-moving creature, that spends most of its life hanging upside down in trees, after this sin. The tree sloth might be cute and cuddly, but the sofa sloth is a tragedy. For Jesus has created us for purpose and redeemed us from sin (including sloth) for adventure and meaning:

For we are God's handiwork, created in Christ Jesus to do good works, which God prepared in advance for us to do. (Eph. 2:10)

Notice with me that Jonathan combats sloth not just in his deeds, but in his thinking as well. He wants to *set [his] heart on things above, where Christ is seated at the right hand of God ... not on earthly things* (Col. 3:1–2). I do find this area of diligence to be a never-ending battle, and the enticement of inertia is constant, but I offer the following thoughts about what I am learning, knowing that there are many examples who will be better than I!

First, I need to recognize that I am not a machine, and that some days will be better than others. No guilt and condemnation are attached to the normal reality of human frailty.

Then, I need to know that, while He has indeed saved me by His grace, it is for purpose and meaning (Rom. 12:2), and for me to submit myself to my Heavenly Father and refuse apathy will bring me into joy and fulness.

Finally, I cannot do anything without Jesus. I *cannot* overcome the inertia of sin and self unless I appeal to God – Father, Son, and Holy Spirit – to supernaturally enable me ... and He is willing and ready to help me! He never wearies of my asking or fails to empower for His service. *I mean that.*

Overcoming apathy and walking in purpose is, for me, often a matter of simply 'doing the next thing'. It does not have to be amazing. I just need to get going: do the dishes, walk the dog. What as-yet-to-be-realized purposes and treasures are just waiting for you to discover and enjoy to the Glory of God and the good of others? Might you be overdue in asking Jesus for yet another helping of grace (He has plenty!) to get going?

Do the next thing.[99] (Elizabeth Elliot)

Take yourself by the scruff of the neck and shake off your incarnate laziness.[100] (Oswald Chambers)

Resolution 62

Resolved to be ever ruled by the Law of Love, cheerfully and willingly serving others, but not so much to please people, as to please the Lord Himself, knowing that the good that a Christian does to a person in need is simply enabled by the Lord and is in the end done unto the Lord.

Serve wholeheartedly, as if you were serving the Lord, not people, because you know that the Lord will reward each one for whatever good they do ... (Eph. 6:5–8)

Dear Friends,

Are you a 'people server' or a 'people pleaser'? There is a big difference!

Martin Luther came out with a zinger when he rightly reminded us that, '[a] Christian man is the most free lord of all and subject to none; [b] a Christian man is the most dutiful servant of all and subject to everyone'.[101]

Free and subject to no-one.

Slave and servant of all.

A servant of Christ who will bow in homage to no person.

A servant of Christ who will wash the feet of any person.

Jonathan resolves to be ruled by one great law, the Law of Love. Jesus summed up the Law of Love – the *Royal* Law of Love – as:

Love the Lord your God with all your heart and with all your soul and with all your mind and with all your strength. The second is this: Love your neighbour as yourself. There is no commandment greater than these. (Mark 12:30–31)

That is radical freedom. That is radical slavery.

The Christian life is meant to be *simple*. I did not say *easy*. It is meant to be uncomplicated. I am to be ruled not by a ledger of edicts, but by the Law of Love. The love of Christ is to motivate, constrain, control, and empower me. But hear this: It is *supernatural*. It is the result of the regenerating act of God's Spirit filling the heart of the believer. I *cannot* love without divine empowerment. But God is ready and willing to empower! He *wants* to enable indeed; He never asks *without* enabling. He wants to give what He commands. And when we are ruled by love, it is inevitable that our lives will spill over into service for others.

But – (and this is a *big* But!) – with the goal of pleasing the Lord, and not those whom we serve.

If we do not get this clear and right, we will become slaves, not to those whom we serve, but to the *opinions* of those whom we serve. Being slaves to their opinions, to what they *think* of our service, will eventually and inevitably lead to bitterness and sourness in our service. Please hear this! The Royal Law of Love leads us to *serve* people, but not to be people *pleasers*. Being a people pleaser is an impossible bondage. People pleasers serve out of obligation. Soon, service becomes a drudgery and resentment sets in. We feel unappreciated. It all becomes a chore. Relationships suffer and the spirit sags.

It is nice to be appreciated, and by all means we should show appreciation toward those who serve us, but when we serve people with a *goal* of being appreciated, we are setting ourselves up for bitterness and disappointment. Think about this: when we serve others to gain their approval, we are actually ... serving *ourselves*. People may see and appreciate, or they may not. *Their* opinion must not be our goal.

Here is the freedom formula in the Royal Law of Love:

We serve *people* with the goal to please the *Lord*.

And – good news – God is easy to please! He is far easier to please than people.

He is impossible to impress. (Don't even try. He made the Universe.)

But he is easy to please.[102] (For He loves us through His perfect Son.)

When we serve with an eye toward our Heavenly Father, we see His smile and bright countenance towards us. He is moment by moment empowering; we are moment by moment receiving. He has already ordained the work; we are now walking in the work. He has brought the need to our attention; we are obeying Him in serving to meet that need. The people we serve may or may not 'get it'. They may or may not appreciate what we do. You might please them, or you might not. They may be quite hard to please. You might feel as though you never can do enough.

But ... (another *big* But!) ...

God is not like them (or us!) and the Law of Love sets you free from trying to please them. It invites you to serve with an eye to your wonderful Heavenly Father who, through your union with His Son, is happy to say to *you* the very words He said to Jesus:

This is my Son [daughter], whom I love; with him [her] I am well pleased. (Matt. 3:17)

Breathe this in. Stop striving. This entire Christian life is an enterprise in grace. We live in the unmerited favour of our super-abundant God and we serve in the crystal current of that favour.

Let's go live, love, and serve, all under the watchful and smiling face of our Heavenly Father.

Whatever you do, work at it with all your heart, as working for the Lord, not for human masters, since you know that you will receive an inheritance from the Lord as a reward. It is the Lord Christ you are serving. (Col. 3:22–24)

One of the principal rules of religion is to lose no occasion of serving God. And, since he is invisible to our eyes, we are to serve him in our neighbour, which he receives as if done to himself in person, standing visibly before us.[103] (John Wesley)

Resolution 63

Resolved, understanding that there is not, nor never has been, one person who in every respect is a shining and true example of a faithful follower of Jesus, but imagining that at a given time there is *one* such person in all of the earth, I resolve – with all my strength – to live as though I might be that one.

Teach me Your way, O Lord; I will walk in Your truth;unite my heart to fear Your name. I will praise You, O Lord my God, with all my heart, and I will glorify Your name forevermore. (Ps. 86:11–13)

Dear Jesus-Following Friend,

In the 1870's the American evangelist D.L. Moody was visiting and preaching in England when he was arrested by an observation from the British preacher Henry Varley: 'Moody, the world has yet to see what God will do with a man fully consecrated to him.'

Moody later recalled how those words pierced his heart:

Ah ... those were the words sent to my soul ... from the Living God. As I crossed the wide Atlantic, the boards of the deck of the vessel were engraved with them, and when I reached Chicago, the very paving stones seemed marked with 'Moody, the world has yet to see what God will do with a man fully consecrated to him.'[104]

Now I love that story and have for many years been affected by it for my good. But I have to temper it with some wisdom born of years following Jesus, wisdom that is found in Jonathan's magnificent *Resolution* given at the top of the page.

So, in wanting Jonathan's *Resolution* – and Varley's words to Moody – to have their full effect upon us, please consider first the following truths:

– No-one has ever been, or will ever be, fully consecrated to Jesus in this life. In the best hearts, there are always dark corners where sin lurks, and battlefronts yet to be conquered and claimed for Jesus.

– The most consecrated followers of Jesus are actually desperately aware of their remaining sin, of the divisions in their hearts, and of the inconsistencies of their lives.

– We are not saved by being fully consecrated to Jesus, but by His mercy to ruined sinners like us who have approached Him with weak, faulty faith.

– As our Saviour and Shepherd, Jesus is fully consecrated to us and that is why we can be assured that we are safe in His care in the midst of our broken, flawed discipleship.

Those things being said: It is *a good thing* to want to be, and to strive to be, as consecrated – as all out for Jesus – as we can be this side of Heaven.

The grace of God, His undeserved favour poured out to us through Jesus, not only brings salvation from the *penalty* of sin, but from its *power*. We are supernaturally given a new life and, therefore, we cannot help but begin to want to please God and to walk in a new way. Salvation is not just 'going to Heaven' (or 'not going to Hell'). It is the ongoing restoration of the Image of God within us, which was so tragically marred by sin. It, therefore, follows that a true Child of Grace will *want* to be as like Jesus as she can be this side of Heaven and will want to be all that she can be for Jesus during her brief sojourn here on Earth.

All of the Christian's life is sustained and fuelled by the grace and power of God so that, '*[t]he life I now live in the body, I live by faith in the Son of God, who loved me and gave himself for me*' (Gal. 2:20), '*with all the energy Christ so powerfully works in me*' (Col. 1:29).

My response to God's unceasing flow of undeserved favour is often so paltry and pathetic. It is not compatible with the goodness

He continually shows me. It is incongruous. It does not fit. It does not make sense.

Jonathan's fits.

Dwight Moody's makes sense.

The Apostle Paul's is compatible.

I can hear these guys in their misunderstood zeal (misunderstood by everyone except Jesus!) spurring one another on:

'I'm all in!'

'I want to be that 100% Jesus-follower the world needs!'

'Let's go for it with all we have!'

Jesus, to borrow from baseball, does not mind you or me striking out. What he does mind is if we do not even want to step up to the plate and swing the bat. Jonathan is swinging for the fence!

I want, by the grace of God, to be all that *I* can be for Jesus this side of Heaven. I must not let fear of failure or love of ease hold me back. I live under the banner of God's love (Song 2:4), and under that banner I can risk, stretch, fail, get back up, try again, make a mess of things, start over, keep going, stumble, strike out, and dream big.

What I cannot do is not bother.

Thank you, Jonathan, Dwight, and Paul for spurring me on and for stirring me up. Without friends like you (and I could add Joni Erickson-Tada, Amy Carmichael, Hudson Taylor, Gladys Aylward, George Verwer, and many others to this list), I would lapse into offering Jesus my second-hand love and my leftover strength ... after I had given my best to this world.

> *[O]ne thing I do: forgetting what is behind and straining towards what is ahead, I press on towards the goal to win the prize for which God has called me heavenwards in Christ Jesus. (Phil. 3:13–14)*

I wasn't God's first choice for what I've done in China ... I don't know who it was ... it must have been a man ... a well-educated man. I don't know what happened. Perhaps he died. Perhaps he wasn't willing ... and God looked down ... and saw Gladys Aylward ... and God said, "Well, she's willing."[105] (Gladys Aylward)

Resolution 64

Resolved never to ignore, but to act upon the 'groanings' and 'longings' of my deep soul, embracing them fully and not tiring of the soul work of pouring out my deepest heart to God, knowing that I am sure to reap a great benefit.

My soul yearns for you in the night; in the morning, my spirit longs for you. (Is. 26:9)

Dear Friend,

God wants your heart. He is not just interested in your service. He is not interested only in your outward obedience. He is not interested in your money.

Those things are not unimportant, but they are no replacement for your heart.

God the Holy Spirit indwells every believer. He moves our spirits toward God the Father. God orders our lives to create in us a soul-thirst, that we might embark upon a pursuit of God at heart-level. Every Christian should live in dread of the words uttered by Jesus, lest they be found to be true of them: *These people honour me with their lips, but their hearts are far from me* (Matt. 15:8).

Do not be satisfied with the shallows. God is inviting you to the depths. God is inviting you to step out where your feet cannot touch bottom. I am not just talking about 'doing' things for God. I am referring to our hearts being drawn out by Him and toward Him. I am speaking of realizing that every lesser love, every rival for our heart's affection, is a pretender to the throne and must be banished. When we sense these deeper longings, when we recognize an emptiness and a dissatisfaction with all that is about us, *God* is summoning us onward, outward, deeper. The challenge from Jonathan is to *respond* to those inconsolable longings, and not just numb them or ignore them. That groan from your heart may well be God trying for your deeper attention. That sigh in your spirit is probably God's Spirit summoning yours to Himself.

Deep calls to deep (Ps. 42:7)

We need to learn to pay attention to the deep groans of the soul, knowing that God is graciously wooing us to himself.

The little book, Song of Solomon, is given to us by God to be, among other things, a picture of the love Jesus has for the simple believer. In that wonderous book, the bridegroom's heart is actually *affected* by the response of the bride. He yearns; she sometimes disregards. He invites; she sometimes refuses. He pursues; she retreats. But the love song gives us a portrait of the very heart of God for us. It is a heart that seeks response. It is a heart that provokes a response. Listen to the bridegroom (Jesus) and imagine yourself to be the beloved bride:

You have stolen my heart, my sister, my bride; you have stolen my heart with one glance of your eyes ... (Song 4:9)

Can it be? Can it be that God, the Eternal Uncreated, the All-Sufficient *God* of the Universe has so ordered things that He actually wants a deep relationship with you and me? That it is actually a part of His essential being to love deeply and to be *affected* by those whom He has created in His image and redeemed through the blood of His Son?

Lord, can I really touch your heart when the eyes of my soul look in love toward You?

Augustine rightly said that God has made us for Himself and that our hearts are restless until they find rest in Him.[106] But dare I venture to say that this God, who made us for Himself, likewise is restless until we rest in Him?

As a bridegroom rejoices over his bride, *so will your God rejoice over
you.* (Is. 62:5)

We believe that the transient things that we can see, feel, taste, buy,
build, and touch will satisfy our deepest desire. So we acquire, we
date, we build, we marry, we invest, we procreate. But, if we will be
still for a moment, can we not still hear that inward groan and feel
that inconsolable longing? *God* put that there. It is Jesus calling. Deep
calls unto deep. Stop and listen! Respond to the invitation:

> 'You, God, are my God, earnestly I seek you; I thirst for you, my whole
> being longs for you, in a dry and parched land where there is no water.'
> (Ps. 63:1)

God repeatedly arranges things so that the visible and transient
disappoint and decay. He does this for our good. He does this because
He loves us. Otherwise, we will be satisfied at a mere 'animal level'
and forget we even have a soul, and that there is a wooing God for
whom we have been created and redeemed.

Blaise Pascal (1623–1662), the French mathematician and
theologian, though he managed only 39 years on this planet, left his
mark, not the least of which is this great observation:

> What else does this craving, and this helplessness, proclaim but
> that there was once in man a true happiness, of which all that now
> remains is the empty print and trace? This he tries in vain to fill
> with everything around him, seeking in things that are not there
> the help he cannot find in those that are, though none can help,
> since this infinite abyss can be filled only with an infinite and
> immutable object; in other words, with God himself.[107]

Don't ignore the inner longing. Don't pacify it. Turn it into a relentless
pursuit of God. It is soul work, and it will reap the wonderful reward
of a deep and real knowledge of the Holy One.

> *Arise, come, my darling; my beautiful one, come with me.'*
> (Song 2:10–13)

All of humanity's problems stem from man's inability to sit quietly in
a room alone.[108] (Blaise Pascal)

Resolution 65

Resolved, in all of my life, and for all of my life, to lay my heart and soul open to God – meaning, all of my temptations, my sins, my sadness, my fears, my hopes, and my desires – holding nothing back from my Lord in any and every circumstance.

But the Lord God called to the man, 'Where are you?' He answered, 'I heard you in the garden, and I was afraid because I was naked; so I hid.' (Gen. 3:9–10)

Dear Friend in Jesus,

Since the dawn of time, we have been hiding. God has been looking. Since Adam and Eve, we have shied away from God, from being real, from coming clean. Their attempt to cover their nakedness with scratchy fig leaves (Gen. 3:7) was the first 'religious' event in human history. It did not work. God saw right through it.

We are forever holding back; God is forever coming forth.

All through the Bible we find a seeking God and a hiding sinner. Finally, we encounter Jesus who plainly and wonderfully tells us that he came 'to seek and to save the lost' (Luke 19:10).

Jonathan wants to be done with hiding, with lurking, with the excuses, with the shadows. He knows the character of God toward him. He knows that the God of the Bible (the only God that there is!) is a *willing, consistent* God, not a capricious, grudging God. He knows that God only has Jonathan's best in mind, and that it is foolish to hide *anything* from such a God (as though it were possible to do so). David, who knew as well as any of us the folly of covering-up and the wonder of opening-up, counsels us: *Blessed is the one ... in whose spirit is no deceit.* (Ps. 32:2) There is a freedom to being open with God. There is a freshness of spirit for the one who daily, even moment by moment, brings all that they are before their loving and all-knowing Heavenly Father.

Your view of God, your understanding of His character and of His heart toward you, is vital in all of this. I cannot be 'open' with God if I am not sure of His heart toward me. Is He really good? Does He truly always have my best in mind? Does He care about the details of my life? Can I pour everything out to Him? Can I tell Him of my hopes and dreams? Can I tell Him of my sins and failures? Does He see me? Does He understand me?

There are many who believe in Jesus, who call themselves Christians, but who have a sad view of God. Many of us think that God, at best, puts up with us. Sure, He has forgiven us through the Gospel, but He does not *like* us. Certainly, He is not *interested* in us. We could never open our hearts to Him. Do you know that God *does have* an open heart for you and that, therefore, you will *not* be rebuffed if you open your heart to Him? It is revolutionary to open up one's entire self to God. Even for a Jesus-follower who knows the forgiveness of his sins and crimes, there can still be a residue of guilt causing an unwillingness to come, a shyness to open oneself, a reticence to let all be seen, born of a wrong view of God and the Gospel. This leads to a spiritual poverty, to distance, to coldness with God.

And – guaranteed – if your heart is not open to Jesus, it is not open to others either. Every human relationship springs from our relationship with God, and to the degree that you are available for intimacy with God, you are available for intimacy with people. (That is why one of the first questions I often ask when counselling friends concerning their human relationships is, 'Tell me about your life with Jesus'.)

Oh, please hear this! Through Christ, because of His blood shed once for our sins, there *need be no hindrance* in our approach to God.

Let us then approach God's throne of grace with confidence, so that we may receive mercy and find grace to help us in our time of need.
(Heb. 4:16)

We will spend eternity marvelling at this wonderful God who, though uncaused and without any need, has chosen to want us and desires to walk in intimacy with us. So many of the word pictures in the Bible describing Jesus' relationship with us depict intimacy, union, friendship, openness:

– Shepherd and sheep,
– Vine and branches,
– Bridegroom and bride,
– Friend and befriended,
– Head and body.

He understands when no one else tries to. He forgives when no one else wants to.

He feels when no one else cares to. He is willing when no one else dares to.

He sees what no one else can see. He hears when no one else will listen.

Wonderful, wonderful Jesus.

Jonathan's *Resolution* is timeless and as needed today in my life and yours as it once was in his. Will you resolve, by the grace of God, to open up your entire self to Jesus? Daily? Yes, even moment by moment? Because of Jesus you will always find a warm welcome, a willing ear, a watchful eye, and a tender voice. Wait not in resolving to lay your heart and soul open to the Lord. Mother-in-law Naomi's advice to the poor widowed Ruth (us) regarding strong Boaz (Jesus) and his heart to redeem her, is a word for us today. Believe it and stop holding back from the One who loves you so!

Wash, put on perfume, and get dressed in your best clothes [open your whole self to Jesus] ... For the man will not rest until the matter is settled today.' (Ruth 3:3; 18)

God is more concerned with winning all of me for Christ than in me winning all the world for Christ.[109] (David Wilkerson)

Resolution 66

Resolved to seek, at all times, to act and speak in a gracious and benevolent manner, in all places and toward all people, unless faithfulness requires otherwise.

Love suffers long and is kind; love does not envy; love does not parade itself, is not puffed up; does not behave rudely, does not seek its own, is not provoked, thinks no evil; does not rejoice in iniquity, but rejoices in the truth; bears all things, believes all things, hopes all things, endures all things. (1 Cor. 13:4–7 NKJV)

Dear Friend in Christ,

Oh, to have a sweet, Christ-like spirit!

Imagine having not one ounce of jealousy, not a grain of ill-will toward another, no grumbling bitterness, no lurking bad attitude. Consider a life with no little twists in your words, no sharp corners in your communications, no raised eyebrows, harrumphs, or rolls of the eye.

Imagine never again tossing in your sleepless bed, rehearsing that 'giving him a piece of my mind' speech over and over. Think of life with no more sour feelings, never another 'Why did I say that?' regret.

Imagine never removing your friend's speck from his smarting eye until you had removed the log from your own. Think of relationships with no arguments, no points to prove, but only engagements arising out of humility, love and a desire to see the other person blessed.

Such a heart, such a life, is what old-timers called ... *Holiness*.

It is not *common* these days. But it is *normal*, sanctified Jesus-following.

My relationship with Jesus has to completely re-wire how I interact with others – both inwardly and outwardly – or it is suspect (1 John 4:7–12). Living the 'crucified life', the life that says 'no' to self and 'yes' to God, inevitably spills over into our actions and attitudes towards others. Holiness is not a feeling one gets when the music is 'just right' and the (short) sermon makes one feel good. It is not a tingling in the spine so much as a trembling in the heart. It is personal but not private. It *must* affect how I relate to people. John Wesley put it simply:

> Solitary religion is not to be found [in the Bible]. 'Holy Solitaries' is a phrase no more consistent with the gospel than Holy Adulterers. The gospel of Christ knows of no religion, but social; no holiness but social holiness. Faith working by love, is the length and breadth and depth and height of Christian perfection.[110]

Holiness of heart and life is not so much a *negative* posture – a posture of *not* being sour and bitter – but a *positive* one – of being sweet and tender in spirit. It is about having a heart like Jesus'. It is about being *'gentle and humble in heart'* (Matt. 11:29). This is what Jesus wants to form in us. What Jonathan is resolving is actually to open himself up to a deep and wonderful work in his inner being that will produce a precious outer countenance toward those he walks with. Old-timers did not see this as optional. It was to them the tell-tale proof that God was making them like Jesus. They not only *believed* their Bibles; they *behaved* them. They wanted to be made like Jesus, demonstrating the fruit of the Spirit: *'love, joy, peace, forbearance, kindness, goodness, faithfulness, gentleness and self-control* '(Gal. 5:22–24): being *'completely humble and gentle; … patient, bearing with one another in love'* (Eph. 4:2).

Sometimes faithfulness will require that we share a hard word with another. At such times it can actually be *un*loving not to speak. How thankful I am for those who have ventured to confront me when I have needed it! You can tell when someone has your best in mind, when their heart is gentle towards your heart, when their words are well chosen and seasoned with salt. Perhaps they have wept first for your situation. Certainly, they have prayed before they have spoken.

The account of Jesus' cleansing of the Jerusalem Temple from those merchandising in God's house is instructive for us:

> As he approached Jerusalem and saw the city, he wept over it ... When Jesus entered the temple courts, he began to drive out those who were selling. (Luke 19:41; 45–6)

Do you see the order of events here? Jesus *wept* before He *whipped*. His heart, defined by gentleness, broke before He bruised. Kindness and gentleness are Christ's 'natural work; judgement and rebuke, while necessary, are His 'strange work'.[111] So should it be with us. What is to be natural to us (in fact, *super*naturally natural!) is to be kind, sweet, and gentle. What is to be strange to us – though sometimes necessary – is to express judgement and rebuke.

Alas! How often with us it is our 'natural work' to be negative, cross, corrective, and censuring, and our 'strange work' to be gracious, edifying, sweet, and gentle!

Lord Jesus! Change me! Work in me a transformation that makes me like You. May there be in me a true and genuine sweetness of spirit that controls my thoughts, words, and actions toward others. By your grace, do a *supernatural* work in me that causes love, sweetness, and kindness toward others to be *natural* to me!

> For he does not willingly bring affliction or grief to anyone. (Lam. 3:33)

> The tongue of the righteous is choice silver ... The lips of the righteous nourish many ... (Prov. 10:20–21)

> Growing up involves the work of the Holy Spirit forming our born-again spirits into the likeness of Christ.[112] (Eugene H. Peterson)

Resolution 67

Resolved, after suffering afflictions and trials, to discover in what ways I am now better for having experienced them. I will ask, 'What good have I received from them? What new insights do I now have because of them?'

It was good for me to be afflicted so that I might learn your decrees.
(Ps. 119:71)

Dear Friend in Jesus,

God wants to make us like Jesus. His love is real and purposeful, and when He takes on 'projects' – you and me – He intends to do a perfect job. We can be confident of this: *'that he who began a good work in you will carry it on to completion until the day of Christ Jesus'* (Phil. 1:6).

His transformation of us, from creatures accustomed to lurking in dark corners to sons and daughters of the Light, usually requires major work. This does not happen without pain, trial, and affliction. But His purposes are sure, and His hand is steady (even if ours is trembling). He is a master artist, a most skilful surgeon, an expert craftsman, a precision builder. There is *purpose* in all that God does in our lives, including sufferings and afflictions. When we kick against Him, we only delay His purposes.

Sadly, I think almost every western Christian has been poisoned by the 'prosperity gospel'. By that I mean, we all have been infected by the notion that if we are following Jesus, everything should go well with us most, if not all, of the time. We think, 'Certainly, God wants us healthy and wealthy, doesn't He? He would not put us through tough trials, would He?

Ah, but we forget that He has *eternal* purposes for us. We forget that our addiction to sin and self has warped every faculty of ours, and that salvation is God restoring us to glory and preparing us to inhabit eternity with Him.

We need to learn to learn from afflictions and trials.

We need to learn to submit to His skilful, precise, purposeful work in our lives.

How well I remember being with a dear friend on the day he was diagnosed with the cancer that would kill him. I can never forget his words: 'I am not going to waste this!' His determination was that if God had ordered this hard providence, he was going to let it do its good work of refining his soul. How well I remember watching this refinement during that last year of his earthly life! How can I ever forget his final days when he freely confessed that God had been *good* to him in weaning him from sin and making him more like Jesus? He told me without hesitation that he would not want to turn back the clock and be the strong young man he had been just a year ago, because now he was in fact a 'new man' ready to be with Jesus. Reciting 1 Peter 4:1 to me the last time I was with him, he rejoiced that *finally* he was free from sin. (To my friend, being free from sin was a greater victory than being hale and hearty.)

Trusting God's goodness in the midst of afflictions is a faith issue. Can we really believe that '... in all things God works for the good of those who love him, who have been called according to his purpose' (Rom. 8:28)? Can we truly 'lean in' to God's providential workings in our lives? Can we trust? Jonathan's resolve not to waste his trials reveals his confidence in God's goodness toward him, and his trust in God's long-range purposes concerning him. He is not kicking and squirming. He is trusting and submitting. He is allowing the Artist to work His master strokes. He is submitting to the Surgeon's necessary knife. He is letting the Potter work the lump of clay. He is trusting the Builder to demolish and build.

Remember that Jonathan recited this *Resolution* weekly until his death at the age of 55: and what a seemingly untimely death it was! Having just become president of what was to become Princeton University, he received an inappropriately dosed small-pox vaccination, and contracted the deadly malady. For weeks he suffered an excruciating sickness and then a painful death. But grace had well-instructed His soul! I cannot explore this *Resolution* without quoting from his attending physician, Dr. Shippen.

Please read these words slowly and let the truth of them sink in. In a letter to Jonathan's daughter, Sarah, he writes:

> This afternoon, between two and three o'clock, it pleased God to let [your father] sleep in that dear Lord Jesus, whose kingdom and interest he has been faithfully and painfully serving all his life. And never did any mortal man more fully and clearly evidence the sincerity of all his professions, by one continued, universal, calm, cheerful resignation, and patient submission to the divine will, through every stage of his disease, than he; not so much as one discontented expression, nor the least appearance of murmuring, through the whole ...[113]

And to another daughter, Lucy, he communicates Jonathan's encouragement to his soon-to-be-fatherless children. ' ... [S]ubmit cheerfully to the Will of God' and '... seek a Father who will never fail you ...'[114]

Jonathan's dear wife, Sarah, was later able to write to a daughter: 'My God lives; and he has my heart. O what a legacy my husband, and your father, has left us! We are all given to God; and there I am, and love to be.[115]

Beloved, learning to learn from afflictions is not optional if you want to grow in Christlikeness, and live fearlessly and joyfully until you enter Heaven! God is good. His ways are good. His mysteries are good. His designs are good. Let us learn to learn.

For our light and momentary troubles are achieving for us an eternal glory that far outweighs them all. (2 Cor. 4:17)

Trust in God, and ye need not fear.[116]
(Jonathan Edward's last words in this life)

Resolution 68

Resolved to be honest with myself regarding my own weaknesses and sins, being diligent regarding my spiritual health, to confess my whole heart to God, asking for, and trusting Him for His needed help.

For we do not have a high priest who is unable to feel sympathy for our weaknesses, but we have one who has been tempted in every way, just as we are – yet he did not sin. Let us then approach God's throne of grace with confidence, so that we may receive mercy and find grace to help us in our time of need. (Heb. 4:15–16)

Dear Friends,

Do you know that we have a *willing* God? He is actually motivated to help His children through their weaknesses and failures. His desire for us is that we live lives that honour Him, know fulness and blessedness, and bring blessing to our world. It is this desire that motivated Jesus to leave Heaven and come on His saving errand to this rebel planet.

Because of the heart of God to alleviate our guilt and lift us from our shame, there is no reason for us to hesitate for an instant to be honest about our sins, and to bring our whole hearts often before Him for cleansing and help. Confession and repentance are the meat and potatoes of the Christian life. But ... the sad fact is that sin has so deceived us, so perverted our view of God and His goodness, that we hide in the shadows rather than come out into the light. We hold on to our sins as though they were of benefit to us when, in fact, they are killing us. We shy away from God. We deceive ourselves. We make up excuses. We cast blame. All the while God is ready, willing and waiting, saying, *'All day long I have held out my hands to an obstinate people, who walk in ways not good, pursuing their own imaginations'* (Is. 65:2). God wants us to know that *'the one who confesses [their sins] finds mercy'* (Prov. 28:13). There is *freedom* in confession. There is *joy* in repenting. There is *liberty* in bringing one's messed up heart before a willing God. His grace is an inexhaustible river, not a muddy little puddle (Zech. 13:1).

When we are willing to 'walk in the light' (1 John 1:7), we are willing to see our sins and confess them. Then and there, we are cleansed by the blood of Jesus which was once shed for all sins for all time. *And* – BONUS – there in the light, where we are confessing and being cleansed, 'we have fellowship with one another'. For there, while we are confessing, we find others doing the same. What sweet fellowship exists between repenting believers as Christ cleanses and restores! This is nothing short of revival and the more repenters join in, the farther the revival spreads. Families, churches, whole nations have experienced such wonders.

But – let me say this again – the only heart I have any jurisdiction over is my own. So, as far as *I* am concerned, revival needs to begin with me – with me being ready and willing to be real with myself and with God regarding my sin and coming without delay to Him. When *I* deal with *my sin* before Jesus, *my* world changes. Everything can be transformed when *one* person deals with their hearts before their welcoming God.

I cannot say this better than Roy Hession does in his remarkable little book *The Calvary Road*. I recommend (again!) that you get his wonderful book and read it over and over.

Roy, forgive me for quoting you at length! You say it better than I can!

> The only basis for real fellowship with God and man is to live out in the open with both. *'But if we walk in the light, as He is in the light, we have fellowship one with another.'* To walk in the light is the opposite of walking in darkness ... As far as God is concerned, this means that we are willing to know the whole truth about ourselves, we are open to conviction ... Everything He shows us to be sin, we will

deal with as sin – we will hide or excuse nothing ... and we shall see things to be sin which we never thought to be such before. [And] the verse goes on with the precious words, '*and the Blood of Jesus Christ, His Son, cleanseth us from all sin.*' Everything that the light of God shows up as sin, we can confess and carry to the Fountain of Blood and it is gone, gone from God's sight and gone from our hearts.

But the fellowship promised us here is not only with God, but 'one with another', and that involves us in walking in the light with our brother too. In any case, we cannot be 'in the open' with God and 'in the dark' with him. This means that we must be as willing to know the truth about ourselves from our brother as to know it from God ... That means we are not going to hide our inner selves from those with whom we ought to be in fellowship; we are not going to window dress and put on appearances; nor are we going to whitewash and excuse ourselves. We are going to be honest about ourselves with them. We are willing to give up our spiritual privacy, pocket our pride and risk our reputations for the sake of being open and transparent with our brethren in Christ ... As we walk this way, we shall find that we shall have fellowship with one another at an altogether new level, and we shall not love one another less, but infinitely more.[117]

Oh, let us learn the holy habit of dealing with our own sins quickly. Let us each have a path worn to the cross. May Jesus find us often there, for there He will always be ready to receive us.

In repentance and rest is your salvation, in quietness and trust is your strength. (Is. 30:15)

Life changing repentance begins when blame shifting ends.[118]
(Tim Keller)

Resolution 69

Resolved, when I see others do something admirable which I wish
I had done, to make it my habit to do it.

One who walks with wise people will be wise ... (Prov. 13:20 NASB)

Dear Friends,

We saw in an earlier *Resolution* that envy is destructive, but
admiration can be constructive. To see something good in another's
character or actions, and to desire it in your life, can be the beginning
of transformation.

There is humility and a teachable spirit in this *Resolution*. It is
quite remarkable that it comes from the pen of such a young man.
Young men can be hard to teach, but grace is clearly at work in young
Jonathan. His humble spirit, seeing something admirable in another,
doesn't resort to envy but wants to learn all he can as he applies
himself to being all that he can be for Jesus. This is as rare as it is
beautiful.

But, beware! If youngsters can be brash and unteachable, older
men (and women!) can be crusty, stuck, and unwilling to learn, grow,
and change. The story of Saul in the Old Testament is instructive
here. Instead of admiring the gifts and deeds of young David, he
allowed jealousy and a mean spirit to grow within him, which would
eventually destroy him.

When the men were returning home after David had killed the
Philistine, the women came out from all the towns of Israel to meet
King Saul with singing and dancing, with joyful songs and with

tambourines and lyres.

As they danced, they sang:

'Saul has slain his thousands, and David his tens of thousands.'

Saul was very angry; this refrain displeased him greatly. 'They have credited David with tens of thousands,' he thought, 'but me with only thousands. What more can he get but the kingdom?' (1 Sam. 18:6–8)

No humble, teachable, spirit there! Go read the sad story of Saul and see where his envious heart took him ...

A teachable spirit is a peaceful spirit, with which God can do great things. To look on another's good accomplishments and 1) praise God for them, 2) desire them in your own life, and 3) emulate them with a humble spirit, is a remarkable accomplishment of grace in the soul. Think about this with me: a good athlete wants to be in the presence of a great one; journeyman craftsman wants to be in the workshop with a master; second-chair violinist wants to learn all she can from the first chair. Translate that into the Kingdom:

Who can I run with?

Who is excellent in prayer and godliness?

Where is a better preacher than I from whom I can learn?

Where is that godly grandmother who can teach me to be a godly mother?

Where is the young man who is running hard after God, overcoming lust and bad habits, that I can grab onto?

Timothy had his Paul.

Mary had her Elizabeth.

Elisha had his Elijah.

Ruth had her Naomi.

Joshua had his Moses.

Look at Paul's instruction to young Timothy. He urges Timothy to *'[f]lee the evil desires of youth and pursue righteousness, faith, love and peace, along with those who call on the Lord out of a pure heart'* (2 Tim. 2:22). 'Timothy! Find those sold-out Jesus followers, grab on, and then hang on for dear life!'

Let me ask you, and let's be honest with one another: Do you have a teachable spirit? When you see someone exceed you in some desirous area, or when someone does something excellent or praiseworthy, is your reaction one of joy and praise to God, soon followed by a desire for God to work something of that into you, or does that horrible feeling of envy steal into your heart?

Jonathan's *Resolution* has a sweet freedom to it. We have all been around those ... bores ... who just cannot handle someone else doing something they wish they had done or something better than they can do it. They always have to come up with a better story. Behind them is insecurity and a sense of inferiority. But, as Jesus' followers, we can be secure in who we are in Him, and thus be delivered from such destructive complexes. This liberates us to rejoice in the good things others do and desire to do them with a free spirit that enables a lifetime of growth! I remember hearing the story of Billy Graham, that great and wonderful evangelist, when he was well over eighty years of age, having preached all over the world, having written endless books ... sitting in the front row of a meeting, with Bible open and notebook and pen in hand!

Teach me!

What can I learn?

I am ready!

I want such a child-like spirit of teachable humility to follow me through to the very end of my days on earth.

It is good to ask God the Holy Spirit the following questions:

Lord God, as I engage with this person, will You please grant me a humble and teachable spirit?

Lord, what is it in this person that You would like to work in me? And, if needed,

Lord, why is my spirit disturbed over their good work? Why am I envious? Please grant me a spirit of repentance here and now!

This is really just about being sanctified, growing in grace, and walking in the purposes for which God has created and redeemed us (Eph. 2:10). Growing in grace cannot happen without a humble spirit which always seeks to be learning and is willing to be challenged and inspired by the beautiful qualities evidenced in those around us.

May the Lord Jesus grant us humble, teachable, godly spirits that are easily encouraged by His wonderful work in others.

When pride comes, then comes disgrace, but with humility comes wisdom. (Prov. 11:2)

No one has a corner on wisdom ... Our acute need is to cultivate a willingness to learn and to remain teachable.[119] (Charles Swindoll)

Resolution 70

Resolved that there be something good and helpful for others in everything that I speak.

A good man brings good things out of the good stored up in his heart, and an evil man brings evil things out of the evil stored up in his heart. For the mouth speaks what the heart is full of. (Luke 6:45)

Dear Friends,

This is the last of Jonathan's *Resolutions*. Here is his final 18th century promise to himself. What final encouragement and challenge does it hold for his 21st century readers – you and me?

We are people of words. Our inner life, thoughts and feelings are mediated outwards through words. And once out, like the feathers from the burst pillow, or the toothpaste from the tube, it is very hard – impossible – to get them back in again.

Oh, to be a channel of goodness and grace to all whom I encounter! Every day, in countless scenes, we have opportunity to bring life or death, healing or pain, hope or despair into the lives we rub up against through the words we speak. So much harm can be done with words. Indeed, the abuse of speech, the poison, the vitriol we hear all around us, proves the fallenness of our race. Paul references all of humanity when he says:

Their throats are open graves; their tongues practise deceit. The poison of vipers is on their lips. Their mouths are full of cursing and bitterness.
(Rom. 3:13–14)

But as redeemed people, those who have been transferred from the kingdom of darkness to light, our words should – *must* – reflect the wonders of our redemption. We have an opportunity with our speech to bring life into a world of death, grace into a culture of anger, hope into an age of despair. If '*[t]he words of the reckless pierce like swords… the tongue of the wise [can] bring healing* (Prov. 12:18). As Jesus said, '*Out of the abundance of the heart [the] mouth speaks*' (Luke 6:45), and a true work of grace in the heart will inevitably change the words that spring out of our mouths. If I want my words to bless and not blast, then Jesus and His Word need to be present and pre-eminent in my heart.

I have an opportunity to be a world-changer. Every day. In every encounter. It is actually *fun* to speak words of grace and goodness into lives: '*[A] person finds joy in giving an apt reply – and how good is a timely word!*' (Prov. 15:23). I am not talking about flattery. Flattery is manipulative and ungodly. I am talking about truly trusting Jesus to use little old me as a channel of life into lives. This is supernatural because it is not who I am naturally! Left to myself I will snipe and cut. But with Jesus in my heart, *I can* become a gospelling grace-spreader in countless encounters day in and day out.

Even when I have to speak a 'hard word' into someone's life (and we have seen that this, too, is a part of having a benevolent heart toward others), if my words are sourced in a Jesus-filled heart, they are going to be appropriate and medicinal. I can then trust the Holy Spirit to bring the right result, using my words to do His work in the heart of one whom He loves with an everlasting love:

> *Blessed are those whose strength is in you ... As they pass through the Valley of Baka, they make it a place of springs ...* (Ps. 84:5–6)

The use of our words for good or for evil is too big an issue to ignore. It is not an 'elective subject' for some Christians to specialize in. It is integral to who God is, and to who we are as those made in His image. God is a speaking God. From the dawn of creation to the incarnation of Jesus, The Word Made Flesh – God – speaks life into being. Being Divine image-bearers, we, as the crown of His creation, are most like Him when we are speaking. Nothing else, in all creation, save the angelic host, uses words. Words are the privilege and domain of God and humanity. Is it any wonder that Satan wants to work his mischief with our words, and cause us to use words to destroy and tear down? Is it any wonder that God will hold us accountable for the things we say? (see Jas. 3:9–12 and Matt. 12:35–37).

If we want to, we can submit our words to Jesus and allow Him to speak through us into this broken world. We can refuse to let our tongues be instruments of destruction and stop doing the devil's work! We can view our fellows – *everyone* – through the lens of the Gospel and seek supernatural power to speak beneficial words into their world – words inspired by the Holy Spirit to bring truth and life into lives which have been battered and beaten.

As we come to the end of this challenging list of *Resolutions*, perhaps nothing will better demonstrate how fully we are engaging with the beautiful change God wants to effect within us (with our full consent and partnership) than how we use words:

'Lord Jesus! Fill my heart with Your love, Your Spirit, and Your Word until it spills its banks in life-giving words to each and every person I encounter. Make me good at grace-spreading. May my words be a source of joy and life in a weary world. For the sake of the Gospel, for the sake of people, for the sake of your Glory in this day of need.'

May these words of my mouth and this meditation of my heart be pleasing in your sight, Lord, my Rock and my Redeemer. (Ps. 19:14)

Let nothing be said about anyone unless it passes through the three sieves: Is it true? Is it kind? Is it necessary?[120] (Amy Carmichael)

**If you don't quit...
you win.**

Heidi Baker

The *Resolutions* of Jonathan Edwards[121]

1722–1723

> "Being sensible that I am unable to do anything without God's help, I do humbly entreat him, by his grace, to enable me to keep these *Resolutions*, so far as they are agreeable to his will, for Christ's sake."

Remember to read over these *Resolutions* once a week.

1. *Resolved*, That *I will do whatsoever* I think to be most to the glory of God, and my own good, profit, and pleasure, in the whole of my duration; without any consideration of the time, whether now, or never so many myriads of ages hence. *Resolved,* to do whatever I think to be my *duty*, and most for the good and advantage of mankind in general. *Resolved,* so to do, whatever *difficulties* I meet with, how many soever, and how great soever.

2. *Resolved*, To be continually endeavouring to find out some *new contrivance* and invention to promote the forementioned things.

3. *Resolved*, If ever I shall fall and grow dull, so as to neglect to keep any part of these Resolutions, to repent of all I can remember, when I come to myself again.

4. *Resolved*, Never *to do* any manner of thing, whether in soul or body, less or more, but what tends to the glory of God, nor *be*, nor *suffer* it, if I can possibly avoid it.

5. *Resolved*, Never to lose one moment of time, but to improve it in the most profitable way I possibly can.

6. *Resolved*, To live with all my might, while I do live.

7. *Resolved*, Never to do anything, which I should be afraid to do if it were the last hour of my life.

8. *Resolved*, To act, in all respects, both speaking and doing, as if nobody had been so vile as I, and as if I had committed the same sins, or had the same infirmities or failings, as others; and that I will let the knowledge of their failings promote nothing but shame in myself, and prove only an occasion of my confessing my own sins and misery to God. *Vid.* July 30.

9. *Resolved*, To think much, on all occasions of my dying, and of the common circumstances which attend death.

10. *Resolved*, when I feel pain, to think of the pains of martyrdom, and of hell.

11. *Resolved*, When I think of any theorem in divinity to be solved, immediately to do what I can towards solving it, if circumstances do not hinder.

12. *Resolved*, If I take delight in it as a gratification of pride, or vanity, or on any such account, immediately to throw it by.

13. *Resolved*, To be endeavouring to find out fit objects of liberality and charity.

14. *Resolved*, Never to do anything out of revenge.

15. *Resolved*, Never to suffer the least motions of anger towards irrational beings.

16. *Resolved*, Never to speak evil of anyone, so that it shall tend to his dishonour, more or less, upon no account except for some real good.

17. *Resolved*, That I will live so, as I shall wish I had done when I come to die.

18. *Resolved*, To live so, at all times, as I think is best in my most devout frames, and when I have the clearest notions of the things of the gospel, and another world.

19. *Resolved*, Never to do anything, which I should be afraid to do, if I expected it would not be above an hour before I should hear the last trump.

20. *Resolved*, To maintain the strictest temperance in eating and drinking.

21. *Resolved*, Never to do anything, which if I should see in another, I should count a just occasion to despise him for, or to think any way the more meanly of him.

22. *Resolved*, To endeavour to obtain for myself as much happiness in the other world as I possibly can, with all the power, might, vigour, and vehemence, yea violence, I am capable of, or can bring myself to exert, in any way that can be thought of.

23. *Resolved*, Frequently to take some deliberate action, which seems most unlikely to be done, for the glory of God, and trace it back to the original intention, designs, and ends of it; and if I find it not to be for God's glory, to repute it as a breach of the fourth Resolution.

24. *Resolved*, Whenever I do any conspicuously evil action, to trace it back, till I come to the original cause; and then, both carefully endeavour to do so no more, and to fight and pray with all my might against the original of it.

25. *Resolved*, To examine carefully and constantly, what that one thing in me is, which causes me in the least to doubt of the love of God; and so direct all my forces against it.

26. *Resolved*, To cast away such things as I find do abate my assurance.

27. *Resolved*, Never wilfully to omit anything, except the omission be for the glory of God; and frequently to examine my omissions.

28. *Resolved*, To study the Scriptures so steadily, constantly, and frequently, as that I may find, and plainly perceive, myself to grow in the knowledge of the same.

29. *Resolved*, Never to count that a prayer, nor to let that pass as a prayer, nor that as a petition of a prayer, which is so made, that I cannot hope that God will answer it; nor that as a confession which I cannot hope God will accept.

30. *Resolved*, To strive every week to be brought higher in religion, and to a higher exercise of grace, than I was the week before.

31. *Resolved*, Never to say anything at all against anybody, but when it is perfectly agreeable to the highest degree of Christian honour, and of love to mankind, agreeable to the lowest humility, and sense of my own faults and failings, and agreeable to the golden rule; often, when I have said anything against any one, to bring it to,

and try it strictly by, the test of this Resolution.

32. *Resolved*, To be strictly and firmly faithful to my trust, that that, in Prov. xx. 6. 'A faithful man, who can find?' may not be partly fulfilled in me.

33. *Resolved*, To do always what I can towards making, maintaining, and preserving peace, when it can be done without an overbalancing detriment in other respects. Dec. 26, 1722.

34. *Resolved*, In narrations, never to speak anything but the pure and simple verity.

35. *Resolved*, Whenever I so much question whether I have done my duty, as that my quiet and calm is thereby disturbed, to set it down, and also how the question was resolved. Dec. 18, 1722.

36. *Resolved*, Never to speak evil of any, except I have some particular good call to it. Dec. 19, 1722.

37. *Resolved*, To inquire every night, as I am going to bed, wherein I have been negligent,— what sin I have committed,— and wherein I have denied myself;—also, at the end of every week, month, and year. Dec. 22 and 26, 1722.

38. *Resolved*, Never to utter anything that is sportive, or matter of laughter, on a Lord's Day. Sabbath evening, Dec. 23, 1722.

39. *Resolved*, Never to do anything, of which I so much question the lawfulness, as that I intend, at the same time, to consider and examine afterwards, whether it be lawful or not; unless I as much question the lawfulness of the omission.

40. *Resolved*, To inquire every night before I go to bed, whether I have acted in the best way I possibly could, with respect to eating and drinking. Jan. 7, 1723.

41. *Resolved*, to ask myself, at the end of every day, week, month, and year, wherein I could possibly, in any respect, have done better. Jan. 11, 1723.

42. *Resolved*, Frequently to renew the dedication of myself to God, which was made at my baptism, which I solemnly renewed when I was received into the communion of the church, and which I have solemnly re-made this 12th day of January, 1723.

43. *Resolved*, Never, henceforward, till I die, to act as if I were any way my own, but entirely and altogether God's; agreeably to what is

to be found in Saturday, Jan. 12th. *Jan.* 12, 1723.

44. *Resolved*, That no other end but religion shall have any influence at all on any of my actions; and that no action shall be, in the least circumstance, any otherwise than the religious end will carry it. Jan. 12, 1723.

45. *Resolved*, Never to allow any pleasure or grief, joy or sorrow, nor any affection at all, nor any degree of affection, nor any circumstance relating to it, but what helps religion. Jan. 12 and 13, 1723.

46. *Resolved*, Never to allow the least measure of any fretting or uneasiness at my father or mother. *Resolved,* to suffer no effects of it, so much as in the least alteration of speech, or motion of my eye; and to be especially careful of it with respect to any of our family.

47. *Resolved,* To endeavour, to my utmost, to deny whatever is not most agreeable to a good and universally sweet and benevolent, quiet, peaceable, contented and easy, compassionate and generous, humble and meek, submissive and obliging, diligent and industrious, charitable and even, patient, moderate, forgiving, and sincere, temper; and to do, at all times, what such a temper would lead me to; and to examine strictly, at the end of every week, whether I have so done. Sabbath morning, May 5, 1723.

48. *Resolved,* Constantly, with the utmost niceness and diligence, and the strictest scrutiny, to be looking into the state of my soul, that I may know whether I have truly an interest in Christ or not; that when I come to die, I may not have any negligence respecting this to repent of. May 26, 1723.

49. *Resolved,* That this never shall be, if I can help it.

50. *Resolved,* That I will act so, as I think I shall judge would have been best, and most prudent, when I come into the future world. July 5, 1723.

51. *Resolved,* That I will act so, in every respect, as I think I shall wish I had done, if I should at last be damned. July 8, 1723.

52. I frequently hear persons in old age say how they would live, if they were to live their lives over again: *Resolved,* That I will live just so as I can think I shall wish I had done, supposing I live to old age. July 8, 1723.

53. *Resolved,* To improve every opportunity, when I am in the

best and happiest frame of mind, to cast and venture my soul on the Lord Jesus Christ, to trust and confide in him, and consecrate myself wholly to him; that from this I may have assurance of my safety, knowing that I confide in my Redeemer. July 8, 1723.

54. *Resolved*, Whenever I hear anything spoken in commendation of any person, if I think it would be praiseworthy in me, that I will endeavour to imitate it. July 8, 1723.

55. *Resolved*, To endeavour, to my utmost, so to act, as I can think I should do, if I had already seen the happiness of heaven and hell torments. July 8, 1723.

56. *Resolved*, Never to give over, nor in the least to slacken, my fight with my corruptions, however unsuccessful I may be.

57. *Resolved*, When I fear misfortunes and adversity, to examine whether I have done my duty, and resolve to do it and let the event be just as Providence orders it. I will, as far as I can, be concerned about nothing but my duty and my sin. June 9, and July 13, 1723.

58. *Resolved*, Not only to refrain from an air of dislike, fretfulness, and anger in conversation, but to exhibit an air of love, cheerfulness, and benignity. May 27, and July 13, 1723.

59. *Resolved*, When I am most conscious of provocations to ill nature and anger, that I will strive most to feel and act good-naturedly; yea, at such times, to manifest good nature, though I think that in other respects it would be disadvantageous, and so as would be imprudent at other times. May 12, July 11, and July 13.

60. *Resolved*, Whenever my feelings begin to appear in the least out of order, when I am conscious of the least uneasiness within, or the least irregularity without, I will then subject myself to the strictest examination. July 4 and 13, 1723.

61. *Resolved*, That I will not give way to that listlessness which I find unbends and relaxes my mind from being fully and fixedly set on religion, whatever excuse I may have for it—that what my listlessness inclines me to do, is best to be done, &c. May 21, and July 13, 1723.

62. *Resolved*, Never to do anything but my duty, and then, according to Eph. vi. 6–8. to do it willingly and cheerfully, as unto the Lord, and not to man: knowing that whatever good thing any man doth, the same shall be receive of the Lord. June 25, and July 13, 1723.

63. On the supposition, that there never was to be but one individual in the world, at any one time, who was properly a complete Christian, in all respects of a right stamp, having Christianity always shining in its true lustre, and appearing excellent and lovely, from whatever part and under whatever character viewed: *Resolved*, To act just as I would do, if I strove with all my might to be that one, who should live in my time. Jan. 14, and July 13, 1723.

64. *Resolved*, When I find those '*groanings which cannot be uttered*,' of which the apostle speaks, and those '*breathings of soul for the longing it hath*,' of which the psalmist speaks, Psalm cxix. 20. that I will promote them to the utmost of my power; and that I will not be weary of earnestly endeavouring to vent my desires, nor of the repetitions of such earnestness. July 23, and Aug. 10, 1723.

65. *Resolved*, Very much to exercise myself in this, all my life long, *viz.* with the greatest openness of which I am capable, to declare my ways to God, and lay open my soul to him, all my sins, temptations, difficulties, sorrows, fears, hopes, desires, and every thing, and every circumstance, according to Dr. Manton's Sermon on the 119th Psalm, July 26, and Aug. 10, 1723.

66. *Resolved*, That I will endeavour always to keep a benign aspect, and air of acting and speaking, in all places, and in all companies, except it should so happen that duty requires otherwise.

67. *Resolved*, After afflictions, to inquire, what I am the better for them; what good I have got by them; and, what I might have got by them.

68. *Resolved*, To confess frankly to myself, all that which I find in myself, either infirmity or sin; and, if it be what concerns religion, also to confess the whole case to God, and implore needed help. July 23, and August 10, 1723.

69. *Resolved*, Always to do that, which I shall wish I had done when I see others do it. Aug. 11, 1723.

70. Let there be something of benevolence in all that I speak. Aug. 17, 1723.

Notes

1. Trace Thurlby, former president Global Orphan Project and radical world-Christian.

2. Throughout, I have modernized Jonathan's wording. The originals are in the Appendix. Scriptures underneath each modernized Resolution have been added by myself.

3. C. S. Lewis, *The Weight of Glory* (Grand Rapids: Zondervan 2001), p. 1.

4. G. A. Müller, *Narrative of Some of the Lord's Dealings with George Müller, Pt. II* (London: Nisbet & Co, 1874), p. 417.

5. M. Henry, *The Life of the Rev. Philip Henry, AM* (London: Wm Ball, 1839), p. 138.

6. Jim Cymbala, *Fresh Faith: What Happens When Real Faith Ignites God's People* (Grand Rapids: Zondervan, 1999), p. 126.

7. N. Grubb, *C.T. Studd: Cricketer and Pioneer* (Cambridge: The Lutterworth Press, 2014), p. 179.

8. Cited in many texts by many authors.

9. I heard this quotation from the godly and manly Rev Geoffrey Sharp, pastor, Plymouth Methodist Central Hall, during a drive in his car to a prayer meeting in 1987. I recall it from memory as I have never found it in print.

10. Widely attributed.

11. Quotations are from the Joe DiMaggio Official Website, 2022, http://www.joedimaggio.com/the-legacy/quotes-from-joe/

12. E. Elliot, *Through Gates of Splendor* (Wheaton: Tyndale House, 1981), p. 18.

13. Ibid. p. 20.

14. C. Miller, *Into the Depths of God* (Minneapolis: Bethany House, 2000), p. 13.

15. A. Begg, *Truth For Life*, 1999, 2023, https://www.truthforlife.org/resources/sermon/approved-god/.

16. J. Elliot, GoodReads, 2023, https://www.goodreads.com/quotes/69071-when-the-time-comes-to-die-make-sure-that-all.

17. T. Keller, *The Prodigal God* (New York: Dutton, 2008), p. 46.

18. R. Hession, *The Calvary Road* (Fort Washington: CLC Publications, 2012), p. 10.

19. C. Johnson, 'Dying Well According to John Wesley', Seedbed 2012, https://www.seedbed.com/dying-well-according-to-john-wesley/

20. J. Owen, *The Death of Death in the Death of Christ*. There are many publications of this book. I recommend one with J. I. Packer's helpful Introductory Essay. See Martino Publishing, Mansfield Centre, CT, 2016.

21. S. Smith, 'Over 900,000 Christians Martyred for Their Faith in Last 10 Years: Report', *Christian Post* 2017. https://www.christianpost.com/news/over-900000-christians-martyred-for-their-faith-in-last-10-years-report.html.

22. E. M. Fitzpatrick, *Comforts from the Cross* (Grand Rapids: Zondervan, 2015), p. 114.

23. Z. Ursinus, (2012). *The Heidelberg Catechism*.

24. Widely attributed.

25. J. I. Packer, *Knowing God* (Downers Grove: IVP, 2021), p. 34.

26. C. H. Spurgeon, (1855) 'The Immutability of God' The Spurgeon Center, 2017, https://www.spurgeon.org/resource-library/sermons/the-immutability-of-god/#flipbook/ See also J. I. Packer, *Knowing God* (Downers Grove: IVP., 2021), p. 18.

27. J. Edwards, 'A Narrative of the Revival of Religion in New England: With Thoughts on that Revival', *The Works of Jonathan Edwards, Vol. 1* (Edinburgh: The Banner of Truth Trust, 1974), p. 399.

28. Z. Van Zant, 'The Radical Budget of John Wesley', 2016, https://www.zackvanzant.com/blog/john-wesley-budget.

29. E. Elliot, (2013) Leaving Self behind. Radio Broadcast.

30. A. Carmichael, *If: What Do I Know of Calvary Love?* (Fort Washington: CLC Publications, 2003), p. 35.

31. C. ten Boom, *Tramp for the Lord: The Story that Begins Where The Hiding Place Ends* (Fort Washington: CLC Publications, 1974), p. 57.

32. Ibid.

33. F. Faber, *Kindness* (London: R. & T. Washburn, 1901), p. 84.

34. Stephen Olford was known as 'The Preachers' Preacher'. Billy Graham said he was the man who most influenced his ministry.

35. J. Edwards, 'The Portion of the Righteous', *The Works of Jonathan Edwards, Vol. 2* (Edinburgh: The Banner of Truth Trust,1974), p. 902

36. S. Pauley, 'Christians You Should Know: Jim Elliot', *Enjoying the Journey*, 2023, https://enjoyingthejourney.org/christians-you-should-know-jim-elliot/.

37. It was A. W. Tozer who first arrested me with this truth in his Preface to my now dog-eared copy of *The Knowledge of the Holy*: 'What comes into our minds when we think about God is the most important thing about us.'

38. Widely attributed.

39. C. S. Lewis, *Surprised by Joy* (Glasgow: Collins, 1955), p. 181.

40. R. I. Wilberforce, & S. Wilberforce, *The Life of William Wilberforce*, Vol 3, (London: J. Murray 1839), p. 295.

41. J. Elliot, (1949) Journal: Entry for October 28.

42. Widely attributed to William Faulkner.

43. http://en.wikipedia.org/wiki/Roy_Riegels

44. James P. Geldstone, (1871) *The Life and Travels of George Whitefield* (London, Longmans, Green, and Co.), p. 406

45. A. W. Tozer, *Worship: The Missing Jewel of the Evangelical Church* (Christian Publications, 1961).

46. J. Piper, Sermon Quotes, 2017, https://sermonquotes.com/identity/10833-we-werent-meant-to-be-somebody.html.

47. Widely attributed.

48. From the – nearly forgotten – hymn *Let Earth and Heaven Combine*.

49. J. Piper, 'William Tyndale – The Underground Translator', Desiring God 2023, https://www.desiringgod.org/articles/the-underground-translator.

50. J. Wesley, *A Man of One Book, in English Prose* Vol IV Eighteenth Century edited by Craik, H, (1916): see Bartleby, 2023, https://www.

bartleby.com/209/750.html.

51. C. H. Spurgeon, Prayer Coach, 2022, https://prayer-coach.com/prayer-quotes-charles-spurgeon/.

52. C. ten Boom, *Reflections of God's Glory* (Grand Rapids: Zondervan, 1999), p. 25.

53. J. C. Ryle, *Expository Thoughts on the Gospels: St Luke* Vol 1 (New York: Robert Carter and Brothers 1859), p. 193.

54. E. Elliot, 'The Vice of Self-Esteem', Newsletters: Sept 1st, p 1. 2023, https://elisabethelliot.org/resource-library/newsletters/the-vice-of-self-esteem-2/.

55. A. Kuyper, Center for Faith and Culture, 2018, https://intersectproject.org/faith-and-culture/abraham-kuyper-quotes-on-faith-and-culture/.

56. F. Schaeffer, *Art and the Bible* (L'Abri Fellowship: IVP, 1973), p. 94.

57. A. Kuyper, Center for Faith and Culture, 2018, https://intersectproject.org/faith-and-culture/abraham-kuyper-quotes-on-faith-and-culture/.

58. G. K. Chesterton, Illustrated London News: January 14. 1911.

59. A. Solzhenitsyn, *The Gulag Archipelago 1918–1956*. GoodReads, 2023, https://www.goodreads.com/quotes/9054930-one-man-who-stopped-lying-could-bring-down-a-tyranny.

60. R. Hession, *The Calvary Road* (Roy Hession Book Trust, 1950), p. 8.

61. A. Carmichael, *Candles in the Dark: Letters of Hope and Encouragement* (Fort Washington: CLC, 1981), p. 56.

62. C. R. Swindoll, *Great Days With Great Lives: Daily Insight From Great Lives of the Bible* (Nashville: Thomas Nelson, 2005), p. 201.

63. J. Bloom, 'Lord Keep Me From Wasting My Life'. Desiring God (2016) See https://www.desiringgod.org/articles/lord-keep-me-from-wasting-my-life.

64. *The Confessions of Saint Augustine: Books I–X* (London: Griffith, Farran, Browne and Co. Limited, 1886), p. 183.

65. See J. I. Packer, *Among God's Giants* (*Brighton:* Kingsway Publications, 1991), chapter 2 'Why We Need the Puritans.'

66. E. Elliot, *Discipline, the Glad Surrender* (Grand Rapids: Fleming H. Revell Company, 2006), p. 111.

67. Attributed to John Wesley and a partial match to quotes from the 1799 work 'Sermons on Several Occasions': Sermon 36, p. 486, and Sermon 50,

p. 675.

68. Z. Ursinus, (2012). *The Heidelberg Catechism.*

69. See also Resolution 1.

70. T. Trahern, *Centuries of Meditations* (London: Dobell, P.J. & A.E., 1908), p. 31.

71. Widely attributed to Emerson. Brought to my attention by a helpful friend, Steve Johnston, in 1986.

72. Widely attributed to C.T. Studd and Oswald J. Smith. I first heard it from my old Cornish farmer mentor Stuart V. Pearce in 1987.

73. H. Taylor, cited in George, D. *The Daily Thought Shaker* (Bloomington: West Bow Press, 2014), p. 191.

74. Quoted in Dane Ortlund's wonderful book *Gentle and Lowly*, (Wheaton: Crossway, 2020), p. 81.

75. J. Bunyan, (1658), *A Few Sighs from Hell...* p. 1. Printed by Ralph Wood for M. Wright at the Kings Head in the Old Bailey, London.

76. See also Resolution 17.

77. G. K. Chesterton, *What's Wrong with the World* (London; Toronto: Cassell, 1912), p. 22.

78. C. S. Lewis, *Mere Christianity* (Grand Rapids: Zondervan, 2001), p. 143.

79. C. S. Lewis, *Joyful Christian* (New York: Simon and Schuster, 1996), p. 138.

80. Author unknown.

81. J. Bunyan, *Pilgrim's Progress* (Edinburgh, Scotland: Nelson and Sons, 1857), p. 191

82. M. Muggeridge, in conversation with William Buckley cited by Mathwin D. A Stick in the Mud blog (Feb 18, 2021).

83. Widely attributed.

84. R. Ebert, (2009) 'I'm a Proud Brainiac', https://www.rogerebert.com/roger-ebert/im-a-proud-brainiac.

85. J. Wesley, *Sermons on Several Occasions: Volume One*, Preface. (1747)

86. L. Schmucker, 'The Uncomfortable Subject Jesus Addressed More Than Anyone Else', The Gospel Coalition, 2017, https://www.thegospelcoalition.org/.

87. R. Baxter, *The Saints Everlasting Rest* (Leeds: Davies and Booth, 1814), p. 222.

88. Thankfully, James Bell has recently provided us with a far more 'useable', Daily Readings from *The Christian in Complete Armour*, (Chicago: Moody Press, 2015).

89. John Newton is believed to have said, 'If I might read only one book beside the Bible, I would choose *The Christian in Complete Armour*'.

90. My paraphrase from W. Gurnall, *Christian in Complete Armour*, (Edinburgh: Banner of Truth Trust, 1964), p. 13.

91. My paraphrase from Book VIII Augustine, *The Confessions*, Ed: Clark, G. (University of Liverpool, 1876), pp. 201–02.

92. From John Bunyan's Dying Sayings in *Miscellaneous Pieces*, (2021).

93. E. Sherill, B. Andrew, & J. Sherrill, *God's Smuggler* (London: Hachette, 2015), p. 70.

94. J. Gillespie, *The New Life of God in the Soul of Man* (Overland Park: Myrrh Books, 2017), p. 102.

95. E. Elliot, *Passion and Purity* (Grand Rapids: Revell, 2002).

96. R. Hession, *The Calvary Road* (Fort Washington: CLC Publications, (2016), p. 8.

97. Ibid.

98. Resolution 38.

99. From an anonymous poem referenced by Elizabeth Elliot in her series of radio talks, Gateway to Joy, 2023, https://elisabethelliot.org/resource-library/gateway-to-joy/do-the-next-thing-practical-holy-living/

100. O. Chambers, *My Utmost for His Highest*, 'Can You Come Down?' (Uhrichsville, 1963), April 16th.

101. M. Luther, *The Freedom of a Christian: Concerning Christian Liberty* (Pennsylvania: Fortress Press, 2008), p. 1.

102. See also Resolution 27.

103. J. Wesley, *A Plain Account of Christian Perfection* (New York: G. Lane & P.P. Sandford, 1844), p. 53.

104. M. Fackler, Christianity Today, 2023, https://www.christianitytoday.com/history/issues/issue-25/world-has-yet-to-see.html.

105. For her story see A. Burgess, *The Small Woman* (London: Pan Books, 1972).

106. Augustine, *The Confessions*. Paraphrase of il, p. iii. Ed, G. Clarke, (University of Liverpool, 1876).

107. B. Pascal, *Pensées* (New York: Penguin Books, 1966), p. 75.

108. B. Pascal, *Pensées and Other Writings* (Oxford University Press, 1999), p. 44.

109. I heard David Wilkerson speak these penetrating words from a pulpit in 1983. I have never forgotten them.

110. J. Wesley, *Hymns and Sacred Poems*, p. viii. (Bristol: Felix Farley, 1739).

111. From Dane Ortland's *Gentle and Lowly* (Wheaton: Crossway, 2020), p. 144.

112. E. Peterson, *Practice Resurrection: A Conversation on Growing Up in Christ* (Cambridge: W.B. Eerdman's, 2010), p. 2.

113. J. Edwards, *The Works of Jonathan Edwards, Vol. 1.* (Edinburgh: Banner of Truth, 1974), p. clxxix.

114. Ibid, p. clxxviii.

115. Ibid. p. clxxix.

116. Ibid. p. clxxviii.

117. R. Hession, *The Calvary Road* (Fort Washington, PA: CLC Publications, 1990), p. 38.

118. T. Keller, tweet @timkellernyc, Dec 11, 2018.

119. C. Swindoll, "Servant-Hearted Leaders" in *Day by Day,* (Nashville: Thomas Nelson, 2005).

120. Widely attributed.

121. J. Edwards, *The Works of Jonathan Edwards, Vol. 1.* (Edinburgh: Banner of Truth, 1974), p xx.

Also available from Christian Focus Publications ...

Jonathan Edwards and the Christian Pilgrim:
Our Journey Towards Heaven

by Deborah Howard

978-1-5271-0978-0

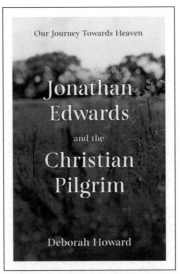

Wisdom from Jonathan Edwards on the journey towards death, with application for modern life.

Death is inevitable. Whether we're facing the death of a loved one, or our own passing from this world to the next, we cannot avoid it. Death is something we never get used to. But it is something that we can get ready for.

Deborah Howard has taken Jonathan Edwards' intensely encouraging sermon on the Christian Pilgrim and, drawing on her own experiences as a hospice nurse, has written this book to encourage us to live with our final destination in mind.

Focussing on scripture truth, the reader is encouraged to think about the journey that leads us towards our final destination. How are we spending our lives, as we live in the light of eternity? This combination of classic sermon and modern application makes this book an essential addition to any Christian's bookshelf.

A New Inner Relish:
Christian Motivation in the Thought of Jonathan Edwards

by Dane Ortlund

978-1-8455-0349-9

What made Jonathan Edwards tick? Dane Ortlund shows us that Edwards was gripped, spellbound by what he saw in God – and that underscored everything he did. Such motivation is essential to authentic Christian living.

A Call to United, Extraordinary Prayer:
An Humble Attempt...

by Jonathan Edwards

978-1-8579-2860-0

Jonathan Edwards was the foremost leader of the Great Awakening in North America in the 18th Century. His writings continue to have a marked influence today on the life of the church, his example stands as a beacon to guide us from the shallows of our low levels of spirituality to the deeper waters of life. This classic book by Jonathan Edwards was first published to promote unity in prayer amongst all believers.

Christian Focus Publications

Our mission statement –

STAYING FAITHFUL

In dependence upon God we seek to impact the world through literature faithful to His infallible Word, the Bible. Our aim is to ensure that the Lord Jesus Christ is presented as the only hope to obtain forgiveness of sin, live a useful life and look forward to heaven with Him.

Our books are published in four imprints:

CHRISTIAN
FOCUS

Popular works including biographies, commentaries, basic doctrine and Christian living.

CHRISTIAN
HERITAGE

Books representing some of the best material from the rich heritage of the church.

MENTOR

Books written at a level suitable for Bible College and seminary students, pastors, and other serious readers. The imprint includes commentaries, doctrinal studies, examination of current issues and church history.

CF4·K

Children's books for quality Bible teaching and for all age groups: Sunday school curriculum, puzzle and activity books; personal and family devotional titles, biographies and inspirational stories – because you are never too young to know Jesus!

Christian Focus Publications Ltd,
Geanies House, Fearn, Ross-shire,
IV20 1TW, Scotland, United Kingdom.
www.christianfocus.com